In the air, their only enemy was defeat . . .

Here are the true stories of the aces of World War II—dozens of pilots from both sides who were the best of the best in the air—the valiant battles they fought, the incredible victories they won, and, for some, their violent ends, including:

- Legendary Marine aviator Gregory "Pappy" Boyington, the unpredictable, unconventional, cigar-chomping "bad boy" ace, who led his Black Sheep Squadron to victory after victory in the Pacific . . .

- Hans-Joachim Marseille, regarded by many pilots and experts as the best fighter pilot in the Luftwaffe and possibly the best ever . . .

- Japan's Tetsuzo Iwamoto, who started his wartime career at Pearl Harbor and finished by shooting down a B-29 bomber over Japan during the war's final days . . .

- Katya Budanova and Lidiya Vladimirovna "Lilya" Litvak—Russia's two women aces, both of whom were killed in action . . .

D0012912

ACES

True Stores of Victory and Valor in the Skies of World War II

William Yenne

BERKLEY BOOKS, NEW YORK

ACES

A Berkley Book / published by arrangement with
the author

PRINTING HISTORY
Berkley edition / October 2000

All rights reserved.
Copyright © 2000 by William Yenne.
Book design by Beth Kessler.
Cover design by Steven Ferlauto.
Cover photographs by Bettman/Corbis.
On the cover (bottom photo): Tommy McGuire
(with cap and moustache, second from right) and
Dick Bong (no cap, third from right).
This book, or parts thereof, may not be
reproduced in any form without permission.
For information address:
The Berkley Publishing Group, a division of Penguin Putnam Inc.,
375 Hudson Street, New York, New York 10014.

The Penguin Putnam Inc. World Wide Web site address is
http://www.penguinputnam.com

ISBN: 0-425-17699-1

BERKLEY®
Berkley Books are published by The Berkley Publishing Group,
a division of Penguin Putnam Inc.,
375 Hudson Street, New York, New York 10014.
BERKLEY and the ''B'' design
are trademarks belonging to Penguin Putnam Inc.

PRINTED IN THE UNITED STATES OF AMERICA

10 9 8 7 6 5 4 3 2 1

CONTENTS

INTRODUCTION

FIGHTER PILOTS HAVE ALWAYS BEEN described as the knights of the air. Since World War I, they have been seen as a breed apart, fighting their battles high above the mud and muck of the battlefield, engaging one another man-to-man like the knights of medieval jousting tournaments. A special folklore grew up around the knights of the Middle Ages, and the code of chivalry that defined knighthood created a special vocabulary. This was the case with the knights of the air as well. Most important in this modern lexicon is the term "ace," which was coined to describe the pilot who had achieved a level of expertise beyond that of his peers.

What is an ace? Technically it means a pilot of a fighter aircraft who has shot down, or destroyed in the air, a total of *five* enemy aircraft. An ace is defined as a fighter pilot who has achieved five aerial *victories*. Alternately, an ace can be described as a fighter pilot who has dueled to the death with five other fighter pilots, and survived to tell the tale.

As with the knights of old, however, the knight of the air does not necessarily seek literally to *kill* his opponent, but rather to destroy his aircraft just as in the joust the medieval knight would seek primarily to knock his opponent off his horse. If he dies in the process, he dies a heroic death, but if he survives, the code of the ace abhors the fighter pilot who would shoot at a man hanging helpless in a parachute. While this did occur, it is, and always has been, roundly condemned by fighter pilots everywhere. It was much more common to see the victorious pilot fly past his victim with a salute or a wave.

Other examples of the kind of chivalry shown by aces occurred in 1941 and 1942, when the British aces Douglas Bader and Robert Tuck were shot down over France. In both cases, the German ace Adolf Galland, who was also a Luftwaffe group commander, invited the men to dine with him at his officers' mess. In the air, Galland would have considered them enemies. Elsewhere, they were respected colleagues. After the war, Galland and Bader were reported to be close friends. For many years after the war, numerous surviving aces from opposing sides met and mingled at reunions and other events, as though they were all members of the same brotherhood.

The Origin of the Term "Ace"

The term was coined in April 1915 to describe the French daredevil-aeronaut-turned-military-pilot Roland Garros when he had succeeded in becoming the first man to successfully score five aerial victories.

Before Garros, the crews of aircraft had been shooting at one another for several years. Balloons had been used for observation in the various conflicts of the nineteenth century, and airplanes were used in Italy's war with Turkey in 1911, but World War I was the first war in which airplanes became an integral part of battlefield action.

Before World War I, there had been the problem of aiming a gun from a moving airplane. Shooting straight ahead was the best for aiming, but it was hard to do this because it meant shooting through the propeller arc and probably shooting off the propeller. Garros solved this difficulty by having metal deflection plates attached to the propeller. Within three weeks, Garros had downed five German aircraft, and the French media hailed him as hero, an "ace."

Later, the Germans developed a method of synchronizing the gun with the engine driveshaft and the era of aces began. Aces were popular in World War I because of the glamour involved. They fought high above the filth of the terrible trenches and they fought one-on-one like the knights of old. They inspired just about the only chivalrous tales to come out of that terrible war.

In World War II, aces were equally colorful, though aerial combat had become more sophisticated technologically, more routine, and much more deadly. Far more individuals were involved in aerial combat and far more became aces. Also in World War II, the recording of aerial victory data became an official part of air-force record keeping. It had been so with the German and the French in World War I, but was much more informal with the air services of other countries.

Precisely Defining Aces

While the maintaining of data relative to aerial victories was more formalized in World War II, there were still differences and variations from one air force to another. An ace was universally accepted as someone who has scored five aerial victories, but each of the air forces involved in World War II had a different method for calculating exactly what constituted an aerial victory.

Germany had the most precise definition. In World War II, as in World War I, it was a strict "one pilot, one victory" rule. One pilot was given a victory credit for each enemy aircraft shot down. If he was assisted by another pilot, the other pilot got no credit to his overall score for the "assist." If two pilots shared equally, then the credit went to the staffel (squadron) and to the overall tally of neither pilot. To claim a victory in the German Luftwaffe, the claimant had to have a witness—preferably two—and he had to formally fill out a comprehensive victory report which was followed by a combat report. These had to be signed off by the gruppe (group) commander and the intelligence officer. For this reason, German victory totals in World War II are considered very accurate, and in cases where there might have been a discrepancy, the totals are definitely on the low side.

The Germans even went so far as to be the only country to officially downgrade "ace" status in favor of recognizing only those with ten or more victories. Such a pilot would be referred to as an "experte."

The Americans are also considered to have been very accurate in their accounting, because, through most of World War II, American fighters were equipped with gun cameras, and no scores were recognized as "confirmed" without gun camera film footage as proof. American victory totals are often qualified by the mention of "probables" or "damaged" enemy aircraft, which are those that were "probably" shot down but cannot be "confirmed." These are often mentioned parenthetically, but are not included in official victory totals.

In World War I, the U.S. Army Air Service didn't get its squadrons assembled until the last months of the war, so American pilots who had flown with foreign squadrons had used the latters' methods of counting scores. When American squadrons were formed, the practice of recording victories was much more flexible in the counting of probables and damaged aircraft than it would be in World War II.

In World War I, there was a tendency toward giving out several whole numbers to several pilots participating in downing a single enemy, but this practice was not followed in World War II. Whereas the German practice was to simply not award any scores for "assists," the Americans developed a system for giving appropriate credit for "assists" by calling them "shared" victories.

The American system of "shared" victories that was used in World War II was much more precise and accurate than the system in place during the earlier conflict. It was also more complicated than the German system, it was certainly more fair, and it certainly encouraged teamwork. German "shared" victories were allocated only to one of the "sharees" or to nobody, but American "shared" victories were divided among the "sharees." If two Americans worked together to shoot down one enemy aircraft, then each American would have a half point added to his victory total. If three pilots were involved, then each pilot would officially have .33 added, and so on.

Since 1957, the U.S. Air Force Historical Research Agency at Maxwell AFB has carefully researched aerial victory for U.S. Army and U.S. Air Force aces in World War I, World War II, and the Korean War, updating and correcting data as much as possible. For the Vietnam War and subsequent conflicts, the data has been collected and maintained as soon as possible after the victories were scored. The data thus collected is probably as historically accurate as is possible.

In World War II, Britain's Royal Air Force formally

adopted the same method of counting "confirmed" and "shared" victories as the Americans, although, early in the war, shared victories were often counted with whole numbers, as had been the practice in the First World War. Like the Americans, the system the British used in World War I was unofficial and tended to give credit for enemy aircraft "driven down" to a lower altitude or forced to land, even if it was behind their own lines. The counting of "probables" (and even "improbables") in the final totals definitely inflated scores. The practice was officially abandoned by the British relatively early in World War II.

Finland, where precise records were kept, also maintained the practice of using fractions to credit shared kills.

During World War I, the French used a method of calculation that was nearly as strict as that used by Germany. Verification and witness statements were essential in order for scores to count. "Probables" were absolutely disallowed, but, as with the British, "shared" victories were often counted as whole numbers.

In World War II, however, the French Armée de l'Air counted everything in whole numbers. When France was invaded, such desperate times probably led to desperate measures. In 1940, scores were credited for actually shooting down an enemy, but full scores were also given for "assists" and for "probables." Shared victories always got full scores and were often allocated to more than two or three pilots who were present at the time. This was almost certainly a propaganda measure designed to ensure that the French media would report good news about the battle. During World War II, the Italian Regia Aeronautica used the same method, so the victory totals for most pilots of both air forces are drastically inflated.

In Eastern Europe, especially in Romania and Bulgaria, the tendency to officially inflate scores reached an extreme.

The Royal Romanian Air Force formally adhered to the practice of awarding multiple points depending on the type of aircraft shot down. This practice called for awarding three "victories" to a pilot that claimed a four-engine bomber, and two victories for downing a twin-engined aircraft. Shooting down a fighter in a dogfight, however, counted merely as one. As in France and Italy, the purpose of this practice was obviously for domestic consumption, to keep morale up. However, this would lead to the strange circumstance of a Romanian pilot getting a score of 12 for shooting down four bombers, while a Luftwaffe pilot operating from the same base might only get a score of 3 for the same effort, if the pilot didn't happen to have his paperwork in order for one of the four. The Bulgarians also officially used the multiple point system to inflate scores.

Just the opposite was true a bit farther east in the Soviet Union, where the effort of the individual was officially subordinated to the collective effort. Early in the war, there was a deliberate and official practice of *not* recognizing individual scores, but the propaganda value of having aces as heroes of what the Soviet Union called the "Great Patriotic War" was soon recognized and the situation changed. Still, the unofficial nature of keeping the counts has led to some uncertainty about the exact numbers, and regarding exactly how many aces there were.

With the Japanese, it was an official practice in the field to credit victories to the group or squadron rather than to the actual pilot. Such individual scores which do exist were kept informally and are not always accurate. Even for all of the important Japanese aces, there is a wide spread of numbers that are mentioned in the literature as their possible final score.

With Japan, as with the Soviet Union, the highest-scoring aces are well known, but the exact numbers for these men are not known for certain, although, with the Soviet aces, the numbers given for the major aces are probably more accurate. For both countries, the scores, and even the names of all the lesser aces, will probably never be known for certain.

Qualifying and Quantifying the Aces of World War II

The highest-scoring ace of World War II was the German pilot Erich Hartmann, who scored 352 well-documented aerial victories. Behind him, there were over 100 aces in the German Luftwaffe who scored more than 100 victories. No other country had any aces who are confirmed to have scored more than 100 victories.

The highest number of confirmed victories outside the Luftwaffe is the score of 94.17 credited to Eino Ilmari Juutilainen of Finland. Next in line are the Japanese aces. Tetsuzo Iwamoto is credited with having scored 80 victories in World War II and 14 during the Sino-Japanese War for a total of 94. Hiroyoshi Nishizawa is credited with 87 in World War II alone. However, because of Japan's official record-keeping practices—or the lack thereof—these totals are regarded as "best guesses." Some sources credit Iwamoto with as many as 250 victories or as few as 66, and Nishizawa with as many as 202.

The highest-scoring Soviet ace is known to have been Ivan Kozhedub, and his score of 62 is generally accepted by most sources. The highest-scoring British Commonwealth ace is known to have been Marmaduke "Pat" Pattle, but his exact score is not known. The reason is that the relevant records for his unit, Royal Air Force No.33 Squadron were lost in the British evacuation of Greece in 1940, and Pattle himself was killed during this operation.

His score is known to have been at least 40, which is enough to earn him the top slot, but it was almost certainly higher and may have been as high as 51. The highest-scoring American ace was Richard Ira "Dick" Bong. Well-kept records confirm that his score was exactly 40.

The total numbers of aces for most countries are known to a reasonable degree of certainty, but at least some records for every air force were lost, so some aces with smaller scores, such as below ten, may not have been counted, and some scores may be missing or incorrect. For example, someone who was killed in action with an official score of 4.5 would not have been included on a list of aces, so if it was found later that he had an additional victory, his name would not be on the list, upgraded to 5.5. Other discrepancies still remain in many ace lists because the Royal Air Force began the war with the liberal policy of crediting whole numbers for shared victories, and it then converted to using fractions without exhaustively revising all the numbers that were already in the records.

Just as they had the highest-scoring aces, the Luftwaffe also led in the total number of aces. The number is at least 5,000, although many records are lost, and so perhaps are the names and numbers of some aces with smaller scores that would have been in the shadow of the well-known and widely reported scores of the aces with more than 100 victories. The number of Luftwaffe aces with more than 20 aerial victories is probably more than 950.

The combined total number of American aces in the USAAF, the U.S. Navy and the U.S. Marine Corps stands at about 1,280, but even with the Americans, names and numbers from the early part of the war are uncertain. The combined total number of aces for the British Commonwealth air services of Australia, Canada, New Zealand, South Africa, Britain itself, and all others is also above

1,200. The Soviet Voenno-Vozdushnie Sily may have had
as many as 2,000 aces or as few as 300. Italy and Japan
are probably the only other countries with more than 100,
but Italy's totals are inflated by an especially liberal count
of shared victories and Japan's numbers are just the opposite. If some victories by leading aces could be overlooked, then all or most victories by less prominent aces
were probably ignored.

The statistics, however, are really just a trivial part of
the story. For fighter pilots to do battle, one-on-one, with
other fighter pilots, was an act of courage and dedication
that linked them with the timeless tradition of the classic
warrior. Whatever can be said about the statistics, the var-
iables, and the numbers, nothing can subtract from the
skill, bravery, and devotion to duty that was exemplified
by those pilots who became aces in mankind's biggest
global conflict.

1

THE U.S. ARMY AIR FORCES

WHEN WORLD WAR II BEGAN in 1939, the entity that evolved into today's U.S. Air Force was merely a corps within the U.S. Army. In terms of men and aircraft, it was smaller than the Luftwaffe, Britain's Royal Air Force, or the Soviet Union's Voenno-Vozdushnie Sily. However, thanks to the efforts of its chief, General Henry Harley "Hap" Arnold, the U.S. Army Air Corps would expand into the largest air force in history—in less than four years. Arnold was part of a generation of Air Corps leaders who had entered the U.S. Army Aviation Section at a time when it was still part of the Signal Corps, but who had seen the promise and the possibilities of military airpower in World War I. Through the 1920s and 1930s, Arnold had been one of a number of young officers who believed in the idea that airpower was an effective means of waging war and defending the United States.

Gradually, U.S. Army aviation grew in importance within the service. After World War I, the Aviation Section became the Air Service, and in 1926, it became the U.S. Army Air Corps. Still, Hap Arnold and his generation believed that the Air Corps should not be a corps of the

Army, but rather an independent "air force," equal in official status to the Navy and the army itself.

In 1938, when he became chief of the U.S. Army Air Corps, that service had fewer than 2,000 airplanes and 21,000 people. In 1941, Arnold won, if not independence, at least autonomy, from the army. On June 20, 1941, the U.S. Army Air Forces (USAAF) were created. By now, most of the world was at war, and Arnold faced the even bigger challenge of preparing for the inevitable United States entry into the war. The United States government had lagged behind on national defense until Germany swallowed all of Western and southeastern Europe, as well as Scandinavia. Suddenly there was an urgency in the wind. President Franklin D. Roosevelt called for a doubling, then a quadrupling, of American airpower.

At the beginning of 1941, the Air Corps had grown to 3,961 aircraft and 51,165 personnel, but it was still dwarfed by the German Luftwaffe, and inferior to most of the world's major air forces. By the time that the United States entered World War II, Arnold had increased the new USAAF to more than 9,000 aircraft and nearly 150,000 personnel, but the miracle of mobilization was yet to come. In the next two and a half years, the USAAF would grow ninefold in aircraft and 16-fold in manpower. At the time of the Normandy Invasion on June 6, 1944, the USAAF had a peak wartime strength of 78,757 aircraft and 2,372,292 people in uniform.

It was a herculean effort. Three years after World War II began, there was 100 times as many personnel in Arnold's air force as there had been when he became chief. Not only were there 35 airplanes in USAAF markings for every one in Air Corps insignia, they represented a vast qualitative and technological change. Reflecting Arnold's own intense interest in technology, the USAAF went from biplanes to jets in a few short years.

Ironically, history's largest air force was always under U.S. Army command, although Arnold wore five stars and operated autonomously. The service would not become the independent U.S. Air Force until September 1947. By that time aircraft strength had withered to 20,000 and personnel strength was down to 305,827.

USAAF Air Forces and Aces

During World War I, the fledgling Air Service of the U.S. Army's American Expeditionary Forces had been in action for less than a year, but it managed to produce 21 aces with ten victories or more. Two of these, John Malone and Frederick Gillette, had scores of 20, while William Lambert had 22. America's ace of aces in World War I was the dashing former race-car driver and future airline executive, Edward V. "Eddie" Rickenbacker. During the early years of American involvement in World War II, Rickenbacker's 26 victories became the Holy Grail of aspiring fighter pilots.

Getting into the spirit of the times, Rickenbacker offered to buy a case of Scotch whiskey for the first Army pilot to top his score. Ironically, the first American to match Rickenbacker's score in World War II was not an Army pilot, but a Marine—Joe Foss.

In World War I, the Army Air Service fought in the skies over a small corner of France, but General Arnold realized that World War II would be a true global war, with American aircraft flying and fighting in the skies over every continent but Antarctica. For this task, he created a global force on a scale never previously imagined. Arnold organized the USAAF into numbered air forces, each one

assigned a specific task in a specific theater. He started
with 7, added 6 in 1942, and ended the war with 16.

The first four air forces were located in the continental
United States, where the former Northeast Air District became the First Air Force, the former Northwest Air District
became the Second Air Force, the former Southeast Air
District became the Third Air Force, and the former Southwest Air District became the Fourth Air Force. Also in
North America, the Caribbean Air Force became the Sixth
Air Force and the former Alaskan Air Force became the
Eleventh Air Force. Because of the nature of their geographic locations, none of these air forces would produce
any aces.

In the European and Mediterranean theaters, the Eighth
Air Force was created in England in January 1942 for strategic operations against German-occupied Europe, the
Ninth Air Force was created in England in December 1942
for tactical operations against German-occupied Europe,
and the Twelfth Air Force was created in August 1942 for
operations in the Mediterranean Theater. The Fifteenth Air
Force was created in Italy in November 1943 for strategic
operations against German-occupied Europe from bases in
Italy. There would be more USAAF aces among these air
forces, especially the Eighth, than in any other region.

In the European Theater, the Eighth Air Force began its
offensive against Germany in 1942 and in early 1943, the
first escort fighter units became operational at bases in
Britain. These included the 4th Fighter Group, 56th Fighter
Group, and the 78th Fighter Group. Initially, these units
were equipped with P-47 Thunderbolts, but by 1944, the
more effective P-51 Mustang had arrived with its ability
to escort the heavy bombers all the way to Berlin.

The top two USAAF aces in the European Theater were
Francis "Gabby" Gabreski, who scored 28 victories while

flying with the 56th Fighter Group, and Robert S. Johnson, who scored 27 with the 56th Fighter Group. Both men did so while flying the P-47 Thunderbolt.

Other top Thunderbolt aces in the European Theater were David C. Schilling, who scored 22.5 victories; Fred J. Christensen, with 21.5 victories; and Walker M. "Bud" Mahurin, with 20.8 victories. All of these men flew with the 56th Fighter Group. Dominic "Don" Gentile, who scored 21.8 victories with the 4th Fighter Group, started out in the P-47, but scored many of his victories after the group switched to the P-51 Mustang.

The top European Theater Mustang aces were George Preddy, who scored 26.8 victories while flying with the 352th Fighter Group; John Meyer, with 24 victories while flying with the 352th Fighter Group; and Ray Wetmore, with 22.6 victories while flying with the 359th Fighter Group. Of the European Theater aces, Gabreski, Johnson, Schilling, Gentile, Christensen, Preddy, and Meyer would be awarded the Distinguished Service Cross.

The Twelfth Air Force and Fifteenth Air Force pilots who flew in the Mediterranean Theater found enemy aircraft strength to be significantly less than in northern Europe. The Germans abandoned North Africa in 1943 and the Italians surrendered in 1943. Thus, Axis fighter opposition came principally from the Germans still based in Italy through 1945 and that which was encountered on long-range escort missions to Munich, Vienna, and the oil fields of Romania.

Unlike northern Europe, the Allies thoroughly outnumbered the Axis in the Mediterranean and southern Europe after the summer of 1943. There were many aces, but the scores were smaller. The two leading aces were John Voll, who claimed 21 victories while flying P-51s with the 31th Fighter Group, and Herschel "Herky" Green, who scored

18 victories while flying P-47s with the 325th Fighter Group. Green was awarded the Distinguished Service Cross.

In the Pacific Theater, the formerly Philippines-based Far East Air Force (FEAF) became the Fifth Air Force, the formerly Hawaii-based Hawaiian Air Force became the Seventh Air Force, and the new Thirteenth Air Force was created in the Solomon Islands in December 1942. These would be loosely united as the new Far East Air Force under General George Kenney, and would produce the USAAF's highest-scoring aces.

In the Asiatic Theater, the Tenth Air Force was created in India in 1942 for logistical operations in support of China, while the prewar American Volunteer Group in China became the China Air Task Force in July 1942, and in turn became part of the Fourteenth Air Force in March 1943.

The last USAAF Air Force activated was the Twentieth, which was designed specifically for the strategic bombing of Japan with Boeing B-29 Superfortresses, and it had no fighters. Fighter escorts for the B-29s would be supplied by Seventh Air Force units based on Iwo Jima and Okinawa.

As noted above, the Fifth Air Force was the home to America's top-scoring aces of all time, and most of the highest-scoring aces of the Pacific Theater. Decimated in the fall of the Philippines in December 1941, it was reorganized in Australia and placed under the umbrella of the FEAF. Units assigned to it, especially the 49th Fighter Group and 475th Fighter Group, carried the heaviest workload among USAAF fighter units during the 1942–1944 period when the Imperial Japanese Navy Air Force was at the apogee of its strength in the Solomons, New Guinea, and the Netherlands East Indies (now Indonesia). As the P-51 Mustang would become the signature USAAF fighter in Europe, the P-38 Lightning was that aircraft for the FEAF in the Southwest Pacific.

The two leading American aces of the war were Richard Ira "Dick" Bong, who scored 40 victories while flying with the 49th Fighter Group, and Thomas "Tommy" McGuire, who had 38 victories while flying with the 475th "Satan's Angels" Fighter Group. Both men would be recipients of the Congressional Medal of Honor, but neither would survive the war. Another Medal of Honor recipient was tied with two others as the fourth-highest-scoring USAAF ace in the Pacific Theater. This man, Neel Kearby, scored 22 victories while flying P-47s with the 348th Fighter Group. He was the only ace in the top eight in the Pacific Theater *not* to score his victories in the Lockheed P-38.

Other USAAF aces with scores of 20 or more in the Pacific Theater were Charles MacDonald, who scored 27 victories while flying with the 475th Fighter Group; Gerald R. Johnson, with 22 victories while flying with the 49th Fighter Group; Jay T. Robbins, with 22 victories while flying with the 8th Fighter Group; Robert Westbrook, with 20 victories while flying with the 18th Fighter Group (of the Seventh Air Force); and Thomas J. Lynch, who had 20 victories while flying with the 35th Fighter Group. MacDonald, Johnson, and Robbins all were awarded the Distinguished Service Cross.

Also worth noting is the Texan Lance Wade, who scored 25 victories while flying in North Africa with Britain's Royal Air Force (see British Commonwealth). Unlike other men such as Don Gentile, who scored victories with the Royal Air Force as well as the USAAF, Wade never flew with the USAAF.

USAAF Fighter Aircraft

When World War II began in 1939, the Curtiss P-40 Warhawk was the standard frontline fighter in the U.S. Army Air Corps. In fact, from 1940 to 1942, more P-40s were produced in the United States than all other fighter types combined. Warhawks saw action at Pearl Harbor and they went on to serve in combat in every theater of the war where the United States was involved. They were also exported to Allied services, especially to China and to Britain's Royal Air Force.

During the 1920s and early 1930s, Curtiss was one of the leading builders of fighters for both the U.S. Army and U.S. Navy. These aircraft were primarily radial-engined biplanes for which Curtiss established a solid reputation. By 1934, the Air Corps was making the transition to monoplanes, and the Curtiss entry, while not the first monoplane fighter, was among the first generation of Air Corps monoplane fighters. The Curtiss Model 75 Hawk was powered by a Pratt & Whitney R-1830 radial engine. It first flew in May 1935 and was soon being delivered to the U.S. Army Air Corps under the designation P-35. Eventually the Hawk would be the first American airplane of which over 1,000 would be produced.

Based on the Hawk, the Warhawk was similar in size and appearance to the Hawk, but it was equipped with a supercharged in-line engine for better high-altitude performance. First flown in October 1938, the Warhawk was delivered to the Army for evaluation in January 1939. Orders for 524 P-40s were forthcoming, and an export version was also sold to France.

Deliveries began in the spring of 1940, with the Air Corps assigning theirs to Langley Field, Virginia; Hamilton Field, California; and Selfridge Field, Michigan.

France was invaded by Germany in May, and defeated in June, before any of their deliveries could be made. Britain took over the French contracts, and between September and December 1940, 558 aircraft were delivered to the Royal Air Force under the British-assigned name "Tomahawk."

Meanwhile, the U.S. Army Air Corps was beginning to take delivery of its own version of the newer Tomahawk-type aircraft under the appellation P-40B Warhawk. These were followed by the Tomahawk II/P-40C series in the spring of 1941. The British immediately sent 300 Tomahawk IIs into combat in North Africa, and they achieved their first aerial victory there on June 8, 1941. Against the legendary German Messerschmitt Bf-109, the Tomahawks did reasonably well. Though they were slower in the climb, they could outmaneuver the Messerschmitts.

In May 1941, Curtiss introduced the P-40E type, of which over 2,000 were built, including 1,500 to be delivered to the Royal Air Force as the Kittyhawk I. The Curtiss P-40E Warhawk had a wingspan of 37 feet 4 inches, and a length of 31 feet 2 inches. It weighed 8,280 pounds fully loaded and fueled. It was powered by an Allison 1,150-hp, liquid-cooled V-1710-39 engine that gave it a top speed of 354 mph. It had a service ceiling of 29,000 feet and a range of over 700 miles. Armament consisted of six wing-mounted .50-caliber machine guns.

When the Japanese attacked the Hawaiian Islands on December 7, 1941, the USAAF Warhawks performed well, with Lieutenant George Welch shooting down four of the attackers in a P-40B. Welch would add to his score to become an ace. He ended the war with 16 total victories.

In the weeks after Pearl Harbor, five outnumbered Warhawk squadrons (mostly equipped with P-40Es) faced the Japanese in the Philippines, where Lieutenant Boyd Wagner became the *first* American ace of World War II.

The need for better high-altitude performance led Curtiss to replace the Allison engine with the Rolls-Royce-designed, Packard-manufactured 1,300-hp V-1650 Merlin engine in the P-40F through P-40L. These aircraft were then sent to the North Africa and Mediterranean theaters with the USAAF in the latter half of 1942. They also were supplied to the Royal Air Force in the same theaters as the Kittyhawk II. Merlin-powered Warhawks were also widely active in the Pacific during 1942–1943, serving in combat from Guadalcanal to New Guinea.

The most widely produced Warhawk was the P-40N, of which over 5,000 were produced. They began to enter USAAF service in March 1943, and although the superior P-47 and P-51 were coming on line at the same time, P-40Ns were being produced so rapidly, they gave the USAAF a chance to concentrate large numbers of aircraft in the field, while waiting for production momentum on the P-47 and P-51 assembly lines to build up.

The P-40N Warhawk had a wingspan of 37 feet 4 inches, and a length of 33 feet 4 inches. It weighed 7,400 pounds fully loaded and fueled. It was powered by an Allison 1,360-hp, liquid-cooled V-1710-81 engine that gave it a top speed of 378 mph. It had a service ceiling of 38,000 feet and a range of over 1,000 miles. Armament consisted of six wing-mounted .50-caliber machine guns and there were wing racks for bombs or extra fuel tanks.

By 1944, the P-40 was gradually phased out of service with the USAAF and the Royal Air Force, although exports to Australia, Russia, China, and Brazil increased until 1944. The last of over 13,700 P-40s was delivered in November 1944, and except for northern Europe, where their role had been entirely usurped by the P-51D, they continued in service on most fronts until the end of the war.

The Lockheed P-38 Lightning was one of the most important fighters in the USAAF arsenal through most of World War II. Development of the aircraft began in June 1937 when the Air Corps called for a very fast, twin-engine air superiority fighter. Lockheed's Hall Hibbard and Kelly Johnson (later the head of the legendary Lockheed Skunk Works) gave the P-38 its unusual configuration to accommodate its twin 1,150-hp Allison V-12s (later Lightnings would sport yet more powerful engines), complete with General Electric superchargers, and its awesome armament. The ingenious contra-rotating propellers erased the often troublesome prop torque effect.

The XP-38 prototype's top speed of 417 mph, demonstrated in 1939, made the Lightning the fastest fighter of its day. It was armed with four .50-caliber machine guns and a cannon that ranged from 20mm to 37mm, depending on the model of the aircraft.

The definitive Lightnings were the P-38D, with a top speed of 400-plus mph, a ceiling of 39,000 feet, and a range of 1,425 miles; and the P-38J, with a top speed of 414 mph, a ceiling of 44,000 feet, and a range of 2,260 miles.

The P-38 saw its first full deployment in Europe in 1942, where the Germans called it the "Fork-Tailed Devil." In the Pacific Theater, the Lightning proved itself to be fast, powerful, maneuverable, and extremely deadly. It also had the range that the USAAF needed to cover the vast distances between the islands.

The Republic P-47 Thunderbolt was used as often in World War II as a fighter-bomber as it was an air superiority fighter, and it was often overshadowed by the P-51 Mustang. However, the highest-scoring USAAF aces in the European Theater all flew Thunderbolts.

The P-47 evolved from the prewar Republic Aviation

P-43 Lancer, which was delivered to the USAAF in 1941. By then, however, the USAAF was concentrating on development of the heavier and more powerful P-47. While the P-43 was powered by a 1,200-hp Pratt & Whitney R-1830-47, the first P-47 (designated XP-47B) was designed around a 2,000-hp Pratt & Whitney R-2800 Double Wasp. The first production P-47B was delivered immediately after Pearl Harbor and several squadrons were active by the spring of 1942. The first of over 600 P-47Cs went into combat over Europe in September 1942.

The definitive Thunderbolt was the P-47D, of which over 12,000 would be produced. The P-47D had a wingspan of 40 feet 9 inches, and a length of 36 feet 1 inches. It weighed 14,500 pounds fully loaded and fueled. The basic P-47D powerplant was the 2,300-hp, air-cooled Pratt & Whitney Double Wasp series, including the R-2800-59 and the R-2800-63, among others. It had a top speed of about 430 mph, a service ceiling of 42,000 feet, and a range of up to 1,700 miles, although its operational radius fully armed was less. Armament consisted of eight .50 caliber machine guns. All P-47Ds were equipped to carry 500-pound bombs, and later production blocks had underwing launching stubs for ten five-inch rockets.

The first P-47Ds, like the earlier Thunderbolts, had a tall rear fuselage—with no direct rear view from the cockpit—and were nicknamed "Razorbacks." After April 1944, most P-47Ds, as well as the subsequent P-47M and P-47N, had bubble canopies and were known affectionately as "Jugs."

Because of their long range, the USAAF earmarked the first batches of P-47s for assignment to the Eighth Air Force in England, where they were badly needed to escort bombers on raids into the heart of Germany. The first aerial victory by a P-47 came in April 1943, and by the end of the war in Europe, Thunderbolts would claim 3,082 kills in battle and 3,202 destroyed on the ground.

By the end of 1943, there were ten fighter groups in England that were equipped with P-47s, a truly formidable force. By that time, however, the North American P-51D Mustang was also present in large numbers. Because the Mustang was better suited for long-range air-to-air combat missions and the Thunderbolt was heavily armed and armored, the USAAF began to transfer the P-47s to the IX Fighter Command of the Ninth Air Force, which was conducting tactical sweeps over northern France in preparation for the invasion of Europe.

By D-Day, June 6, 1944, there were 17 Thunderbolt groups on hand for ground attack missions and for air superiority missions over the battlefield. By this time, a large number of Thunderbolts had also been assigned to 12 combat groups in the Twelfth Air Force in Italy for similar tasks. The later P-47Ds had the capability of carrying two 1,000-pound bombs. In operations in Europe, P-47s dropped 113,963 tons of bombs, more than any other fighter and more than all but three bomber types.

Thunderbolts were assigned to two fighter groups with the Fourteenth Air Force in China, and to the 1st Air Commando Group in India. In the Pacific, Jugs were sent into combat during the Saipan invasion in 1944, being flown off U.S. Navy escort carriers.

The first of over 1,600 P-47Ns were introduced at the end of 1944. They were the heaviest single-engine fighter of the war, could carry three 1,000-pound bombs, and had a combat radius of 1,000 miles. The P-47N had a short but intense career, being used extensively in the final four months of the war against Japan. In addition to their ground attack capability, they were an excellent air superiority weapon. On May 25, 1945, for example, P-47Ns of the 318th Fighter Group shot down 43 Japanese aircraft with no losses to themselves.

When production ended three months after the war itself, over 15,600 P-47s had been manufactured. Most served with the USAAF, but they were also delivered to the Royal Air Force (mainly in India), the Soviet air force, the Free French air force, the Brazilian air force (which flew combat missions in Italy), and to the Mexican air force (which flew combat missions in the Philippines).

After World War II, P-47s remained in the USAAF inventory, being redesignated as F-47s in 1947 when the USAAF became the U.S. Air Force. They were the only Air Force fighters on hand in Europe when the Berlin Blockade began in 1948. Gradually they were transferred to the Air National Guard or sold to foreign governments under the Military Assistance Program. Today, a relative handful remain on the air race and air show circuit in the United States.

The North American P-51 Mustang is remembered today as perhaps the greatest American fighter of World War II, but it ironically began its career as a ground attack bomber that the British Royal Air Force wanted and the USAAF did not. The idea for the Mustang even came about as a result of the customer wanting something else. In 1940, British aircraft manufacturing capacity was pushed to the limit and they needed more aircraft. They were buying large numbers of Kittyhawks (P-40Ds) from Curtiss, but they needed more than even Curtiss could produce. For this reason, North American Aviation was asked whether they could build Kittyhawks. The answer was to the affirmative, but North American countered with what they sold as a better idea.

North American proposed to the British that they could design a better airplane—using the same Allison V-1710 engine—and they could design it and build a prototype in four months. This was done and the prototype first flew in October 1940. The US Army Air Corps took a passing interest in the sleek new plane and ordered a couple for tests under the designation XP-51.

Production aircraft, known as Mustang I, reached England in April 1941, and tests showed them to be superior to the Kittyhawk, and they even outflew the great Spitfire in low-altitude operations. Armed with four 20mm cannons, the first Mustang Is were used in the ground attack role. When the United States entered the war, the first USAAF orders for the Mustang saw it in the photoreconnaissance aircraft role rather than as a fighter. In another twist in the Mustang story, the first large order was for it to be configured as a dive-bomber under the designation A-36 Apache. The A-36 began combat operations against targets in Italy from Tunisia and continued these activities from bases in Italy until the middle of 1944.

Meanwhile, in parallel development with the A-36, the USAAF was almost reluctantly putting the P-51 fighter into production. The Achilles' heel of the early Mustangs—as discovered by the British and confirmed by the Americans—was the relative weakness of the Allison engine. Britain began using the Rolls-Royce Merlin, and the results were so good that the Packard Motor Company started building the Merlin in the United States under the designation V-1650.

Powered by the 1,595-hp Packard V-1650 Merlin, the first production P-51B was finally delivered to the USAAF in May 1943. It was a moment of profound revelation for those who had doubted the Mustang's promise. Not only was it fast and maneuverable, it had the range to accompany Eighth Air Force bombers to any target in Germany. The P-51B had a wingspan of 37 feet, and a length of 32 feet 3 inches. It weighed 8,350 pounds fully loaded and fueled. The Merlin gave it a top speed of 440 mph at 30,000 feet, and it had a service ceiling of 42,000 feet and a range of 2,200 miles. Armament consisted of four .50-caliber machine guns.

Over 3,700 P-51Bs and P-51Cs would be built before the P-51D came on line in the spring of 1944. The P-51D represented a major design change. The high-topped rear fuselage was cut down and the greenhouse canopy was replaced by a bubble canopy, giving the pilot a 360-degree field of view. The P-51D became the definitive Mustang, and over 8,000 would be manufactured at the two North American Aviation plants at Inglewood, California, and Dallas, Texas. Most would go to the USAAF, but a few went to the Royal Air Force—who had been first to realize the Mustang's potential—as the Mustang IV.

The P-51D/Mustang IV had a wingspan and length matching those of the P-51B, but it had a gross weight of 10,000 pounds. It was powered by a 1,720-hp, liquid-cooled Packard V-1650-7 engine that gave it a top speed of 440 mph at 25,000 feet and the ability to climb 3,450 feet in one minute. It had a service ceiling like that of its older sibling and a range of 2,300 miles. Armament consisted of six, rather than four, .50-caliber machine guns.

By the time the war ended, the largest P-51 user was the USAAF Eighth Air Force, with 14 fighter groups, among them the 357th, which had scored 609 aerial victories with P-51s. The Mustang scored more such kills than any other Allied aircraft of the war, with 4,950 confirmed kills in the European Theater alone. Mustangs also saw service with the Fifth Air Force in the Pacific, with the Tenth Air Force in India, and with the Fourteenth Air Force in China. During the final offensive against Japan, three groups of P-51Ds were based on Iwo Jima to escort the B-29 bombing missions against Japanese targets.

The P-51 continued to evolve, with the most significant "post-D" Mustang being the P-51H, which appeared in February 1945, and of which only 555 were built. It was probably the fastest piston-engine aircraft to be in production during the war, with its V-1650-9 Merlin giving it a speed of 487 mph. Ultimately, over 15,400 Mustangs—more than half P-51Ds—were produced, most of them during the last two years of the war. After the war, the Mustang was retained in a frontline role until finally replaced by jets. Redesignated as F-51s in 1947 when the USAAF became the U.S. Air Force, they were delegated to the Air National Guard, but recalled to active duty when the Korean War started in 1950. Used primarily in a ground support role, the F-51s flew over 62,000 missions and remained in service with the air forces of South Korea, South Africa, and Australia, as well as the United States, until the last year of the war.

Baumler and Tinker: The Volunteers

The Spanish Civil War, which raged from 1936 to 1939, pitted Spain's Republican government against the eventually victorious Nationalist insurgents led by General Francisco Franco. This war was seen at the time as a sort of dress rehearsal for the weapons and tactics that would be used in World War II, particularly with regard to the use of airpower. Germany and Italy sent fully organized "volunteer" air-force contingents to help Franco, and the Soviet Union did the same to aid the Republicans.

Meanwhile, there were large numbers of actual volunteers who arrived in Spain to fight for one side or the other. Among these were many young Americans who wanted to fight with the Republicans against the evils that they could see in the fascist dictatorships of Hitler, Mussolini, and, potentially, Francisco Franco.

The Americans arrived in force in 1937 to join the Abraham Lincoln and George Washington battalions, which were part of the 15th International Brigade. This brigade also contained volunteers from Britain and Canada. Many American pilots also flew with the Republican air force and associated Soviet squadrons, where they were paid a base salary, plus $1,000—a considerable sum in the Depression era—for every Nationalist aircraft they shot down. The two most successful Americans in the Republican air force would be Albert J. "Ajax" Baumler, who scored 13 victories in Spain, and Frank Glasgow Tinker, who claimed eight. They flew Polikarpov I-15s, and later I-16s, with the Soviet squadron, Escuadrilla Tarkhov, as well as with Escuadrilla Lacalle and 1 Escuadrilla de Caza. Tinker also flew with the Soviet Escuadrillas de Moscas.

Ajax Baumler arrived in Spain on December 27, 1936, and scored his first victory, an Italian Fiat CR-32, on March 16, 1937, while on a patrol near Madrid. On March 20, Baumler claimed another Fiat near Brihuega, when his unit broke up a bombing mission conducted by an Italian strike force with fighter escort. On April 17, while flying out of Sarrion, he scored one confirmed and one "probable" in an encounter with some Heinkel He-51 fighters of Germany's Condor Legion.

By the end of May, Baumler and Tinker were flying the Polikarpov I-16s, and Baumler scored his first victory in this type on June 2 near Segovia. His final victory in the Spanish Civil War came on July 8, when he destroyed a Fiat during a large battle in which his flight intercepted a bomber strike against Quejormas. Ajax Baumler went on to score one victory while flying with the American Volunteer Group in China, and 3.5 with the USAAF 75th Fighter Squadron during World War II.

Frank Tinker, who first began flying in Spain on January 7, 1937, scored his first Fiat CR-32 on March 14. In April, he moved to the Escuadrillas de Moscas, with whom, on July 12, he became the first American to shoot down a Messerschmitt Bf-109. He shot down a second on July 17, and scored his last victory, a Fiat, the following day.

Hill: Flying with the Tigers

If the Spanish Civil War presented a "dress rehearsal" for World War II in Europe, the Sino-Japanese War that began in 1937 was certainly a precursor to World War II in the Far East. Indeed, when Japan went to war with the United States and Britain in 1941, the Sino-Japanese War simply became the Asiatic Theater of World War II. Just as Germany, Italy, and the Soviet Union sent organized air forces of "volunteers" to fight one another in Spain, the United States had sent a "volunteer" air force to China to help the Chinese fight Japan. The American Volunteer Group (AVG) that fought in China was the brainchild of General Claire Chennault.

Chennault had quit his job as a Texas high-school principal to become a flyer in World War I, but the war ended before he earned his wings. He decided to remain in the Army after the war and by 1925, he was commanding a pursuit squadron in Hawaii. Chennault became one of the Air Corps' rising stars in the field of combat tactics for fighters and he was named to head the Pursuit Section. In 1934, he organized an aerobatic team called Three Men on a Flying Trapeze to demonstrate his ideas.

Chennault retired from the Army in 1937, and was hired by China's first lady, Madame Chiang Kai-shek, to set up a school in China to train military pilots. China was then involved in a losing war with the Japanese, and Chennault watched the situation deteriorate from bad to worse. The Chinese air force was losing badly at the hands of the Japanese. In 1940, with the clandestine approval of the United States State Department, Chennault put together the American Volunteer Group. It was a fighter squadron composed of American civilian volunteer pilots who'd been trained in the U.S. Army Air Corps, some of them by Chennault himself.

Better known as the "Flying Tigers" because of the jagged teeth they painted on the cowlings of their Curtiss P-40 aircraft, the AVG pilots achieved amazing results against the Japanese because of the tactics they practiced. Some of the pilots who served with the AVG were Ajax Baumler, the top-scoring American in the Spanish Civil War; Robert Scott, who wrote the book *God Is My Co-pilot;* and Gregory "Pappy" Boyington, who scored six victories with the AVG while on leave from the U.S. Marine Corps. He later went back to the Marines during World War II, where he would score 22 victories and earn the Congressional Medal of Honor.

The highest-scoring ace with the AVG was David Lee "Tex" Hill, with 12.75 victories (some sources list 11.25). Born in 1914, the son of American missionaries in Korea, Hill was an aviator with the U.S. Navy during the 1930s. He flew Douglas SBD Dauntless and Vought SBU scout bombers on board the USS *Yorktown,* USS *Ranger,* and USS *Saratoga.* Hill joined the AVG in April 1941, flying missions out of Toungoo, halfway between Rangoon and Mandalay in Burma. Here, the Flying Tigers operated from a crude landing strip and lived with insects and unbearable heat and humidity. However, for Hill it meant trading his $125 per month ensign's pay for a $750 monthly salary, plus a bonus of $500 for each Japanese aircraft destroyed.

Chennault had studied Japanese aircraft and tactics and he taught the Tigers how to win. He instructed them not to get into a dogfight with the more maneuverable Japanese A6M Zero, but to use the P-40's speed to their advantage in fast, slashing attacks. The AVG was quite successful against the numerically superior Japanese, and their attacks on Japanese bombers are credited with keeping the Burma Road, China's critical overland supply route, from being destroyed or falling into Japanese hands during the dark days before the United States and Britain entered the war against Japan. On July 4, 1942, the American Volunteer Group was incorporated into the newly formed USAAF China Air Task Force as the 23rd Fighter Group. General Chennault was brought back into the USAAF to command the Task Force, which later became the Fourteenth Air Force. Robert Scott would become the commander of the 23rd Fighter Group and Tex Hill would command the 75th Fighter Squadron. During World War II, Hill added six victories to his score and Scott scored five.

Wagner: The USAAF's First Ace

World War II began for the United States as a rude wake-up call on the morning of December 7, 1941. The primary target of the Japanese strike force was the U.S. Navy base at Pearl Harbor in Hawaii, but the Japanese launched simultaneous attacks on American facilities in the United States Commonwealth of the Philippines. Since the Philippines is located across the international date line, it was already December 8 when the attacks came. The attack on Hawaii had been a hit-and-run, but the attack on the Philippines was the opening blow of a campaign. The Japanese meant to invade and occupy the Philippines. The American and Philippine forces fought back with all they had—which was not much, compared with the well-armed Japanese invaders.

One of the Americans' most potent weapons in the futile defense of the Philippines turned out to be a young USAAF pilot named Boyd D. "Buzz" Wagner.

He had studied aeronautical engineering at the University of Pittsburgh for three years before joining the Air Corps and completing flight training in June 1938. In December 1940, he was assigned to the 24th Pursuit Group, based at Clark Field, north of Manila in the Philippines. He was later assigned to command the group's 17th Pursuit Squadron, which was equipped with Curtiss P-40s.

When the Japanese struck, nearly half the USAAF strength in the Philippines was destroyed on the ground, and the remainder were badly outnumbered. On December 11, Buzz Wagner was on patrol toward the beaches on the northern part of the Philippine main island of Luzon, where the Japanese invasion forces were coming ashore. The Japanese had already begun landing troops and aircraft at Aparri, a base that they would use to support their ground attack on Manila and the rest of Luzon.

Lining up for a strafing attack on the airfield, Wagner came under fire from Japanese ships offshore and he was attacked by five Imperial Japanese Navy Air Force A6M Zeros. He managed to elude the attackers long enough to make two attacks on parked enemy aircraft. Having destroyed ten on the ground, Wagner shot down two of the Zeros that were after him. He thought he had shaken the rest, and he headed back to Clark. However, two of the Zeros tried to ambush him. He managed to down both. His score now stood at four.

On December 15, Wagner led an early-morning, low-level, three-P-40 strike on another airfield at Vigan that the invaders were using. After a bomb run in which one P-40 was lost, Wagner attacked with his guns, destroying nine enemy aircraft before one Zero managed to get airborne. As the A6M came up behind him, Wagner chopped the throttle, let the pursuer overshoot, then shot him down. Buzz Wagner had his fifth, and a week after the attack on Pearl Harbor, America had its first ace. He would later be awarded the Distinguished Service Cross for this action.

A few days later, an antiaircraft artillery shell exploded dangerously close to Wagner's aircraft, shattering his windshield and leaving glass fragments in his face and left eye. He was evacuated to Australia for medical attention. The Philippines was conquered by Japan before Wagner could fly again, but as soon as he was able, he was back in action, flying P-39 Airacobras in the campaign in New Guinea. The air battles over New Guinea in 1942 were some of the biggest of the Pacific Theater, and they were battles in which the Imperial Japanese Navy Air Force held the upper hand.

In his last air combat action, Wagner was involved in a huge fight in which Japanese aircraft jumped a flight of P-39s, destroying four of them. The remaining Americans fought back, destroying a like number of Japanese. Of this total, Wagner claimed three.

In April 1942, the USAAF brought Buzz Wagner and his valuable experience back to the United States, where he would help to train future fighter pilots. Ironically, his last flight was a routine one. En route from Eglin Field in Florida to Maxwell Field at Montgomery, Alabama, on November 29, 1942, Wagner suffered a mechanical failure and crashed to his death. Wagner High School at the post-war Clark Air Base was named for him.

Bong: America's Ace of Aces

Richard Ira "Dick" Bong was the highest-scoring American ace of World War II, and indeed of all time. He was born in Superior, Wisconsin, on September 24, 1920, the first of nine children born to Swedish immigrant Carl Bong and Dora Bryce Bong. He grew up on the family farm in northwest Wisconsin, near Poplar, where he learned self-reliance, an ethic of hard work, and—when predators came calling—good marksmanship. He entered the Superior State Teachers College in the autumn of 1938, but he was anxious to learn to fly, so he joined the government-sponsored Civilian Pilot Training Program at the college and earned his pilot's license in a Piper Cub.

In May 1941, Dick Bong enlisted in the Army Air Corps Aviation Cadet Program. After basic flight training at Gardner Field near Taft, California—where he soloed in a Vultee BT-13—Bong was assigned to Luke Army Air Field, Arizona, for advanced pilot training in North American AT-6 Texans. His gunnery instructor at Luke was an officer named Barry Goldwater, later the longtime Arizona senator, who would be the Republican candidate for President of the United States in 1964.

He earned his fighter pilot wings—along with high praise from his instructors—and was commissioned into the USAAF in January 1942, a month after the United States entered World War II. Ironically, the USAAF was reluctant to transfer him to an active combat unit because he was such a good instructor. In May, he was sent to Hamilton Field north of San Francisco, where he was assigned to the 49th Pursuit Squadron of the 14th Pursuit Group as a gunnery instructor in the Lockheed P-38.

Faced with the prospect of not getting into action, Bong engineered an infraction of rules so that he would be punished by an overseas assignment. He looped an airplane around the center span of the Golden Gate Bridge in San Francisco, and as a "penàlty," he was sent to join the Fifth Air Force in Australia in September 1942. Actually, his commander at the time was General George Kenney, who was, himself, being reassigned to the Southwest Pacific Theater to command the Fifth Air Force. Kenney has been promised P-38s and he wanted pilots. He wanted Dick Bong.

When Bong reached Brisbane, he was assigned to the 9th Fighter Squadron of the 49th Fighter Group, but he was temporarily detailed to the 39th Fighter Squadron of the 35th Fighter Group. Kenney sent his best pilots where they could fly with experienced units and gain some combat experience themselves. The 35th Fighter Group was in the center of the action in the huge fighter battles that were raging over New Guinea between Allied units based at Port Moresby, and the Imperial Japanese Navy Air Force units based near Lae on the other side of the vast island.

The young pilot from Wisconsin got his New Guinea underfire training and he scored his first two aerial victories in December 1942. By January 8, 1943, Bong had become an ace with a Silver Star and the Distinguished Flying Cross—while still on temporary duty with the 39th Fighter Squadron. By March, he had scored nine, including one Mitsubishi A6M Zero and six Nakajima Ki-43 Oscars.

Reassigned to his "permanent" unit, the 49th Fighter Group, Bong became a double ace by April 14, 1943. Most of his scoring missions resulted in single or double victories, but he had one four-victory mission on July 26, for which he was awarded the Distinguished Service Cross. By now, he had equaled the best score in the Fifth Air Force, with 16, and he continued to work toward his goal of becoming the top USAAF ace in the Southwest Pacific Theater.

In the autumn of 1943, Bong returned home, where he was invited to appear at the Superior State Teachers College Homecoming. In the course of the festivities, he discovered that since all of the men were away at war, there was no Homecoming King—so he was chosen to get the crown. As the story goes, the 1942 outgoing Homecoming Queen was supposed to crown the 1943 Homecoming Queen, but when 19-year-old Marjorie Vattendahl met the handsome young war hero in his uniform and medals, she was so awestruck that Bong had to crown the 1943 Queen.

It was love at first sight both ways. When Bong returned to the Southwest Pacific Theater, he renamed his P-38 *Marge* and mounted a large photo of Marjorie Vattendahl on the side. Soon *Marge* was one of the most recognized Lightnings in the 49th Fighter Group. On February 15, 1944, Dick and *Marge* scored their first victory together, a Kawasaki Ki-61 that went down in flames near Cape Hoskins, New Britain. Not all of their missions were triumphs, however. On March 8, Bong's friend, the 20-victory ace Thomas J. Lynch, was shot down by ground fire while the two men were on a strafing run.

In April 1944, Bong hit the magic 27-victory count, becoming the first USAAF ace of World War II to surpass Eddie Rickenbacker's World War I score. General Kenney sent him a case of champagne, but General Arnold, knowing that Bong was not a drinker, sent two cases of Coca Cola, accompanied by the message "I understand you prefer this type of refreshment to others. You thoroughly deserve to have the kind you want. The Army Air Forces are proud of you and your splendid record. Congratulations!"

Rickenbacker himself sent a congratulatory telegram, telling Dick Bong: "Just received the good news that you are the first one to break my record in World War I by bringing down 27 planes in combat, as well as your promotion, so justly deserved. I hasten to offer my sincere congratulations with the hope that you will double or triple this number. But in trying, use the same calculating techniques that has brought you results to date, for we will need your kind back home after this war is over. My promise of a case of Scotch still holds. So be on the lookout for it."

Bong went back to the United States again in the summer of 1944. Now a celebrity, he was used on a War Bond tour, but he also found time to attend the USAAF gunnery school to perfect his skills even further. When he returned to the Pacific in September, Bong was now officially a "gunnery instructor." His instructions from General Kenney were to avoid combat. The USAAF didn't want to lose the new Rickenbacker. However, gunnery instructor Bong did not stay out of the action. On October 10, General Kenney grounded Bong, whose score had now reached 30. However, by this time, the 49th Fighter Group had relocated to the Philippines, where American forces had just landed. Kenney needed all the help he could get from the 49th Fighter Group to support these operations, so he let Bong talk him into returning to the air.

On November 15, Bong scored his 36th victory, prompting Kenney to recommend him for the Congressional Medal of Honor. In awarding the medal, General Douglas MacArthur, the theater commander and himself a Medal of Honor honoree, commented that Bong "has ruled the air from New Guinea to the Philippines."

The official Medal of Honor citation read: "For conspicuous gallantry and intrepidity in action above and beyond the call of duty in the Southwest Pacific area from 10 October to 15 November 1944. Though assigned to duty as gunnery instructor and neither required nor expected to perform combat duty, Major Bong voluntarily and at his own urgent request engaged in repeated combat missions, including unusually hazardous sorties over Balikpapan, Borneo, and in the Leyte area of the Philippines. His aggressiveness and daring resulted in his shooting down eight enemy airplanes during this period."

In the meanwhile, a competition had begun to develop between Bong and another Fifth Air Force P-38 pilot. Thomas McGuire had been in the Southwest Pacific since March 1943; he had topped the Rickenbacker number and was keeping pace with Bong. In November 1944, Bong and McGuire each scored three to bring their respective scores to 36 and 29.

On the third anniversary of Pearl Harbor, both men scored two victories, and on December 15 and 17, Bong shot down two more to bring his total to 40. Nearly half his victories had now come since he had completed a 158-mission combat tour, and was no longer required to fly such missions. Kenney finally decided to ground Bong again. He was America's top-scoring ace on any front and he had just been awarded the Congressional Medal of Honor personally by General Douglas MacArthur. Kenney sent him home for the last time.

When Dick Bong reached the United States on New Year's Eve, he was still America's top-scoring ace, but McGuire had shot down three Zeros on Christmas, and four more the next day, to bring his score to 38. On January 7, 1945, however, McGuire lost his life (see following section) in combat, having scored no further victories.

Richard Bong and Marge Vattendahl were married February 10, 1945, at the Concordia Lutheran Church in Superior, Wisconsin, and after the honeymoon, the group reported for duty at the Flight Test Section of the USAAF

Air Technical Services Command at Wright Field near Dayton, Ohio. America's ace of aces had been earmarked to be part of the first generation of American jet fighter pilots. By this time, the USAAF was ready to start forming active jet fighter squadrons, using the Lockheed P-80 Shooting Star, the first American jet fighter to go into production. They were anxious to bring the best pilots up to speed in the new weapon, and Bong was the best of the best. At Wright Field, he was briefed on the technical aspects of the P-80, and in June, he was sent to Burbank, California, home of the Lockheed Aircraft Company. Having scored all of his 40 victories in a Lockheed fighter, Dick Bong would now test the newest Lockheed.

Beginning on July 7, Dick Bong logged four hours in 11 flights with the jet, and took off on his 12th on the afternoon of August 6, 1945. Just after the aircraft became airborne, the engine flamed out and the P-80 went down, killing Bong instantly. Ironically, Bong would die one day after the nuclear strike on Hiroshima that hastened the end of World War II. (On August 6 in the United States, it is already August 7 across the international date line.)

Out in the Pacific, General Kenney was on his way to General MacArthur's headquarters when he got the news. "I stopped thinking of the atom bomb which had wiped out Hiroshima that morning," he said. "I even stopped thinking of the capitulation of Japan, which we all knew was about to take place in a few days. Wherever I landed, I found that the whole Fifth Air Force felt the same, that we had lost a loved one, someone we had been glad to see out of combat and on his way home eight months before. Major Richard I. Bong of Poplar was dead. . . . We not only loved him, we boasted about him, we were proud of him. That's why each of us got a lump in our throats when we read that telegram about his death. Major Bong, Ace of American Aces in all our wars, is destined to hold the title for all time. With the weapons we possess today, no war of the future will last long enough for any pilot to run up 40 victories again.

"His country and the Air Force must never forget their number-one fighter pilot, who will inspire other fighter pilots and countless thousands of youngsters who will want to follow in his footsteps every time that any nation or coalition of nations dares to challenge our right to think, speak, and live as a free people." Eddie Rickenbacker commented that Bong was "an example of the tragic and terrible price we must pay to maintain principles of human rights, of greater value than life itself. This gallant Air Force hero will be remembered because he made his final contribution to aviation in the dangerous role of test pilot of an untried experimental plane, a deed that places him among the stouthearted pioneers who gave their lives in the conquest of sky and space."

Richard Ira Bong was buried in the Poplar Cemetery on August 8. Marge remarried several years later and had two daughters. She did not speak publicly about her first husband for four decades, but after 1985, when she attended the dedication of the Richard Ira Bong Memorial Bridge in Minnesota, she became active in veterans' affairs and in the efforts to build the Richard Ira Bong Heritage Center, located on the bay front in Superior, that honors all the Americans, especially from Wisconsin and Minnesota, who served in World War II. The centerpiece of the facility is a Lockheed P-38 that was restored by volunteers at the Minnesota Air National Guard in nearby Duluth and painted to be a replica of Bong's *Marge,* in which he scored his key 1944 victories.

In recalling her generation, the World War II generation, Marge is quoted recently as saying that "I feel that the people in that era were very unique. . . . There was such a sense of pride and patriotism. As far as Richard is concerned, he was one of the most visible heroes of the war. But he didn't feel like a hero. He expressed a sentiment that summed it up so well. He said he was just doing his job."

McGuire: He Died Trying

The second-highest-scoring American ace of World War II, Thomas Buchanan "Tommy" McGuire, Jr., was clearly one of the best combat pilots of World War II, but he spent the last year of his life racing to catch Richard "Dick" Ira Bong. He never succeeded, and he died trying.

Tommy McGuire was a tough and ambitious Irish-American from New Jersey who was a natural when it came to air combat. "Go in close," he would tell the younger combat pilots, echoing the words of legendary aces such as "Sailor" Malan and Erich Hartmann. "And when you think you're too close, go in closer."

He was born in Ridgewood, New Jersey, on August 1, 1920, attended the Georgia Institute of Technology ("Georgia Tech"), and later joined the U.S. Army Air Forces as an aviation cadet at MacDill Field in Florida on July 12, 1941. McGuire trained at Randolph Field and Kelly Field in Texas and earned his pilot's wings in February 1942, two months after Pearl Harbor, and requested a combat assignment. At that time, United States strategic necessity dictated efforts to halt the Japanese advances in the South Pacific and the North Pacific. Lieutenant McGuire was assigned to the latter, as it was assumed that the Japanese were then headed for Alaska.

While they did capture several islands in the Aleutian chain southwest of Alaska, they never launched their invasion the mainland, and duty in Alaska became synonymous with boredom and inaction. After a year of seeing little action, McGuire asked to be reassigned to a theater where he could use his combat flying aptitude. Finally, in March 1943, he was reassigned to the 49th Fighter Group of the USAAF Fifth Air Force in the Southwest Pacific, where aerial combat was furious and constant.

In June 1943, he was transferred to the 475th "Satan's Angels" Fighter Group. Based at Dobodura on New Guinea, it was the first group in the Fifth Air Force to be composed entirely of Lockheed P-38 Lightnings, which were faster and had longer range than the Curtiss P-40s and Bell P-39s, which had previously been the backbone of the Fifth. At last in the air combat environment for which he had yearned, Tommy McGuire achieved his first three aerial victories over Dagua, New Guinea, on August 18, and made ace by the end of the month. By October 17, he would reach "Lucky 13."

It was "Lucky 13" only in that he was lucky to be alive. On October 17, McGuire claimed three Mitsubishi A6M Zeros in one engagement, but as he banked away to help another pilot whose Lightning was damaged, he was bounced by three Zeros that shot up *Pudgy*—one of a series of P-38s that he flew, all named for his wife. As *Pudgy* nosed over and started to go down, and as it passed through 12,000 feet, McGuire tried to jump, but he was caught and couldn't get out. At 5,000 feet, he finally broke free, but discovered that the rip cord on his parachute had torn off. He finally got the parachute open just in time, but spent 40 minutes treading water in Oro Bay hoping that a U.S. Navy patrol boat would reach him before the sharks or the Japanese.

By this time, Tommy McGuire and Dick Bong were the leading USAAF aces in the theater—with Bong eight victories ahead—so a competition naturally ensued. Both men eagerly sought the distinction of being the top-scoring USAAF ace in the Pacific. When Bong went home on leave, McGuire expected to make up the difference, but he wound up grounded by malaria until the end of December. The day after Christmas, he led a 475th Fighter Group force covering a U.S. Navy convoy off Cape Gloucester on New Britain. The convoy came under attack, and McGuire led the counterattack. His formation destroyed ten dive-bombers and three fighters. To Tommy McGuire went three aerial victories and a Distinguished Service Cross for leadership and heroism.

Two of the top-scoring USAAF aces in the Southwest Pacific, Neel Kearby and Tommy Lynch, were shot down early in 1944, leaving Bong and McGuire at the apogee of acedom in the region. Bong pushed his score to 27 in April 1944—becoming the first USAAF ace of World War II to surpass Eddie Rickenbacker's World War I score— and was sent home to take part in a celebrity War Bond tour.

While Bong was stateside, McGuire—now the commander of the 475th Fighter Group's 431st Fighter Squadron—was gaining on him. As an interesting footnote to the history of the 475th Fighter Group, it was in the summer of 1944 that the great aviation hero Charles A. Lindbergh joined the group—unofficially. He was serving as a civilian "consultant" with United Aircraft, makers of the Pratt & Whitney engines used in many American combat aircraft, albeit not in the P-38s, which had General Motors Allison engines. He was in the Pacific to observe, and he wound up teaching techniques for extending the range of the P-38. He did fly a number of combat missions and is known to have scored two aerial victories. These were never officially credited.

The competition between McGuire and Bong—which had reportedly become an obsession with McGuire—resumed when Bong returned to action by September 1944, and continued after the 475th Fighter Group relocated to Leyte in the Philippines after the October invasion. It was in October that the faster, longer-range P-38Ls were delivered to the 475th Fighter Group. McGuire's new aircraft—his fifth P-38—was promptly identified with his wife's nickname as *Pudgy V*.

On October 14, McGuire scored three more victories in his new aircraft, but the goal of reaching Bong's score still eluded him. According to the folklore, the two men were cordial to one another, and are often reported to have been friends. In any case, Bong—who was ahead by a comfortable margin—seems to have taken the competition less seriously than McGuire.

In November, Bong and McGuire scored three each to bring their respective scores to 36 and 29. On the third anniversary of Pearl Harbor, both men scored two victories, and on December 15 and 17, Bong shot down two more to bring his total to 40. With this, Fifth Air Force commander General George Kenney decided to ground Bong. He was America's top-scoring ace on any front and he had just been awarded the Congressional Medal of Honor personally by General Douglas MacArthur. Kenney did not want to lose him, so he was grounded and sent home—permanently.

This left Tommy McGuire—the lanky 24-year-old who grew a black mustache to make himself look older—as the top-scoring USAAF ace still in combat. He was also now the commander of the 431st Fighter Squadron of the 475th Fighter Group.

When Dick Bong reached the United States, he was still America's top-scoring ace, but McGuire shot down three

Zeros during a bomber escort mission on Christmas day, and four more on December 26, to bring his score to 38—two short of Bong. In the latter engagement, he set his sights on one Zero that was attacking a B-24 and shot it down with a 45-degree deflection shot at a range of 400 yards. It was an impossible shot—but he did it.

Dick Bong was due to arrive in the United States on New Year's Eve, and there were plans for him to be greeted as "America's leading ace." General Kenney was under pressure from those who were choreographing the public relations aspect of Bong's arrival. They wanted to be sure that Bong *really was* "America's leading ace." He had been for months, and they wanted it to stay that way—at least until after the homecoming celebrations. With this in mind, Kenney grounded McGuire until January 6, 1945.

On January 7, 1945, McGuire took off before dawn from Marsten Field on Leyte, intending to add to his score and hoping to add three. He was not flying *Pudgy V,* but rather another P-38L that was assigned to fellow pilot Fred Champlin. He was accompanied by his usual wingman, Edwin Weaver, with a second element led by Jack Rittmayer with his wingman, Douglass Thropp. Each of the P-38s carried two 160-gallon external fuel tanks. The mission was to be a fighter sweep of Negros Island, which was known to have Japanese airfields. According to various sources, the mission was not officially authorized.

They made most of the flight at 10,000 feet, but at Negros, the weather forced them to descend to 6,000 feet, and then to 1,400 feet. After failing to engage the enemy over Fabrica, McGuire ordered the flight to proceed to another Japanese base. On the way, Rittmayer experienced engine trouble, and he became separated from the others while flying through a cloud.

Weaver then spotted a Japanese Nakajima Ki-43 fighter

ahead and below the Americans heading in the opposite direction. The aircraft passed one another, and the Japanese pilot, Akira Sugimoto, turned to attack. He scored a hit on Thropp's P-38, but Rittmayer, who had caught up with the others, opened fire on him.

Instead of breaking off his attack, Sugimoto slipped away from Rittmayer and opened fire on Weaver. There was now a serious dogfight going, and the pilots would obviously be inclined to jettison their drop tanks in order to be better able to maneuver. However, at some point early in the fight, McGuire specifically ordered that the tanks not be jettisoned. Dropping their extra fuel would greatly reduce the amount of time that they would have to spend over Negros before making the long flight back. It is theorized that McGuire gave the order because he was anxious to have as much time as possible to hunt for his three decisive kills.

When he came under attack, Weaver called for McGuire to help him. McGuire turned to go after Sugimoto, but his P-38 started to stall. Instead of backing off the tight turning maneuver, McGuire appeared to turn harder. His aircraft stalled, nosed over, and started to go down. Since he was barely more than 1,000 feet above the jungle, McGuire had no time to recover control. The tight, fast turn at low altitude—with the heavy fuel tanks still in place—was what caused McGuire's P-38 to stall and spin. He was too low to recover and he crashed to his death in a ball of fire.

Weaver saw the explosion as McGuire crashed. Rittmayer and Thropp chased Sugimoto's damaged aircraft. Various versions of the story say that Sugimoto crashlanded and either died of bullet wounds suffered in the dogfight or was killed by Filipino guerrillas.

At this point, a second Japanese aircraft, a Nakajima Ki-84 piloted by Mirunori Fukuda, entered the fight. Weaver returned Fukuda's fire, but Fukuda then opened up on Rittmayer, who was trying to turn to get a shot. Rittmayer's P-38—also behaving sluggishly because of its fuel tanks—received a fatal burst from the Ki-84's guns and went down, crashing not far from where McGuire had crashed.

Fukuda then turned his attention toward Thropp, who escaped into a cloud bank with a damaged engine. Weaver then attempted to find Fukuda in the clouds. Failing that, he rendezvoused with Thropp and the two headed for home.

The news of McGuire's loss would not be released to the public for ten days. When he heard the news, Dick Bong is reported to have said sadly, "I was afraid of that."

Major Thomas Buchanan McGuire was posthumously awarded the Congressional Medal of Honor for his heroic actions on December 25 and 26, 1944. General George Kenney personally presented McGuire's Medal of Honor to his widow, Marilynn "Pudgy" McGuire, on May 8, 1946, at the City Hall in Paterson, New Jersey. Charles Lindbergh was reportedly in the crowd of family and friends.

Marilynn McGuire returned to her hometown of San Antonio, Texas, where she had met McGuire when he was in flight school, and later remarried. In September 1949, the former Fort Dix Army Air Field near the New Jersey state capital of Trenton was reopened as a U.S. Air Force facility and renamed McGuire Air Force Base in Tommy's honor. During that same year, McGuire's remains were identified and recovered from Negros Island and interred at Arlington National Cemetery near Washington, D.C.

Kearby: He Also Died Trying

Three of the top two dozen USAAF aces in the Pacific Theater would earn the Congressional Medal of Honor.

Two were the top two aces—Dick Bong and Tommy McGuire—and the third was Neel Kearby, the number-four USAAF ace in the theater. Kearby, like McGuire, had also figured in the Dick Bong story, because, before his "ace race" with McGuire, Bong had been in a similar race with Kearby. In fact, in the months before Bong scored his magic 27th to top Rickenbacker, he and Kearby had been tied several times. This was something that McGuire had never been able to accomplish.

Kearby arrived in Australia on June 30, 1943, assigned to the 348th Fighter Group, the first unit in the area to be equipped with the P-47 Thunderbolt. For a year, the signature USAAF fighter in the region had been the P-38 Lightning and the P-38s showed little respect for the single-engine "Jug."

As the story goes, Kearby demonstrated the P-47's prowess in a mock dogfight with a P-38, but operationally, the Thunderbolts were hindered by their lack of range compared with the Lightnings, a situation that was exacerbated by their lack of external fuel tanks until General George Kenney arranged for them to be manufactured locally.

From Australia, the 348th Fighter Group was forward-deployed to Port Moresby on New Guinea to bide its time until the drop tanks arrived. The unit finally got its first taste of combat on August 16, but Neel Kearby did not score his first aerial victories until September 4. He opened with a double, a fighter and a bomber, and he scored his third on September 15. He had openly stated his intention to be the highest-scoring USAAF ace of World War II, and promised that he would not go home until he had scored 50 victories.

On October 11, Kearby was leading a four-Thunderbolt reconnaissance patrol near Wewak, northwest of Port

Moresby, when he observed a Mitsubishi A6M below them. Kearby attacked, converting his altitude advantage to speed, and destroyed the Japanese fighter. The four USAAF fighters had just resumed their patrol when they observed a huge armada of Japanese warplanes far below. There were a dozen bombers and three times that number of fighters, obviously headed for a raid on Allied positions.

Despite the enemy's numerical superiority, Kearby figured that surprise would convert to even odds, so he ordered an attack. In his first high-speed pass, Kearby claimed three, while Bill Dunham and John Moore each scored singles.

Kearby then ordered his patrol to break contact and return to base, but he observed the fourth American, Raymond Gallagher, under attack by a pair of Kawanishi Ki-61s. He dived into the fray and shot down both of the Japanese fighters. At that point, Dunham and Moore observed Kearby fighting six Ki-61s. He probably downed at least two of these, but his gun camera ran out of film, so his total for the day would be six confirmed and one probable.

For setting an American record for victories scored in a single day, General George Kenney recommended Kearby for the Congressional Medal of Honor. At the time that General Douglas MacArthur personally awarded the decoration, Kearby was tied with Dick Bong as the highest-scoring aces in the USAAF, with 19 confirmed victories.

Bong was first to break the tie, increasing his score to 21. In turn, Kearby scored a double on January 9, 1944. The score was tied again. General Kenney, meanwhile, had grown concerned about these young pilots becoming careless in their rush to pile up victories. He ordered Bong and Kearby to limit themselves to one kill per mission. If they scored, they were to then break off their attack. As it turned out, February came and went with neither man scoring any victories. It was probably inevitable that the first man to get a kill in March would want to keep up the momentum and make up for lost time.

On March 5, Neel Kearby and Bill Dunham, along with Sam Blair, were on patrol to Wewak, the scene of Kearby's October triumph. Now, however, Kenney had forbidden Kearby to repeat the multiple victory action for which he had recommended him for the Medal of Honor. But the Thunderbolts ran into 15 Japanese aircraft.

Kearby claimed one almost immediately and turned back into the enemy formation for more. Suddenly, he was jumped by three Japanese fighters. Dunham and Blair quickly took out a pair of Zeros, but the third nailed Kearby from close range, and his P-47 augered into the hillside far below. At the time of his death, Kearby's score stood at 22.

Gabreski: The USAAF Top Man in Europe

The top-scoring American ace in the European Theater of World War II, Francis Stanley "Gabby" Gabreski, was also the top-scoring American ace to earn victories in two wars. To his 28 victories in Europe, Gabreski would add 6.5 in the Korean War.

Born and raised in Oil City, Pennsylvania, Gabby Gabreski was a medical student at Notre Dame in Indiana when he decided to take flying lessons. In 1941, he joined the USAAF and earned his fighter pilot's wings before the United States entered World War II. He was then assigned to the 45th Pursuit Group, based at Wheeler Field in the territory of Hawaii. It was here that Gabreski met Catherine Cochran, who would later become his wife, and it was here that he heard the wake-up call of war on the morning of December 7, 1941.

On that morning, Gabreski managed to get airborne in his Curtiss P-36, but not until after the attackers had escaped. His combat experience did not begin in the Pacific Theater, or even with the USAAF, however. In early 1942, he was among a number of American pilots who were assigned to Royal Air Force units in Britain so that they could fly with, and learn from, combat-experienced pilots in combat situations. The American son of Polish immigrants, Gabreski had grown up speaking Polish as well as English, so he was assigned to the No.315 Squadron. Based at Northolt, No.315 was a British squadron composed of Polish pilots who had escaped to England when their country was overrun by the German Blitzkrieg three years before.

After 20 scoreless missions flying a Spitfire with the Royal Air Force, Gabreski was reassigned to fly a Republic P-47 Thunderbolt with the USAAF 56th Fighter Group. The unit was then just forming, but it would eventually become one of the most famous in the USAAF Eighth Air Force, and one of the units most feared by the Luftwaffe. Commanded by the legendary Lieutenant Colonel Hubert "Hub" Zemke, the 56th would come to be known simply as "Zemke's Wolfpack," and it would set a record among USAAF units by shooting down a thousand Luftwaffe aircraft.

Gabreski was assigned to the 61st Fighter Squadron of the 56th Fighter Group, which would also include several former Polish air-force pilots, including Boleslaw "Mike" Gladych. The mission of the Wolfpack, as with most fighter groups within the Eighth Air Force, was to escort strategic bombers on their strikes into German-occupied Europe.

In June 1943, Gabreski became commander of the 61st Fighter Squadron, although he would not score his first aerial victory—against a Focke Wulf Fw-190—until August 24. On November 26, he made ace on his 75th mission by shooting down a pair of Messerschmitt Bf-110s, and was awarded the Distinguished Service Cross.

On December 11, the 61st Fighter Squadron made their rendezvous with the B-17 bombers they were supposed to be escorting, only to find that the bombers were under attack by about 40 Bf-110s. In the course of the ensuing dogfight, Gabreski became separated from the other P-47s, but he attacked three Messerschmitts solo and downed one. Noticing that he was low on fuel, Gabreski turned for home. He ran into a Messerschmitt Bf-109, but had no fuel to get into a dogfight, so he decided to make a run for the British coast. He both outran and outmaneuvered the Messerschmitt, and managed to lose himself in a cloud when his turbo-supercharger played out. The engine failed just as he reached Britain.

In January 1944, Gabby Gabreski, now promoted to deputy executive officer of the 56th Fighter Group, would score his tenth victory. On May 22, Gabreski had the best day of his career, shooting down three Fw-190s. During Operation Overlord, the Allied invasion of northern France on June 6, 1944, Gabreski led the 61st Fighter Squadron in air support missions over the beachhead, but soon the unit was back in action against the Luftwaffe. By July 5, Gabreski had exceeded the 26 victories scored by Captain Eddie Rickenbacker in World War I, making him the top-scoring USAAF ace in the European Theater.

On July 20, having completed 193 missions, Gabreski was about to be rotated home, when he chose to fly one more mission, a mission that he did not have to fly. One version of the story tells that he was actually on the field with his bags packed, waiting for the transport that would take him home.

The fateful flight took Gabreski and the 61st Fighter Squadron on a strafing attack against various targets in western Germany, including an air base near Coblenz. Gabreski made one low pass over the field, scoring many good hits on German aircraft. However, capriciousness overcame good sense and he went back for another pass. This time, he was too low and the angle of attack was too high. His tracers were going over the tops of the targets. He nosed down slightly, and as he did so, the tips of his propeller blades clipped the runway and bent. The resulting vibration almost literally shook the plane apart, and it was starting to tear the engine apart. Oil gushed from the Pratt & Whitney R-2800 Double Wasp and splashed over the windscreen.

Gabreski couldn't fly and was too low to bail out, so he decided to try a crash landing. He brought the Thunderbolt down in a wheat field just as German ground troops started shooting at him. Another P-47 attacked the Germans and Gabreski managed to escape into the woods. For five days, with the help of a Polish laborer whom he met, he eluded German patrols. Imported from Poland to work as a slave for the Germans, the man was a prisoner himself, but he risked his life to try to help Gabreski avoid becoming a prisoner.

Finally, however, Gabreski was captured and sent to Stalag Luft I, a prisoner-of-war camp holding Allied air officers that would also be Hub Zemke's home after he was shot down in October 1944. Gabreski, as one of the senior officers in the camp, would be one of the leaders who oversaw operations of a clandestine radio receiver and several tunnel-digging projects, all of which went unnoticed by the guards. After enduring a bitter-cold winter in captivity, Gabreski, Zemke, and their 8,496 fellow prisoners were liberated by the Russians in March 1945, and repatriated.

Back in the United States, Gabby Gabreski and Catherine Cochran were finally married, and Gabby was assigned to the Air Logistics Command Engineering Flight School at Wright Field, Ohio, where he became a test pilot. He left the service in 1946, however, for the greener pastures of private industry, and he spent a year doing promotional work for the Douglas Aircraft Company while studying for a degree in political science at Columbia University.

In September 1947, the USAAF was separated from the U.S. Army to become the independent U.S. Air Force and Gabreski was lured back into uniform as commander of his World War II unit, the 56th Fighter Group. The latter was now based at Selfridge Field, Michigan, and making the transition to jets.

In 1951, a year after the start of the Korean War, Gabreski was assigned to command the 4th Fighter Interceptor Group. Flying North American Aviation F-86A Sabre Jets, the group had been sent to the Korean War under the command of John Meyer, who, like Gabreski, had been an ace in the Eighth Air Force in England during World War II.

In July 1951, Gabreski shot down a MiG-15 to score his first jet-to-jet aerial victory. In December 1951, after two more MiGs, he was placed in command of the 51st Fighter Interceptor Group, which had just become operational at Suwon Air Base with the newer F-86E aircraft. The specific mission of the 51st was to escort B-29 bombers on strikes against targets in North Korea.

Gabreski would continue flying combat missions, becoming a jet ace early in 1953 and ending the Korean War with a score of 6.5 to add to his 28 scored in World War II. With the 34.5 total victories, Gabreski was the third-highest-scoring American ace of all time—after Richard "Dick" Bong with 40 and Thomas "Tommy" McGuire with 38. With his 28 in World War II, he had been in third place among USAAF pilots in World War II, but he was behind the highest-scoring U.S. Navy ace, David Mc-Campbell, who had 34 in World War II, and tied with top U.S. Marine Corps ace Gregory "Pappy" Boyington.

Gabby Gabreski also ended the Korean War with a Distinguished Service Medal and a ticker-tape parade. In 1955, after serving as director of safety air operations and chief of combat operations and finally chief of special projects at Norton Air Force Base in California, Gabreski completed a course at the Command and Staff School, and was named deputy chief of staff operations in the Ninth Air Force.

In 1960, Gabreski received his penultimate operational command as commander of the 18th Tactical Fighter Wing at Kadena Air Base, Okinawa. In 1962, he became the director of the Secretariat for the commander-in-chief of the Pacific Air Forces (PACAF) at Hickam Air Force Base, Hawaii, and later he served as PACAF inspector general. In 1964, Colonel Gabreski accepted his last U.S. Air Force assignment, as commander of the 52nd Fighter Wing on Long Island, New York.

After his retirement in 1967, Gabreski worked in public relations and customer relations at the Grumman Corporation, and later as president of the Long Island Railroad. He also wrote his autobiography, *Gabby, A Fighter Pilot's Life*. Gabreski's son, Donald, followed in his father's footsteps, graduating from the U.S. Air Force Academy in 1966 and later serving as a fighter pilot. Gabreski Airport

at Southhampton Beach on Long Island, New York, is
named for Gabby Gabreski.

Johnson: The Country-Boy Ace

The USAAF's number-two ace in Europe, like its number
one, was a pilot with the legendary 56th Fighter Group,
"Zemke's Wolfpack." The wolf in this case was a baby-
faced country boy who was born in Lawton, Oklahoma,
on February 21, 1920. Robert Samuel "Bob" Johnson had
studied aeronautical engineering at Cameron College, and
boxed in the amateur 112-to-149-pound class in his spare
time. Interested in flying since his childhood, he took lessons and joined the U.S. Army Air Forces in 1941. The
USAAF trained him as a bomber pilot, but reassigned him
to fighters.

Trained in the Republic P-47 Thunderbolt, Bob Johnson
went to England in January 1943 and was assigned to the
56th Fighter Group. He entered combat in April, escorting
bombers across the English Channel or the North Sea.
Johnson scored his first victory, a Focke Wulf Fw-190, on
June 13. In October, he became an ace. Though Johnson
wouldn't know it for half a century, his fifth victory was
one of the Luftwaffe's finest, Oberstleutnant Hans Philipp,
the commander of Jagdgeschwader 1, who had scored 177
victories on the Eastern Front and another 29 in the West.

In the engagement that made him an ace, Johnson had
observed four Fw-190s attacking some USAAF bombers
over France and dove 5,000 feet to attack the lead ship.
Just as he destroyed Philipp's Focke Wulf, Johnson himself was hit and he lost his rudder. Using his trim tabs to
compensate for lost rudder control, he managed to escape
the remaining Luftwaffe fighters and rendezvous with the
P-47s of the 62nd Fighter Squadron, who escorted him

back to England. When they reached Boxsted, the 62nd pilots wanted the crippled Johnson to land first, but in a gentlemanly gesture, he let them go first because if he crashed on landing, it would block the runway.

By the end of 1943, the P-47s had proven themselves to be so effective against the Luftwaffe that the Germans pulled their defensive line back to the limit of the Thunderbolt's operational range, which meant that they withdrew from the French and Netherlands coastlines, to the area roughly between Kiel and Hannover.

It was here that a number of massive aerial battles occurred, including those on March 6, 8, and 15, 1944, when Bob Johnson led a handful of Thunderbolts against more than 100 Luftwaffe fighters sent up to attack American bombers. There were 34 bombers lost on March 8, but on March 15, Johnson used his radio to vector a large number of American fighters into the battle when the Germans attacked, and no bombers were lost to interceptors.

The Country-Boy Ace would fly 91 missions and score 27 victories, with the final two—a Bf-109G and an Fw-190—coming on the 91st mission on May 8, 1944. Some lists credit him with 28 victories, but the 28th was one that was actually scored by *Ralph* Johnson on the same day and later officially corrected. Bob Johnson was the second-highest-scoring American pilot in the European Theater, with one fewer victory than Gabby Gabreski, who scored his 28th after Johnson left the theater.

Bob Johnson returned to the United States in June 1944, just after the invasion of Europe, and was assigned to go on a publicity tour to help sell war bonds. It was during this tour that he met Richard "Dick" Bong, who was the top-scoring USAAF ace in the Pacific Theater, at that time with 27 victories, the same as Johnson.

While Bong would return to combat and push his total

to 40, Johnson left the service—though he remained in the Air Force Reserve—to go to work for Republic Aviation, the makers of the aircraft that he had flown in combat. Johnson's first task with Republic was to redesign the P-47 cockpit to make it more user-friendly for the pilots by clustering the instruments so that they could be seen at a glance.

Johnson traveled to Korea in December 1951, at the height of the Korean War, as a representative of Republic, whose F-84 Thunderjet was in combat there. Two years later, in the uniform of a U.S. Air Force Reserve lieutenant colonel, he was present at the armistice talks at Panmunjom. He was with Republic for 18 years before going into the insurance business. His book, *Thunderbolt! Flying the P-47 with the Fabulous 56th Fighter Group in World War II*, was published in 1997. Robert Johnson died on December 27, 1998.

MacDonald: With Lindbergh in the Pacific

Tied with Bob Johnson for the number-four spot among all USAAF aces of World War II, Charles H. "Mac" MacDonald scored his 27 victories in the Pacific Theater, and had the distinction of being the highest-scoring of the great P-38 aces to survive the war. Dick Bong and Tommy McGuire are the best remembered, and indeed, they were the two highest-scoring American aces, but MacDonald not only survived the war, he was there when it started. Like Gabby Gabreski, he was at Wheeler Field on December 7, 1941.

During the late 1930s, MacDonald had taken his civilian pilot training while he was studying philosophy at Louisiana State University, and he joined the USAAF after having graduated with his degree and pilot's license. Assigned to 20th Pursuit Group at Wheeler Field on the fateful Sunday morning, he was among those who chased the Japanese but got no hits.

MacDonald remained in Hawaii until early in 1943, when he came back to the continental United States to be trained in the P-38 Lightning. He was then assigned to command the newly formed 340th Fighter Squadron of the 348th Fighter Group, which was destined to be sent out to New Guinea, where the most intense confrontations between the USAAF and the Imperial Japanese Navy Air Force were taking place.

Though the 348th Fighter Group moved to New Guinea in June 1943, MacDonald would see no action until October, when he was re-assigned as executive officer of the 475th "Satan's Angels" Fighter Group—Tommy McGuire's unit—at Dobodura.

Shortly after arriving with the 475th Fighter Group, MacDonald was on a patrol that intercepted a Japanese bomber strike force that had been attacking Allied ships. MacDonald dove to attack and claimed his first two aerial victories in a matter of minutes. As he maneuvered to attack a third, his P-38 started taking hits from behind. The Japanese fighter on his tail managed to knock out one of his two engines and damage his hydraulic and electrical systems. The enemy then broke off, probably assuming that he was a goner. Somehow, MacDonald managed to coax the Lightning back to base.

Later in the month, MacDonald earned his first of two Distinguished Service Crosses on a bomber escort mission to the huge Japanese base at Rabaul, New Britain. The escort team included four flights of P-38s, but the one that MacDonald commanded was the only one that managed to stay with the B-24s when the weather became exceptionally ugly. As it was, they would be desperately needed when the Imperial Japanese Navy Air Force fighters came after the bombers. In the ensuing dogfight, MacDonald claimed one of the attacking A6M Zeros himself.

In November 1943, MacDonald was promoted to command the 475th Fighter Group when George Prentice, the previous commander, was rotated back to the United States. Over the course of the next few months, MacDonald raised his score to 10.

On June 26, 1944, MacDonald was playing checkers with his deputy commander in the operations shack at Hollandia, New Guinea, when a man walked in. MacDonald glanced up, saw a man in a naval uniform without insignia of rank—or pilot's wings. The man said he was there to see Colonel MacDonald, but MacDonald told him to wait and went back to the game. When the game was over, MacDonald asked the man what he'd said his name was and what he wanted.

"Charles Lindbergh," came the reply, and he went on to explain that he was a civilian consultant with United Aircraft, makers of the Pratt & Whitney engines used in many American combat aircraft.

Preoccupied with his checkers, MacDonald hadn't caught the name, and now asked the man if he was a pilot. The way that he said yes made MacDonald look up again. It was in fact, the legendary "Lone Eagle." MacDonald dropped everything, and the two men talked flying for hours. It turned out that the great aviator already had a few hours in the P-38, so MacDonald invited him to fly as part of a four-ship patrol the following day. Lindbergh not only flew with the 475th, he showed an intuitive mastery of the P-38. Even deep inside enemy territory, he maneuvered through the antiaircraft fire with ease.

After he had flown a number of missions, the word got around that his plane always returned with more fuel than the others. One night, as MacDonald introduced the "new man" to a number of the other pilots, someone asked why, if they all flew the same mission at the same speed, did Lindbergh always come back with more fuel.

Calmly, Lindbergh explained that by increasing the manifold pressure, the engine's number of revolutions per minute would go down, and with it, fuel consumption. When the pilots looked at him incredulously, he went on to show them that the General Motors Allison engines in the P-38s—like the Wasp family of engines that Pratt & Whitney made—were designed to military tolerances and could handle the increased manifold pressure with ease. He told them to give it a try.

Over the coming weeks, the 475th Fighter Group began making patrols deeper into enemy territory than before, and surprising the Japanese, who did not expect them. Even though he wasn't supposed to go near potential hostile fire, Lindbergh flew on some of the most dangerous missions, usually as MacDonald's wingman. By July 10, when he was suddenly summoned away by General Douglas MacArthur, Lindbergh had flown at least 25 missions and he had logged almost 100 hours with the 475th Fighter Group. The two aerial victories that he scored were never officially credited.

When General George Kenney found out about the time that Lindbergh was jumped by a Japanese fighter that Mac MacDonald had to shoot off his tail, he reprimanded the 475th Fighter Group commander for letting the famous flyer get into harm's way. The reprimand was actually a disguised leave, and MacDonald was back on duty on October 13, four days before the group began operations in support of the United States invasion of the Philippines. On October 28, after American forces had secured a foothold on the Philippine island of Leyte, the 475th Fighter

Group relocated there. In February 1945, when the big USAAF base at Clark Field, north of Manila, was retaken from the Japanese, MacDonald moved the 475th to Clark.

On July 15, with the war almost won, MacDonald returned to the United States. In his years in combat, most of the time spent with the 475th Fighter Group, he achieved a score of 27 victories. Colonel Charles MacDonald remained with the USAAF after the war, and with the U.S. Air Force, until his retirement in 1966.

Preddy: The Top Mustang Ace

Born in 1920, George Preddy began his World War II combat career at age 21 in the Pacific Theater, but moved to the European Theater to become the highest-scoring ace to fly the USAAF's premier air superiority fighter, the P-51D Mustang. Personally, he was recalled as a man who genuinely cared about those who served under him, and who hated to kill, but viewed combat as a game. As a flight leader, he lost his first wingman, and vowed successfully "not again."

He spent the early months of 1942 flying patrol missions along Australia's northern coastline at a time when a Japanese invasion was not only feared, but considered probable. When his 25th Northern Australian mission ended ignominiously in a midair collision on July 12, 1942, Preddy was sent back to the United States to recuperate and prepare for his next assignment. In January 1943, he was posted to the 34th Fighter Squadron, a part of the 352nd Fighter Group that was to be assigned to the Eighth Air Force. They were based at Republic Field on Long Island and taught to fly P-47 Thunderbolts. In July 1943, Preddy finally went overseas a second time, as the 352nd was shipped out to Britain, specifically to a base at Bodney.

Preddy began flying missions with the 34th Fighter Squadron, which was redesignated as the 487th Fighter Squadron shortly after the base opened for business on July 7. He did not score his first victory until December 1, but he would get his second before Christmas. He and Richard Grow, another P-47 pilot, were escorting a B-24 strike force when they observed six Messerschmitt Me-210 "bomber destroyer" aircraft escorted by ten Bf-109s that were attacking a stray bomber that couldn't keep up with the main formation.

As the two P-47s attacked, Grow was shot down almost immediately, but Preddy succeeded in disrupting the attack, and in downing one of the Me-210s. For this action, he would be awarded the Silver Star.

Preddy would score two more victories flying the Thunderbolt, but in April 1944, the 352nd Fighter Group began transitioning to the P-51D, and he scored his fifth in a Mustang on May 13. Now an ace, Preddy racked up additional scores in his new aircraft, which he dubbed *Cripes a'Mighty*. Soon he was the number-three USAAF in the European Theater, behind Francis "Gabby" Gabreski and Robert Johnson. In June, just after the Normandy Invasion, Johnson, who had 27, went home, and on July 20, Gabreski, who had 28, went down and was captured. This left Preddy, with 18.83, as the number one by default. However, he was determined to be number one, period, but he had a ways to go. He had served his 200 hours and had put in for enough extensions to double the time that he could fly in combat.

Colonel John Meyer, the 352nd Fighter Group commander, tasked Preddy with leading a group-strength escort mission on August 6. On August 5, when bad weather forced a cancellation, a party was scheduled. When the weather cleared late that night and the mission was reinstated, Preddy had imbibed to the point where it took some doing to make him fit to fly by the time that the mission had to be launched.

Preddy did fly that day, and he would see the kind of action that he craved—although he had never imagined getting the wish while his head was held in the vise grip of a hangover. When the Luftwaffe intercepted the B-17 heavy bombers that the 352nd Fighter Group was escorting, Preddy was the first to act, diving into the Bf-109s with the other Mustang pilots following. He quickly downed three German fighters and added two more as the dogfight ensued. Finally, one Messerschmitt dived to 5,000 feet to get away. Preddy followed and claimed him as his sixth kill for the day. For his mission fought with a hangover, Preddy would be awarded the Distinguished Service Cross and a chance for a leave in the United States. Nevertheless, he was anxious to get back to Bodney and back into the air war over Europe.

In October 1944, George Preddy was in action again, with a new assignment as commander of the 328th Fighter Squadron of the 352nd Fighter Group. Preddy saw little of the combat he desired until December, when the Germans launched the winter offensive that would result in the Battle of the Bulge. Overhead, the Luftwaffe would contribute Operation Bodenplatte (Base Plate), the most massive air offensive that they had launched in continental Western Europe since the Battle of France in 1940.

Much of the Allied air response to the German attack was hampered by bad weather, but December 25, Christmas Day, dawned bright and sunny across northern Europe and Preddy led elements of the 328th Fighter Squadron into action over southern Belgium, where the Germans were thrusting through the Allied lines. During the fight, P-51Ds were chasing German fighters at low level all over the rolling hills of Belgium. Preddy managed to down two more Bf-109s to bring his score to 26.83, less than a point from topping Bob Johnson's score. One clean kill would make him number two. Two would make him the top USAAF ace in the European Theater.

As such a thought was probably racing through Preddy's mind, he and his wingman, James Cartee, were then vectored to attack a "schwarm" (swarm) of German fighters near the city of Liège. Preddy was observed diving on a Focke Wulf Fw-190, when suddenly the air was filled with the ugly black puffs of antiaircraft fire—American antiaircraft fire. The Focke Wulf slipped away, but George Preddy did not. He died a victim of friendly fire.

Meyer: Most Likely to Succeed

Among the USAAF aces of World War II, John C. Meyer might have been voted most likely to succeed, for succeed he most certainly did. During World War II, he was the fourth-highest-scoring ace and a group commander; while in the postwar U.S. Air Force, he rose through the ranks to a number of important command positions, including commander-in-chief of the Strategic Air Command. As such, he had become one of the two highest-ranking former air aces of all time, the other being General Adolf Galland, who commanded all Luftwaffe fighter assets for more than two years during World War II.

Born in Brooklyn, New York, Meyer graduated from Dartmouth College with a bachelor's degree in political geography. He enlisted in the Air Corps in November 1939, two months after the start of World War II, and he earned his wings in July 1940.

When the United States entered World War II, Meyer was assigned to the 352nd Fighter Group at Mitchel Field, New York. Over the coming months, the 352nd Fighter Group was rotated to a number of fields in the northeast, in preparation for going overseas. In November 1942, after a month at Bradley Field in Connecticut, it moved to Westover Field in Massachusetts, and in January 1943, it was on to Trumball Field in Connecticut. Between March and June, the squadrons rotated through Republic Field on Long Island as the pilots were trained to fly the P-47 Thunderbolt. Finally, in July, the group went overseas to join the Mighty Eighth Air Force in Britain, and to settle in at Bodney Field.

It was here that John Meyer was given command of the 487th Fighter Squadron of the 352nd Fighter Group. Soon, he was leading elements of the 487th Fighter Squadron in combat over Axis-occupied northern Europe. On November 26, he scored his first aerial victory. During the spring of 1944, the 352nd Fighter Group began the transition to the P-51D Mustang, the aircraft that was to change the face of aerial combat in Europe through the end of World War II.

Meyer earned his first of three Distinguished Service Crosses on May 8, 1944, during a bomber escort mission over Germany. He led a flight of eight P-51s on an attack against a force of Luftwaffe interceptors, downing two in one fast run that broke up the attack. En route back to Britain, Meyer encountered and shot down a third Luftwaffe fighter. He had another multiple-victory day on November 11 during another escort mission in which 487th Fighter Squadron Mustangs were jumped by more than German interceptors, including both Messerschmitt Bf-109s and Focke Wulf Fw-190s. Meyer managed to down three of the Messerschmitts and a Focke Wulf. For this, he was awarded an Oak Leaf cluster to the Silver Star.

On November 21, on a mission over Leipzig, 11 487th Fighter Squadron aircraft observed more than 40 enemy fighters. Meyer decided to jump the Germans before they spotted the Americans. The attack worked, and Meyer himself claimed three Fw-190s. At one point, he used the Focke Wulf's own contrail to mask his attack. He came up from below and behind and fired from close range. Awarded a second Distinguished Service Cross, he became deputy commander of the 352nd Fighter Group.

On January 1, 1945, the Luftwaffe launched their huge Operation Bodenplatte (Base Plate) offensive, which was the biggest air attack on Western Europe in over four years. The 352nd Fighter Group had by this time started sending advance units to airfields in recently liberated areas of continental Europe, in preparation for the group's eventual relocation to a base at Chièvres in Belgium.

On New Year's Day, Meyer was with the advanced units in Belgium—assigned to the IX Tactical Air Command—during the opening phase of the Luftwaffe offensive. He was leading a dozen Mustangs that were preparing to take off, when a large number of German aircraft attacked the field. The attack caught Meyer just as his Mustang lifted off the runway. He opened fire and claimed an Fw-190 before he had even gotten his landing gear up.

The American fighters took off and attacked the Germans. Over the course of 45 minutes, the 352nd Fighter Group shot down 23 Luftwaffe aircraft, including a second Fw-190 for Meyer, his 24th victory.

Eight days later, while he was en route to Paris in a U.S. Army vehicle, the icy roads did to Meyer what the Luftwaffe never had. His injuries would keep him out of the air for the remainder of World War II, but they did not keep him down.

After the war ended, Meyer remained in staff jobs as the USAAF went through the metamorphosis into the U.S. Air Force in September 1947. He was assigned to the office of the secretary of the Air Force in Washington, D.C., and in 1948, he became the U.S. Air Force liaison with the United States House of Representatives.

In August 1950, two months after the start of the Korean War, Meyer returned to a tactical flying unit when he assumed command of the 4th Fighter Interceptor Group, then located at New Castle Airport in Delaware. When the Chinese and Soviet pilots entered the war, operating Mikoyan-Gurevich MiG-15 jet fighters, they had routed the United Nations forces. Desperate measures were needed to gain control of the situation. The U.S. Air Force had the aircraft to do the job, the North American F-86 Sabre Jet. The 4th Fighter Interceptor Group would be the unit to fly them, and John Meyer would command them.

In November, Meyer took the unit overseas to Johnson AB in Japan in preparation for operations over Korea. The 4th Fighter Interceptor Group and its F-86 Sabre Jets would be responsible for taking back control of the Korean skies. By March 1951, the unit was able to move to a base at Suwon in Korea. From here, daily patrols into "MiG Alley," the airspace near the Chinese border, systematically compelled the MiG pilots to engage in fights, which, nine times out of ten, were won by 4th Fighter Interceptor Group pilots. During the war, 792 MiG-15s were lost compared with 78 F-86s.

John Meyer remained in command of the 4th Fighter Interceptor Group through May 1951, and the worst of the battle for air supremacy. During that time, he had the opportunity to lead several patrols personally, and he used it to claim a pair of MiG-15s. One of the subsequent commanders of the 4th Fighter Interceptor Group would be

Gabby Gabreski, who would score 6.5 victories in Korea.

Back in the United States, Meyer served as director of operations for the Air Defense Command and the Continental Air Defense Command. After graduating from the Air War College at Maxwell AFB in Alabama in 1956, he remained as an instructor. His next post was with the Strategic Air Command, for whom he commanded two air divisions in the Northeastern United States. The World War II fighter commander was now in the bomber business. In June 1962, he moved to Strategic Air Command headquarters at Offutt AFB in Nebraska as deputy director for planning. While there, he also served as the Strategic Air Command representative to the Joint Strategic Target Planning Staff.

In November 1963, General Meyer made the move from the Strategic Air Command to the Tactical Air Command, returning to fighters as commander of the Twelfth Air Force in Texas, where he coordinated ground support for the U.S. Army. In February 1966, he moved back to Washington, D.C., to serve with the Joint Chiefs of Staff, first as deputy director and later as vice director. In May 1967, he moved across the hall as director of operations for the joint staff under Chief of Staff General John P. McConnell. Between August 1969 and April 1972, now wearing his fourth star, he served as vice chief of staff, the number-two job in the U.S. Air Force, under Chief of Staff General John Dale Ryan.

On May 1, 1972, General Meyer went back to bombers, and back to Offutt AFB to command the Strategic Air Command as its chief of staff. While there, he oversaw the Linebacker II operations against North Vietnam in December 1972 that helped end the War in Southeast Asia. John Meyer retired from the U.S. Air Force at the end of July in 1974. The seventh-ranked all-time USAAF/U.S.

Air Force ace, and a three-time recipient of the Distinguished Service Cross, died of a heart attack on December
2, 1975.

Voll: Top USAAF Ace in the Mediterranean

During the period from 1940 through early 1943, the Mediterranean area had seen some of the most extreme air combat of World War II. Both Marmaduke "Pat" Pattle—the
top Royal Air Force ace—and Hans-Joachim Marseille—
the top Western Front Luftwaffe ace—had fought and died
there. All of the great Italian aces and many Royal Air
Force aces were in action there. By the time that the
USAAF entered the Mediterranean Theater in strength
early in 1943, the intensity had diminished considerably.
However, in late 1944 and 1945, as the Fifteenth Air Force
bombers based in Italy began to make their regular strikes
into the underbelly of the Third Reich, the fighter pilots
that flew as their escorts began to rack up scores.

The top-scoring USAAF in the Mediterranean Theater
did not even arrive in the combat zone until after the great
USAAF Eighth Air Force aces based in England had
scored most of their victories. John Voll didn't even earn
his wings until January 7, 1944.

Voll was assigned to fly P-51D Mustangs with the 308th
Fighter Squadron of the 31st Fighter Group in Italy in
May, and scored his first victory on June 23. Voll was
flying an escort mission during a raid on the big German
oil refinery complex at Ploesti, Romania, when he encountered and destroyed a Focke Wulf Fw-190. Three days
later, the escort mission took the 308th Fighter Squadron
on a mission to Vienna. A large number of Messerschmitt
Bf-109s and Me-210s attacked the B-24s, and Voll dived

to the attack, claiming one each of the two Luftwaffe types.

On June 27, the target was Budapest in Hungary, and Voll claimed his second Bf-109. Five days later, also on an escort mission to the Hungarian capital, he downed a third Bf-109, the victory that made him an ace. On July 18, he would shoot down his second Fw-190.

Returning from another mission to Ploesti on August 17, another 308th Fighter Squadron pilot suffered engine trouble and was forced to ditch. As he followed the man down to observe his landing spot, Voll observed a schwarm of Bf-109s and promptly attacked. He destroyed two and claimed a "probable" on the third.

Through the remainder of August, Voll flew a series of escort missions into Czechoslovakia. On August 25, he destroyed a Fiesler Fi-156 Storch observation plane and damaged a second. Three days later, his victory was a bit more substantial and the Luftwaffe was short one more Fw-190. On the last day of the month, Voll claimed a pair of multiengine transports, probably Junkers Ju-52s, as well as an Italian Macchi MC-202.

On October 17, on an escort mission to southern Germany, Voll was forced to abort because of engine trouble. On his way home, he observed six Bf-109s, which he attacked—despite his malfunctioning Merlin. He dove through them at high speed, blasting away with his guns. The surprised Germans attempted to follow and two of them collided. After he had eluded his quarry, Voll struggled back to his cruising altitude. Here, he crossed paths with a Dornier Do-217, which he shot down.

On November 6, Voll shot down another Bf-109 over Vienna, bringing his total to 17. Ten days later, as the 308th Fighter Squadron was over northern Italy, returning from a mission, Voll observed a Ju-52 and he peeled off to attack. Just as he started pouring rounds into the Junkers, a dozen Luftwaffe fighters—seven Fw-190s and five Bf-109s—jumped him and bounced him. As the Ju-52 went down, he turned into the fighters. Shooting and dodging, he managed to claim a pair of the Focke Wulfs and a Messerschmitt. As he reported later, "It was just a matter of shooting everything that passed in front of me."

This action would make John Voll the top USAAF ace in the Mediterranean Theater, with 21 victories, and the third-highest-scoring P-51 Mustang ace of World War II. When his tour was completed, he returned to the teaching career that he had planned before the war.

Gentile: An American Ace in Two Air Forces

The highest-ranking ace having victories with both the Royal Air Force and the USAAF, Dominic Salvatore "Don" Gentile had scored two victories with the Royal Air Force before going on to raise his overall total to 21.83 while flying with the USAAF Eighth Air Force. Lance Wade, the American who scored 25 victories with the Royal Air Force, never flew with the USAAF (see British Commonwealth section).

Gentile was born on December 6, 1920, in Piqua, Ohio, to Italian-American parents. Dominic Gentile was one of those people who grew up obsessed with flying and who also turned out to be an excellent pilot. Indeed, he was already flying his own biplane when he was in high school. By 1941, with World War II raging in Europe, he had started calling himself "Don" rather than "Dom" because the latter sounded Italian (which it was) and Italy was part of the Axis.

With the war going, Gentile was anxious to get into action and do some combat flying. In 1941, the U.S. Army

Air Corps required two years of college to get into flight training, but British Empire air forces did not, so Gentile crossed the border to join the Royal Canadian Air Force. After finishing an eight-week training program in two weeks, he was sent to England. Early in 1942, Gentile, now a Royal Air Force pilot officer, was assigned to the Royal Air Force No.133 Squadron, one of several "Eagle" squadrons composed of American pilots who had volunteered to fly with Britain against the Germans.

While flying a Spitfire with No.133 Squadron, Don Gentile shot down a Focke Wulf Fw-190 and a Junkers Ju-88 in the space of ten minutes on the August 1, 1942. For this, he was awarded the British Distinguished Flying Cross. By this time, the United States had entered the war and USAAF fighter units were forming in Britain under the organizational umbrella of the Eighth Air Force. As this occurred, the Eagle Squadron pilots were being transferred from the Royal Air Force to the USAAF's 4th Fighter Group.

As part of this administrative transfer, Don Gentile was assigned, in September 1942, to the 336th Fighter Squadron of the 4th Fighter Group based at Debden. The unit was ultimately so successful that Hermann Göring referred to them as the "Debden Gangsters." Within the group a competition soon ensued between Gentile and Duane Beeson over who would ultimately be the highest-scoring ace among the former Eagles. Gentile would win, but Beeson would be second with 19.3.

By the autumn of 1942, Gentile and his wingman, another ex-Eagle named John T. Godfrey (who ended up with 18 victories), were soon recognized as a remarkably potent combat team. In a typical lead-and-wingman situation, there is a designated leader. Gentile and Godfrey decided that whichever man first spotted a target, or whoever was in the best position to take a shot, would take the lead while the other covered him. They would be together for more than six months and nearly 100 missions, during which time Hermann Göring is said to have actually established a "bounty" for their capture.

Gentile, who would be the 4th Fighter Group's leading ace, had some very good days with Godfrey at his wing. On March 8, 1944, he claimed 4.25 German aircraft. On March 29, and again in his last combat action, on April 8, 1944, he shot down three Luftwaffe aircraft. This would bring his overall score to 19.83 with the 4th Fighter Group, plus the two he'd scored with 133 Squadron. He also had seven "ground kills," which the Eighth Air Force assessment board mentioned at that time because they wanted to encourage pilots to destroy enemy aircraft on the ground. He was also awarded the Distinguished Service Cross, the Silver Star, the Distinguished Flying Cross, and the Air Medal, in addition to his British Distinguished Flying Cross.

Don Gentile was rotated back to the United States, and in June 1944, he was assigned to the Air Logistics Command test center at Wright Field, Ohio, where he worked as a test pilot with Lockheed P-80s until his discharge from the USAAF in April 1946. He rejoined in December 1946 and served as a plans and training officer in the Fighter Gunnery Program until September 1948 when he went to the Air Tactical School.

In June 1949, he enrolled at the University of Maryland to earn his undergraduate degree in military science. On January 28, 1951, he took off from Andrews Air Force Base for a short flight in a Lockheed T-33 jet trainer. The aircraft crashed near Forestville, Maryland, and both Gentile and a passenger were killed. The Defense Electronics Supply Center at Kettering, Ohio, which was established in 1962, was named Gentile Air Force Station in his honor. It provided electrical and electronics logistical support to various branches of the United States armed services until it was closed in 1993 as part of a Defense Department cost-cutting exercise.

Zemke: From Wolfpack to Stalag

The most successful USAAF group commander in World War II, Colonel Hubert "Hub" Zemke is also remembered for serving as commander of 8,498 caged Americans in the prisoner-of-war camp known as Stalag Luft I. For two years, he commanded the 56th Fighter Group, which came to be known as "Zemke's Wolfpack" as it racked up 665 aerial victories as the top-scoring fighter group in the European Theater. Zemke himself would score 17.75 confirmed victories in 154 combat missions while building a reputation as one of the leading tacticians in the Eighth Air Force.

A USAAF officer and a fighter pilot before the United States entered World War II, he spent the early part of the war on liaison missions to the British Royal Air Force and the Soviet Voenno-Vozdushnie Sily—learning from the British and teaching the Soviets to operate American Lend Lease equipment. By mid-1942, he was among the officers who traveled to England to begin setting up the framework around which the USAAF would construct its largest-numbered air force—the "Mighty Eighth." The purpose of the Eighth Air Force was to be the strategic bombardment of the German Reich, so the centerpiece of its organization would be the Bombardment Groups with their eventual thousands of Boeing B-17 Flying Fortresses and Consolidated B-24 Liberators. However, the bombers would need escorts and the escorting fighters would be ultimately tasked with nothing short of achieving air superiority over Germany itself. Men like Ira Eaker and Carl "Tooey" Spaatz would create the bomber force, but men like Hub Zemke would create a force of fighters that took them to the heartland of the Fatherland.

Colonel Hub Zemke took command of the 56th Fighter Group in September 1942. The 56th Fighter Group was created as the 56th Pursuit Group at the end of 1940 as an air defense unit, and it was based at various locations throughout the southeast during 1941, moving from Savannah to Charleston to Charlotte. After Pearl Harbor, however, the USAAF decided to make the 56th Fighter Group into one of its first-line operational units for combat action overseas. In July 1942, the 56th was moved to Bridgeport, Connecticut, equipped with P-47 Thunderbolts and told to prepare for war. Zemke took over the 56th Fighter Group in September and he took it to Britain in January 1943.

First based at King's Cliffe, the 56th Fighter Group would move to Horsham St. Faith in April 1943, to Halesworth in July 1943, and finally to Boxted in April 1944 in anticipation of operations related to the Normandy Invasion.

Tactically, the 56th Fighter Group evolved gradually with Zemke constantly defining and redefining tactics. In 1944, after dozens of missions escorting the Eighth Air Force heavy bombers into Europe, Zemke challenged established Eighth Air Force policy. The idea of having the escort fighters stay close to the bombers throughout the mission had never been officially questioned before. He theorized that if part of the fighter force fanned out ahead of the bombers, they could hit and kill or disrupt the interceptors before the bombers arrived.

Zemke successfully convinced his boss, General William Kepner, commander of VIII Fighter Command (the Eighth Air Force's fighter component), to go along, and the "Zemke Fan" was born. The tactic was first implemented on May 12, 1944, with less-than-auspicious results. Zemke led a four-ship patrol ahead of the bomber stream, but one aborted and the remaining three were attacked by seven Messerschmitt Bf-109s, led by the legendary Luftwaffe ace Günther Rall. Rall attacked, downing two of the P-47s and leaving Zemke alone. By putting his Thunderbolt into a steep dive, Zemke was able to get away, but the Zemke Fan had gotten off to a bad start.

Eventually, however, as it was perfected, Zemke's idea greatly reduced bomber losses while increasing the scores for the aces of the 56th Fighter Group—which was now known universally as "Zemke's Wolfpack."

During 1944, there would be a running competition between the Wolfpack, with its P-47s, and Don Blakeslee's 4th Fighter Group, which had converted to P-51s. When the war ended, the 56th Fighter Group was ahead in aerial victories.

In August 1944, after commanding the Wolfpack for two years, Zemke volunteered to take over the morale-challenged 479th Fighter Group. At the time, the Wattisham-based group was transitioning from Lockheed P-38 Lightnings to P-51s, and Eighth Air Force leadership felt that it needed a new boss to get it into line. Zemke was the man.

By the end of October, Zemke had been given orders that would move him upstairs to become the chief of staff at the headquarters of the 65th Fighter Wing at Saffron Walden, England. Flying his last mission before taking the desk job, Zemke ran into severe turbulence over Germany and was forced to ditch over the Reich.

Once on the ground, he was captured and sent to Stalag

Luft I, located on the Baltic Sea at Barth, Germany. At the prisoner-of-war camp, Zemke became reunited with Gabby Gabreski, the Eighth Air Force's leading ace, who had been shot down two months before, also on what might have been his last mission before leaving combat.

At Stalag Luft I, Zemke was the senior officer among more than 8,000 Allied airmen in a stark and miserable prison camp. By the end of 1944, living conditions in Germany had deteriorated. Food was scarce and luxuries non-existent. In the prisoner-of-war camp, things were that much worse. The place was filthy, with poor rations, inadequate sanitation, and virtually no medical attention. Morale and discipline were naturally at very low ebb.

Gradually, Zemke was able to work with prisoners to restore discipline and morale and to work with the camp commandant to improve conditions. He helped restore morale and helped the men get through the last bitter winter of World War II. As it became obvious that Germany was going to lose the war, the Germans became more cooperative, and Zemke was able to negotiate a quiet surrender. On April 30, 1945, with the Soviet armies approaching, the German commandant ordered Zemke to get the prisoners ready to be moved, but Zemke convinced the Germans to just walk away and leave the prisoners in charge of the compound.

The following day, with the Germans gone, Zemke assumed responsibility for maintaining order in the camp and sent out contact parties to meet with advancing Soviet troops. These forces, the 65th Army of the 2nd Byelorussian Front, under Colonel General Pavel Batov, showed little interest in the needs of the former prisoners for food and water, nor did they cooperate with Allied authorities in arranging an evacuation of the camp. Finally, on May

12, the USAAF started sending transport aircraft to airlift the men to the West.

According to the documentation compiled at the time, 8,498 prisoners—1,415 British and 7,083 American personnel—were released and repatriated in the airlift, which was completed on May 15. Rumors persisted of several hundred that remained in Soviet custody, but no proof ever surfaced.

Hub Zemke remained in the USAAF as he made the transition to the independent U.S. Air Force in 1947, and retired in 1966. He eventually moved to Oroville, California, in the foothills of the Sierra Nevada, where he lived until his death on August 30, 1994.

2

THE U.S. NAVY AND
MARINE CORPS

THE UNITED STATES WAS UNIQUE among the major powers in World War II in that it had not one but *three* air forces, and each of them had aces. The U.S. Army technically controlled the USAAF—forerunner to the independent U.S. Air Force—but it was autonomous after 1941. The other two "air forces" were the aviation units of the U.S. Navy and the U.S. Marine Corps—both of which operate under the U.S. Department of the Navy.

Naval aviation in World War II involved both shore-based operations and aircraft-carrier-based operations. The former involved patrol aircraft—both seaplanes and land planes based at facilities with runways. Carrier operations included fighters, patrol aircraft, and attack bombers (including torpedo bombers). The U.S. Navy's carriers typically had a Carrier Air Wing with homogenous squadrons of fighters and various classifications of bombers.

The U.S. Navy has always viewed its carrier bomber squadrons as the core of the carrier's offensive role, while fighters are a defensive component. Fighters have always existed aboard carriers for the primary purpose of protecting the carrier, and the ships of the carrier's battle group, from enemy bombers, whether they be shore-based or carrier-based. The secondary role of carrier fighters is escorting the carrier-based bombers on their missions.

During World War II, the naval aviators who became aces were members of carrier-based fighter squadrons, which were designated by numbers (which originally corresponded to the number of the carrier) accompanied by the prefix "VF." The majority of U.S. Navy air combat operations during World War II were in the Pacific Theater, where the great carrier battles took place, and where all of the U.S. Navy's top flyers became aces.

The leading U.S. Navy ace was David McCampbell, who scored 34 victories while flying F6F Hellcats with VF-15. He is followed by Cecil Harris of VF-9, with 24 victories, and Eugene Valencia of VF-18, with 23. Three aviators are tied for third with 19 apiece. They are Alexander Vraciu, who flew with VF-6 and with VF-16; Cornelius Nooy of VF-31; and Patrick Fleming of VF-80. Douglas Baker of VF-20 scored 16.3, and Ira Cassius "Ike" Kepford had 16 with VF-17.

Like McCampbell, all of these men would score their victories in the Grumman F6F Hellcat, except Kepford, who scored his while flying a Vought F4U Corsair. For all, their highest decoration would be the Navy Cross, except Baker, who was awarded the Silver Star, and McCampbell, who earned the Congressional Medal of Honor, America's highest award for bravery under fire.

The U.S. Marine Corps was conceived as being the U.S. Navy's "ground forces" or "sea soldiers." As such, their role has generally been to go into action in conjunction with U.S. Navy ships. In World War II, this involved the many amphibious operations that were undertaken in capturing islands from the Japanese. U.S. Marine Corps aviation exists primarily to support ground and amphibious operations, either by directly attacking the enemy on the ground or intercepting enemy aircraft before they attack the Marines on land or sea. U.S. Marine Corps squadrons use a designation system similar to that used by the U.S. Navy, but with the letter "M" inserted after the "V" that denotes aviation. Hence Marine fighter squadrons are indicated with the prefix "VMF."

In World War II, U.S. Marine Corps air operations were concentrated in the Southwest Pacific, in the skies over the hundreds of islands that make up such groups as the Bismarck Archipelago, the New Hebrides, and the Solomons. Guadalcanal in the Solomons became one of the most important battlegrounds of World War II, when the Marines landed there in 1942 to stop the tide of Japanese aggression. It was in the Solomons and neighboring islands that the great U.S. Marine Corps aces had their finest hours during World War II.

During the difficult days of 1942 and 1943, Marine aviators fought under difficult conditions against a determined and powerful enemy. Among them, the top four U.S. Marine Corps aces of World War II would all receive the Congressional Medal of Honor. The leading Marine aces were Joseph Foss, who scored 26 victories while flying with VMF-121; Robert Hanson, who scored 25 victories with VMF-215; Gregory "Pappy" Boyington, who scored 22 victories with VMF-214; and Kenneth Walsh, who scored 21 victories while flying with VMF-124. Boyington had also scored six victories while flying with the American Volunteer Group in China before the war, so his total of 28 made him the highest-scoring Marine, although Foss and Hanson scored more while actually flying with the U.S. Marine Corps.

Other World War II Marine aces of note were Donald Aldrich, who scored 20 victories while flying with VMF-

215; John Smith, who scored 19 victories—and earned a Medal of Honor—while flying with VMF-223; Marion Carl, who scored 18.5 victories while flying with VMF-223; and Wilbur J. Thomas, who scored 18.5 victories while flying with VMF-213.

Of these aviators, three of them—Foss, Smith and Carl—scored their victories in the early days of the war with the relatively primitive Grumman F4F Wildcat, while the rest flew the more sophisticated Vought F4U Corsair.

Navy and Marine Corps Fighter Aircraft

The U.S. Navy has always chosen similar types of aircraft for both its own use and for the use of the U.S. Marine Corps. For example, in the years leading up to World War II, the Grumman F4F Wildcat was the standard U.S. Navy carrier-based fighter and it was also the frontline fighter in U.S. Marine Corps service. The Wildcat was the first in a long line of Grumman "carrier cats" that included the F6F Hellcat of World War II and the postwar F8F Bearcat, and which culminated with the F-14 Tomcat, which was the principal U.S. Navy air superiority fighter at the dawn of the 21st century.

The F4F, which dated back to 1935 and entered service in 1940, was an outstanding fighter for its day. It was a versatile and dependable aircraft, but its top speed of 332 mph made it slower than the operationally superior Japanese Zero. Nevertheless, in the hands of a good pilot, such as the Marine Corps pilots who flew it over Guadalcanal, it was a tough and durable fighter. It would serve in the thick of the action in the Pacific until 1943, when the Vought Corsair and Grumman's F6F Hellcat became operational.

The Hellcat was the U.S. Navy's top fleet air superiority

fighter for most of World War II. Of the 147,094 total sorties flown by American carrier-based aircraft of all types during World War II, 62,240 were flown by Hellcats. This included more than 90 percent of all fighter sorties. The Hellcat performed gloriously in what was the biggest dogfight of the Pacific Theater. On June 20, 1944, in the Philippine Sea off the Marianas Islands, the aircraft carriers of U.S. Navy Task Force 58 met a Japanese task force under Vice Admiral Ozawa. In the skies over the ensuing sea battle, another battle raged, one that the Hellcat pilots would remember as "the Great Marianas Turkey Shoot." The Japanese would lose 402 aircraft that day, and Task Force 58 would lose only 29, with half of the pilots rescued.

The process of designing the F6F Hellcat as the successor to the Wildcat was under way at the time that the United States entered the war, and the first flight of the prototype occurred in June 1942. Production aircraft were first delivered at the end of 1942, and by the end of 1943, over 2,500 Hellcats had been delivered, allowing the U.S. Navy to equip every fighter squadron on its entire "fast carrier" force with F6Fs. Meanwhile, the Wildcats were relegated to service on the growing number of convoy escort carriers. The huge preponderance of Hellcat sorties relative to those of other aircraft is indicative of how much action the carriers saw *after* the Hellcats arrived.

By 1943, the standard Hellcat was the F6F-3, which had a wingspan of 42 feet 10 inches, and a length of 33 feet 7 inches. It weighed 12,441 pounds fully loaded and fueled. It was powered by a 2,000-hp, air-cooled Pratt & Whitney R-2800-10W engine that gave it a top speed of 375 mph. It had a service ceiling of 37,300 feet and a range of 1,590 miles. Armament consisted of six wing-mounted .50-caliber machine guns. The F6F-3 was in combat only

14 months after the first flight of the first Hellcat prototype. The first ships to receive Hellcats were the new carriers USS *Yorktown* and USS *Independence,* who were involved in the August 1943 attack on Marcus Island. Eventually, over 4,100 F6F-3s would be manufactured, including over 300 that were sold to the British under the designation Hellcat I.

The definitive Hellcat was probably the F6F-5, which first flew in April 1944, and of which over 7,800 would be built. It featured a modified cowling, more armor and provisions for beefed-up armament that included having two of the .50-caliber machine guns replaced by 20mm cannons, and the addition of attachment equipment for six rockets or two 1,000-pound bombs. The F6F-5 had the same dimensions as the F6F-3, but weighed 12,740 pounds fully loaded and fueled. It was powered by the same Pratt & Whitney R-2800-10W engines, which gave it the same performance as the F6F-3.

Of note are the facts that over 1,400 of the F6F-5s were fitted out as night fighters, and that nearly 1,000 were delivered to the British as the Hellcat II. Though they were inferior to the Vought F4U Corsair in terms of performance, the Hellcats remained the standard carrier-based U.S. Navy fighter through the end of the war.

In the course of its 62,240 carrier sorties, and another 4,116 Navy and Marine Corps land-based sorties, the Hellcat had a remarkable combat record. Of the 9,282 enemy aircraft shot down by U.S. Navy and Marine Corps aircraft during World War II, 5,156—over half—were dispatched by Hellcats. This was against the loss of only 270 Hellcats in aerial combat. Indeed, the Hellcat had a better record overall than the great P-51 Mustang had in the European Theater. As noted above, the top-scoring U.S. Navy aces of World War II achieved all their victories in Hellcats.

Over 12,000 Hellcats were manufactured, but after the war, they were quickly retired in favor of Corsairs. Some retirees were delivered to the French, who used them during their vain effort to reassert control over their lost colonies in Indochina. Others were resurrected during the Korean War to be used as radio-controlled cruise missiles for attacking bridges.

The Hellcat's lasting legacy was its successor, the Grumman F8F Bearcat, which was first delivered in February 1945, and was en route to the Pacific Theater when the war ended in August. It was similar to the Hellcat in most respects, but it had a bubble canopy for 360-degree vision and its Pratt & Whitney R-2800-34W gave it a top speed above 450 mph. Remembered by some as the "best piston-engine fighter of World War II," the Bearcat never fired a shot, and was retired before the Korean War.

The Vought F4U Corsair had the distinction of being the only extensively used American fighter of World War II that remained in production after 1945. It was also the first U.S. Navy fighter to exceed 400 mph. It originated in the late 1930s as the planners at the Navy's Bureau of Aeronautics were beginning to address the need to bring the performance of carrier-based fighters on par with their land-based cousins. To accomplish this, the engineers at Vought designed their new aircraft around the equally new Pratt & Whitney XR-2800-4 Double Wasp, which delivered 1,850 hp. On the Double Wasp, they hung a huge propeller with a diameter of 13 feet 4 inches. This required designing the Corsair with the distinctive "gull" wings that make it instantly recognizable.

The XF4U-1 Corsair made its first flight in May 1940. The Navy liked the Corsair's performance, but requested refinements in the design, such as moving the cockpit aft and beefing up the armament. The first production contract was issued in June 1941, but it would be a year before the first production F4U-1 aircraft would be delivered. Initial carrier tests were not promising, so the Navy decided to earmark them for delivery to U.S. Marine Corps units in the Southwest Pacific Theater.

Arriving in Guadalcanal in February 1943, the Corsairs proved themselves much better than the F4F Wildcats that the Marines had been using, and easily a match for the best that the Japanese had to offer. After a painfully sluggish start, the F4U was finally in combat and doing extremely well. By August, every Marine unit in the Pacific used F4U-1s.

Vought would build almost 4,700 F4U-1s, and two other manufacturers would also be involved in production. Goodyear manufactured over 4,000 and Brewster built another 735. Of these, most went to the U.S. Marine Corps and the U.S. Navy, but almost 2,000 went to Britain's Royal Navy as Corsair I and Corsair II, and over 400 went to New Zealand as Corsair III and IV.

The F4U-1 had a wingspan of 41 feet and a length of 33 feet 4 inches. It weighed 12,039 pounds fully loaded and fueled. The early F4U-1s were powered by the 1,650-hp, air-cooled Pratt & Whitney R-2800-8 Double Wasp engine, but after November 1943, they were manufactured with the R-2800-8W, which had water injection for emergency power. The F4U-1 had a top speed of 417 mph and cruised at 359 mph. It had a service ceiling of 36,900 feet and a range of 2,220 miles. Armament consisted of six .50-caliber machine guns, although some were built with four 20mm cannons instead. They could also carry two 1,000-pound bombs and the last 600 aircraft were equipped with provisions for eight five-inch rockets.

There were a few radar-equipped night fighter aircraft manufactured under the designation F4U-2, and one of these achieved the first-ever radar-only aerial victory by the U.S. Navy, on Halloween night in 1943.

The first major refinement to the F4U-1 was the F4U-4 type, which was delivered for service in December 1944. These were successfully integrated into aircraft carrier operations, and many were also delivered to the Marines. They were generally similar to the F4U-1, but were powered by the 2,100-hp R-2800-18W engine. Over 2,600 were built, all with provisions for bombs and rockets, and some with 20mm cannons instead of machine guns. Of these, only 1,859 were delivered by the end of the war, but the F4U-4 remained in production until 1947.

The Corsair's combat career in World War II included 64,051 fighter and fighter-bomber missions, including 52,852 land-based Marine Corps sorties. As noted above, many top Marine Corps aces, including Pappy Boyington and Robert Hanson, flew the Corsair. The Corsair pilots shot down 2,140 Japanese planes and only 189 of their own were lost in aerial combat.

After World War II, Vought not only continued to produce the Corsair for the Navy, but they also introduced a new model, the F4U-5. This type addressed the continuing need for fighter-bombers and night fighters, roles for which the early Navy jets were not well suited. The F4U-5 was generally similar to the earlier Corsairs, but was powered by a Pratt & Whitney R-2800-32W that gave it a top speed of 470 mph. The Corsair probably played a more important role in the Korean War than any other World War II fighter. The U.S. Navy's only night fighter ace, Lieutenant Guy Bordelon, scored all his victories in an F4U-5N during the Korean War.

McCampbell: The Navy's Top Ace

David S. McCampbell, the U.S. Navy's "Ace of Aces," was the third-highest-scoring American ace of World War II, with 34 victories. On October 24, 1944, during the Battle of Leyte Gulf, he shot down nine Japanese aircraft in a single day. This, in part, led to his being awarded the Congressional Medal of Honor. McCampbell was born on January 16, 1910 in Bessemer, Alabama, and attended Staunton Military Academy in Virginia and Georgia Tech in Atlanta. Appointed to the U.S. Naval Academy at Annapolis in 1929 by Senator Trammell of Florida, McCampbell joined the swim team and distinguished himself as an AAU diving champion in 1931 and Eastern Intercollegiate champion a year later. In 1933, he graduated with a degree in marine engineering. Because regular officer commissions were limited, McCampbell was shunted into the Naval Reserve, and spent the next year working at various civilian jobs.

In June 1934, he finally got an active assignment in the U.S. Navy, aboard the cruiser USS *Portland*. After three years as an aircraft gunnery observer and a year of flight training, McCampbell became a naval aviator in 1938. For two years, he was assigned to the carrier USS *Ranger* and he was later transferred to the USS *Wasp* as a landing signal officer (LSO), which is where he was based when the United States entered World War II. When the USS *Wasp* was sunk by a Japanese submarine off Guadalcanal in September 1942, McCampbell was rescued and sent to Florida as an LSO instructor.

In August 1943, McCampbell returned to combat in the Pacific Theater, first as commander of VF-15, and from February 1944, of Carrier Air Group 15—later known as the "Fabled Fifteen"—aboard the USS *Essex*. He flew his first combat mission in this role on May 19, 1944, during a fighter sweep over Marcus Island and he scored his first aerial victory less than a month later, on June 11, during the American assault on Saipan.

Eight days later, during the Battle of the Philippine Sea, McCampbell led the fighters flying to intercept a vast Japanese bomber armada headed to attack the United States Fleet. In this aerial battle, known to Hellcat pilots as the "Great Marianas Turkey Shoot," the enemy force was completely destroyed and McCampbell personally shot down seven enemy aircraft as well as two "probables." These seven included five on the morning patrol, one during the afternoon patrol, and one that he scored while returning to the USS *Essex* from the afternoon patrol. He and George Duncan, another VF-15 aviator, observed a pair of A6M Zeros attacking a seaplane that was trying to rescue a downed pilot. They attacked and each claimed a Zero.

By October 1944, when Allied forces moved into position for the recapture of the Philippines, McCampbell's score of enemy aircraft destroyed in battle was already an impressive 19. The end of that month would see the largest air and surface naval battle of the Pacific Theater of World War II, and probably the last great naval battle in history— the Battle of Leyte Gulf.

On October 24, during the Battle of Leyte Gulf, McCampbell and his wingman, Roy Rushing, intercepted and attacked a force of approximately 40 enemy fighters. On this day, Carrier Air Group 15 was tasked with launching two strike missions. McCampbell was to lead the fighters escorting the second strike. However, after the first group went out, a Japanese strike force coming toward the USS *Essex* was detected. McCampbell immediately took off, leading the only seven Hellcats that were available.

The Japanese were encountered, now just 22 miles from the USS *Essex*. McCampbell ordered five Hellcats to attack the bombers while he and Rushing intercepted their fighter escort. They each downed one of the A6M Zeros on their first pass, and McCampbell got a second. The Japanese then went into a defensive circle rather than striking back, and finally turned away and started to return to their base in the Philippines. The Hellcats attacked again, and again both aviators scored.

The Americans chased the Japanese until their fuel ran low. By the time that they turned back, McCampbell had shot down nine—plus two "probables"—while Rushing had claimed six. Equally important, they and the other Hellcat pilots had forced the Japanese force into retreat without a single one of them reaching an American ship.

The next day, McCampbell coordinated an air strike by three carrier air groups against Japanese targets in which they sank an enemy aircraft carrier, a light cruiser, and two destroyers. McCampbell's "Fabled Fifteen" continued to serve through November 1944, when the USS *Essex* concluded her cruise, establishing a record unmatched in the history of carrier warfare. They had shot down 318 enemy aircraft (11 percent of these by McCampbell himself) and had sunk 296,500 tons of enemy shipping, including the battleship *Musashi,* three carriers, and a heavy cruiser.

McCampbell is quoted as having said that "Aggressiveness was a fundamental to success in air-to-air combat, and if you ever caught a fighter pilot in a defensive mood you had him licked before you started shooting."

David McCampbell was awarded the Navy Cross as well as the Silver Star, Legion of Merit, and the Distinguished Flying Cross for his part in the seven-month cruise of the Fabled Fifteen. On January 10, 1945, President Franklin D. Roosevelt personally awarded him the Congressional Medal of Honor for his actions on June 19 and October 24, 1944.

His Medal of Honor citation read: "For conspicuous gallantry and intrepidity at the risk of his life above and beyond the call of duty as Commander, Air Group 15, during combat against enemy Japanese aerial forces in the First and Second Battles of the Philippine Sea. An inspiring leader, fighting boldly in the face of terrific odds, Commander McCampbell led his fighter planes against a force of 80 Japanese carrier-based aircraft bearing down on our fleet on 19 June 1944. Striking fiercely in valiant defense of our surface force, he personally destroyed seven hostile planes during this single engagement in which the outnumbering attack force was utterly routed and virtually annihilated.

"During a major fleet engagement with the enemy on 24 October, Commander McCampbell, assisted by but one plane, intercepted and daringly attacked a formation of 60 hostile land-based craft approaching our forces. Fighting desperately but with superb skill against such overwhelming airpower, he shot down nine Japanese planes and, completely disorganizing the enemy group, forced the remainder to abandon the attack before a single aircraft could reach the fleet. His great personal valor and indomitable spirit of aggression under extremely perilous combat conditions reflect the highest credit upon Commander McCampbell and the U.S. Naval Service."

He would see no more combat action after November 1944, but his career in the Navy and in naval aviation would continue until his retirement in 1964. He would serve two years as chief of staff to commander fleet air and as commander of carrier air groups before being assigned to the Armed Forces Staff College in 1947. Between 1948 and 1951, he was the senior naval aviation advisor to the Argentine Navy, and in 1951 he returned to carrier duty as executive officer of the USS *Franklin D. Roosevelt.* After a stint as flight test coordinator at the Naval Air Test Center in Patuxent River, Maryland, he sailed as commander of the USS *Severn,* and later in command of the USS *Bon Homme Richard.* In 1960, he took a staff job at the Pentagon in Washington, D.C., with the Joint Chiefs of Staff, and in 1962, he accepted his final assignment, as assistant deputy chief of staff for operations to the commander-in-chief of the Continental Air Defense Command.

After his retirement in 1964, David McCampbell moved to Palm Beach County, Florida. In 1988, Palm Beach International Airport officially dedicated its David McCampbell Terminal. McCampbell died at his home in Florida on June 30, 1996, after a long illness.

O'Hare: The Most Daring Single Action

In 1942, World War II was not going well for the United States and the Allies. The United States needed something positive. A hero was needed, and a hero was found in Edward H. "Butch" O'Hare. He would be the U.S. Navy ace responsible for what was referred to in 1942 as "the most daring single action in the history of combat aviation."

O'Hare was born in St. Louis, Missouri, on March 13, 1914, but he grew up in Chicago. He considered it to be his hometown when he joined the U.S. Navy, and it was the "Windy City" that paid him his most lasting tribute.

Already a naval aviator at the time that the United States was drawn into the conflict, O'Hare was a fighter pilot with VF-3, commanded by Lieutenant Commander John Thach, aboard the USS *Lexington.* Only two months had passed since the Japanese attack on Pearl Harbor, as the USS *Lexington*'s task force—including cruisers and destroyers—was steaming west toward the Gilbert Islands in February 1942. The objective was to interrupt Japanese shipping in and around the huge Imperial Japanese Navy base at Rabaul on the island of New Britain.

The force was 400 miles from this objective at dawn on February 20, when it was discovered by a Japanese patrol bomber. Thach took off with a force of Grumman F4F-3 Wildcats. They shot down the intruder, but not before the position of the task force was revealed to the Japanese forces at Rabaul. Late in the day, Thach and five other VF-3 pilots—aided by surface fire from the warships—managed to destroy a wave of nine land-based Mitsubishi G4M1 "Betty" bombers. However, a second wave of bombers was detected.

Butch O'Hare was one of the six pilots who went up to confront the second wave, which the Japanese timed to arrive 30 minutes after the first. The Wildcats split up to search for the incoming bombers, and as it turned out, only O'Hare and his wingman were in a position to intercept the enemy when they arrived on the scene. O'Hare's wingman's guns jammed, and O'Hare was forced to face the enemy alone.

Braving defensive fire from the bombers, O'Hare attacked from the right rear of their "vee" formation. He managed to shoot down two of the bombers in rapid succession and switched to the opposite side. He ultimately succeeded in shooting down six of the nine Japanese bombers and disrupting the bombing accuracy of the remaining three, so that no bombs fell on the carrier. It was observed from below that there seemed to have been three of the bombers falling in flames simultaneously.

The U.S. Navy Department official communiqué of

March 3, 1942, observed that "Only three enemy planes of the first formation reached their bomb release point over the aircraft carrier, which avoided all bomb hits by split-second maneuvering. The leading bomber of this group attempted a crash landing on the carrier and was shot down by heavy close-range antiaircraft fire when barely 100 yards from its objective. In the second attack only five bombers of the enemy formation reached the bomb release point. In this instance the salvo of enemy bombs was closer to the carrier than in the first attack, but again no hits were obtained. Sixteen of the 18 attacking enemy bombers were shot down in this action. There was no damage to our surface forces. Lieutenant (j.g.) Edward H. O'Hare, U.S. Navy, fighter pilot, personally accounted for six bombers of the enemy. In the two attacks only two of our fighter planes were lost. The pilot of one was recovered. The next of kin of the lost pilot has been notified. There is nothing to report from other areas."

An after-action examination of O'Hare's guns indicated that he had used a mere 60 rounds for each of the kills. Scoring six victories in his first combat action, O'Hare was recommended for, and received, the Congressional Medal of Honor as well as a promotion to the rank of lieutenant commander. He was also the U.S. Navy's first ace of World War II. He would later be awarded the Navy Cross and the Distinguished Flying Cross with one gold star.

His Medal of Honor citation read: "For conspicuous gallantry and intrepidity in aerial combat, at grave risk of his life above and beyond the call of duty, as section leader and pilot of Fighting Squadron 3 on 20 February 1942. Having lost the assistance of his teammates, Lieutenant O'Hare interposed his plane between his ship and an advancing enemy formation of nine attacking twin-engine heavy bombers. Without hesitation, alone and unaided, he repeatedly attacked this enemy formation, at close range in the face of intense combined machine-gun and cannon fire. Despite this concentrated opposition, Lieutenant O'Hare, by his gallant and courageous action, his extremely skillful marksmanship in making the most of every shot of his limited amount of ammunition, shot down five enemy bombers and severely damaged a sixth before they reached the bomb release point. As a result of his gallant action—one of the most daring, if not the most daring, single action in the history of combat aviation—he undoubtedly saved his carrier from serious damage."

As it turned out, the six bombers that Butch O'Hare shot down that day would constitute half of his total score.

In November 1943, during operations related to the invasion of Tarawa, O'Hare was in charge of the first attempts at intercepting enemy aircraft at night from carriers. This involved a team of two Hellcats and one radar-equipped Grumman TBF Avenger operating from the USS *Enterprise,* led by O'Hare. In operation, the fighters flew wing on the Avenger, and after being vectored to the vicinity of the enemy aircraft by the ship's fighter director, they relied on the Avenger's radar to get within visual range. On the first occasion, no intercepts were made, but on the second, the enemy was engaged. It was the first aerial battle of its type, and it so disrupted the attack that the flight was credited with saving the task group from damage. On the third mission, Butch O'Hare was accidentally shot down.

Meanwhile back in Chicago, suburban Orchard Place Airport was the site of the factory that produced the Douglas C-54 transport in what is said to have been the largest wooden-roofed building in the world. After the war, in 1946, the Chicago City Council authorized the acquisition of 1,080 acres of this property from the War Assets Administration in order to build a second major airport facility in Chicago to supplement the heavily used Chicago Municipal Airport, later called Midway Airport. Commercial aviation was growing so rapidly at the time that another airport would clearly be needed.

In 1949, as expansion of the Orchard Place Airport got under way, there was a search for an appropriate name for the new facility. Various politicians were considered, but in the end, it would be named for Chicago's favorite war hero. Today, Chicago O'Hare International Airport ranks as the busiest airport in the world.

Harris: Penultimate Naval Ace

The number-two ace in the history of the U.S. Navy, Cecil E. Harris, was the only top naval ace to fly combat missions in both the Atlantic and the Pacific. He also flew both the F4F Wildcat and the F6F Hellcat, although he scored all of his aerial victories in the Hellcat.

Born in 1919 in South Dakota—the home state of top U.S. Marine Corps ace, Joe Foss—Harris was at Northern State Teachers College in 1939 when World War II began, and he made the decision to join the U.S. Navy before the United States entered the war in December 1941. After earning his wings as naval aviator at NAS Corpus Christi, he was assigned to VF-27, aboard the small escort carrier USS *Suwanee* in April 1942.

On November 8, 1942, Allied forces launched Operation Torch, landing troops in northwest Africa to gain a foothold for the eventual defeat of German and Italian forces in North Africa. The USS *Suwanee* was part of the armada of warships that supported the invasion. The defenders against the Operation Torch landings were primarily Vichy French forces that put up little resistance. There would be some limited air combat, but Harris would see no combat during the missions that he flew over North Africa.

Early in 1943, the USS *Suwanee* was redeployed to the Southwest Pacific to support operations in the Solomons. To conserve deck space aboard the small carrier, VF-27 was relocated ashore. Harris scored his first two victories here, but was later reassigned to the new, full-sized carrier USS *Intrepid,* which was commissioned in August 1943. He became an ace while flying F6Fs with the USS *Intrepid*'s VF-18, and on September 13, 1944, he downed four Imperial Japanese Navy Air Force aircraft in a single day.

In October 1944, the USS *Intrepid* was part of the massive U.S. Navy force that was involved in the invasion of the Philippines. The ship was assigned to Fast Carrier Task Force 38, which would be given the job of attacking Imperial Japanese Navy Air Force facilities, especially bomber bases, on the Japanese-held island of Formosa (now called Taiwan). The plan called for three days of attacks, beginning on October 12. A 16-plane force from VF-18 was tasked with flying the initial fighter sweeps over northeast Formosa early in the morning of the first day.

Cecil Harris was in the third of four flights of Hellcats as the attack began. They reached a Japanese base just as five bombers were taking off. In a fast attack, four of these were shot down, two of them by Harris. Then the Zero fighters were observed high above and diving to attack. One Hellcat went down, but another Hellcat attacked his killer. A second Zero wormed into the fight and Harris went after him. Out of the four aircraft involved in this dogfight, both Hellcats scored. As they headed back to the USS *Intrepid,* Harris encountered a stray Zero and shot him down, making it four in one day.

During his mission over Formosa on October 14, Harris claimed three Yokosuka D4Y Suisei "Judy" dive-bombers. On October 29, VF-18 was on patrol over the main Philippine island of Luzon, when a large mass of Imperial Japanese Navy Air Force fighters were observed, stalking a U.S. Navy strike force of bombers and torpedo bombers. Harris led the attack on the enemy aircraft. The attack was disrupted and Harris claimed four victories. For this action, he would be awarded the Navy Cross.

On November 25 off Luzon, the USS *Intrepid* was badly damaged in a kamikaze attack, ending her cruise. As she limped home for repairs, Cecil Harris also headed home. He had ended his combat career with 24 confirmed victories. In addition to his Navy Cross, he was awarded the Distinguished Flying Cross, a Silver Star, and two Gold Stars. When World War II ended, Harris left the U.S. Navy to pursue his teaching career in South Dakota.

Valencia: Kamikaze Killer

The third-highest scoring U.S. Navy ace of World War II, Eugene Valencia was born in San Francisco in 1921, joined the U.S. Navy in 1941, and earned his wings in April 1942. Like many of the best student pilots in 1942, he was retained by the Air Operational Training Command (predecessor of the Naval Air Training Command) as an instructor, but like most naval aviators in this situation in 1942, he was anxious to get into action. He finally got his wish, shipping out aboard the new USS *Essex* in February 1943 as she departed on her first cruise after being commissioned on the last day of 1942.

Sailing for the Southeast Pacific, the USS *Essex* was sent into action off New Britain, and it was over the big Imperial Japanese Navy base at Rabaul on the island that

Valencia scored his first three kills. On November 20, the USS *Essex* was part of the task force involved in the invasion of the island of Tarawa, and here Valencia scored his fourth.

Early in 1944, the USS *Essex* was involved in launching strikes against the Imperial Japanese Navy base on the heavily fortified island of Truk. On February 16, Valencia was on patrol over Truk when he became separated from his wingman, Bill Bonneau. Flying alone, he was jumped by A6M Zeros. He managed to outmaneuver them without taking any hits, so he turned to the attack, assuming the enemy not to be good marksmen. He was right, and he claimed three.

Now an ace, Valencia completed his time aboard the USS *Essex,* and was sent to NAS Pasco in Washington state to develop and train an elite fighter unit. The idea was to start with experienced pilots and allow them the opportunity for extensive training and practice of proven air combat techniques. The technique that they developed, known as the "Mowing Machine," would prove very effective in the final months of the war.

In February 1945, Valencia's handpicked division, known as "Valencia's Flying Circus," was assigned to VF-9, which shipped out aboard the USS *Lexington.* On February 16, VF-9 led the first carrier-based air strike against Tokyo since the Doolittle raid in 1942. They experienced rain and snow over the Japanese capital, but Valencia observed a Nakajima Ki-44 Shoki "Tojo," which was shot down by Harris Mitchell, another Circus pilot. In all, the Circus would claim six confirmed kills on their first mission.

The Circus transferred to the new fast carrier USS *Yorktown* in March, as part of Task Force 58, which was organized for operations against Okinawa. It was at Okinawa that the Japanese launched the most massive of their desperate kamikaze ("Divine Wind") suicide attack operations against the United States Fleet. Strong Japanese air opposition developed on April 6 in the first wave of a series of mass suicide attacks involving some 400 aircraft. In seven mass raids—and many smaller ones—between April 6 and May 23, the Japanese expended some 1,500 aircraft, principally against naval forces supporting the campaign. In the three-month struggle against the kamikaze force, the U.S. Navy took the heaviest punishment in its history. Although Task Force 58 lost no ship during the campaign, eight heavy carriers and one light carrier were hit. On April 16 alone, over 100 kamikaze attacks were launched, sinking the destroyer USS *Pringle,* and hitting 11 other ships. Among the badly damaged was the USS *Intrepid,* with a 12-by-14-foot hole in the flight deck, 40 planes destroyed, and 9 men killed.

On the following day, April 17, VF-9 was on patrol, watching for kamikazes or other enemy action against U.S. Navy ships, when the radar operator aboard the USS *Yorktown* vectored them against a Japanese force of at least 35 aircraft. The force was composed primarily of bomb-laden Nakajima Ki-84 Hayate "Frank" fighters, although there were some A6M Zeros included as well. They were all kamikazes.

The Circus attacked in pairs, but the Japanese aircraft did not vary from their course to fight them. Rather they continued on their suicide run toward the United States Fleet offshore. The Circus destroyed nine of the attackers, including three by Valencia, when the Japanese finally broke formation. Valencia and Mitchell had each claimed a Ki-84, when the Japanese began to strike back. Valencia got one more and then attacked another one that had jumped a Hellcat. He downed this one, bringing his tally for the day to six.

At this point, with fuel running low, the Circus broke off to return to the USS *Yorktown*. Valencia spotted a lone Japanese fighter and attempted to attack, only to discover that he was out of ammunition. Valencia would not score his seventh, but the Circus bagged 17. It was their best one-day score ever, although their "Mowing Machine" would clip 11 kamikazes on May 4 and 10 during the May 11 suicide attack.

When the war finally ended, Valencia's Flying Circus had destroyed 50 Japanese aircraft and had lost none of their own. Eugene Valencia ended the war with 23 victories.

After the war, he commanded VF(AW)-3 a naval air defense fighter unit equipped with Douglas F4D Skyray jet fighters. It was the only U.S. Navy unit to be assigned to the North American Air (later Aerospace) Defense Command (NORAD). Nevertheless, under Valencia's leadership the lone U.S. Navy unit twice won NORAD's highest honors for efficiency and readiness, winning over the other squadrons assigned to NORAD, all of which were U.S. Air Force or Royal Canadian Air Force units.

Foss: A Marine Matches Rickenbacker

During the early days of World War II, when aerial combat was discussed, whether it was on a street corner in Seattle or on an American airstrip in some remote land, talk always turned to speculation about who, if anyone, would be the first fighter pilot to equal the 26 victories that were the World War I score of the great Eddie Rickenbacker. The answer came on January 13, 1943.

In addition to being the first ace to reach the magic 26,

Joseph Jacob "Joe" Foss was one of the U.S. Marine Corps' first aces, and one of a handful of Marine aviators to be awarded the Congressional Medal of Honor.

Born in Sioux Falls, South Dakota, on April 17, 1915, Joe Foss took an interest in aviation at the age of 12 when he saw Charles Lindbergh perform during one of the Lone Eagle's barnstorming trips through the Dakotas. Foss enrolled at the University of South Dakota in 1934, but it was the trough of the Great Depression, and among those hardest hit were Dakota farmers—and this included the Foss family. Joe Foss left school to help at home, but returned, and finally graduated with a business administration degree in 1940.

Foss had learned to fly during his years at the University of South Dakota, and he even went so far as to help establish a civilian pilot training program at the university. After graduation, he joined the U.S. Marine Corps Reserve as an aviation cadet. He received his wings and officer's commission in 1941 and was working as a flight instructor when the United States entered World War II.

Initially assigned to a reconnaissance squadron, Foss requested a transfer to a fighter squadron. Because of his advanced age—he was 26—the request was denied. Foss lobbied hard and was finally sent to a training squadron to learn to fly the F4F Wildcat. After logging 150 hours in the F4F during June and July 1942, he was finally sent overseas with VMF-121, aboard the escort carrier USS *Copahee*, bound for the Solomon Islands, where the Allies were digging in to halt the Japanese advance against Australia.

The ship arrived off Guadalcanal, and on October 9, Joe Foss made his first and only carrier takeoff, landing at Henderson Field, a rugged landing strip hacked out of the Guadalcanal jungle. At this time, the Marines had captured only part of the island, so Japanese snipers were still active, and Japanese air attacks against Henderson Field were also frequent. This, combined with primitive living conditions, rounded out the difficult situation in which the men of VMF-121 found themselves.

Foss was assigned as executive officer of VMF-121 and flew his first mission on October 13. On this, he scored his first victory and was, himself, almost shot down. He was attacked by Japanese A6M Zeros, but as one overshot him, he opened fire, destroying it. In turn, other Zeros shot him up and he was forced to make a dead-stick landing at Henderson Field. Having scored his first victory on his first mission, he went on to get his second the following day.

Over the next few days, the Imperial Japanese Navy Air Force launched a major offensive aimed at destroying Henderson Field. On the ground, the damage was tremendous. Offshore, a barge carrying aviation fuel was destroyed, so VMF-121 was forced to drain fuel from wrecked aircraft in order to keep flying. The Marine aviators on Guadalcanal were flying obsolescent Grumman F4F Wildcats against a Japanese force equipped with the superior Mitsubishi A6M Zero, but they nevertheless achieved impressive results.

On October 18, Foss had an impressive day. His flight engaged a flight of Zeros, and in the ensuing dogfight, he managed to jump three from above, destroying two quickly and pursuing the third into a twisting, turning fight that ended with the Zero's engine aflame.

Having waded through three of the enemy fighters, Foss turned to the bombers that they were escorting. He attacked a flight of Mitsubishi G4M1 Betty bombers, diving on one and pulling up to destroy a second from below.

In just nine days, Foss had become an ace, but he would follow this up with three sets of double victories by October 25. On November 4, he shot down two enemy aircraft while participating in an American attack on Japanese ships that were shelling American shore positions. Returning to base, however, Foss's Wildcat went down at sea when its engine failed.

He swam part of the five miles to Guadalcanal, but he was finally picked up by a some local islanders and an Australian mill operator and taken to another island. The next day, he was collected by a U.S. Navy flying boat and returned to Guadalcanal. By now, Foss's reputation had spread, and for his actions thus far, he was awarded the Distinguished Flying Cross. It was awarded personally by Admiral William "Bull" Halsey, who paid a visit to Henderson Field.

During the latter days of 1942, VMF-121 came to be called "Joe's Flying Circus" in honor of Joe Foss. It would, in fact, become a squadron of aces, with five in addition to Foss, and a combined score of 72 kills against the Imperial Japanese Navy Air Force. For example, on November 12, they destroyed 21 out of 22 bombers in a Japanese strike force.

After a bout with malaria in December, Foss returned to action, and on January 13, 1943, he shot down three Japanese aircraft. This brought his total score to 26, making him the first American ace to match the 26 aerial victories officially credited to Rickenbacker in World War I.

After matching Rickenbacker's record, Foss was shipped home. The Navy Department wanted the publicity value of a live hero rather than risking the chance that he might be unlucky one day as he ran up further aerial victories in the Pacific. Back home, Foss was tasked with participating in a publicity and war-bond-selling tour. Now a high-profile celebrity, Foss made radio broadcasts, toured the Grumman factory on Long Island, New York, and made appearances at the U.S. Naval Academy and numerous bases.

On May 18, 1943, President Franklin D. Roosevelt presented him the Congressional Medal of Honor. The citation read: "For outstanding heroism and courage above and beyond the call of duty as executive officer of Marine Fighting Squadron 121, 1st Marine Aircraft Wing, at Guadalcanal. Engaging in almost daily combat with the enemy from 9 October to 19 November 1942, Captain Foss personally shot down 23 Japanese planes and damaged others so severely that their destruction was extremely probable. In addition, during this period, he successfully led a large number of escort missions, skillfully covering reconnaissance, bombing, and photographic planes as well as surface craft.

"On 15 January 1943, he added three more enemy planes to his already brilliant successes for a record of aerial combat achievement unsurpassed in this war. Boldly searching out an approaching enemy force on 25 January, Captain Foss led his eight F4F Marine planes and four Army P-38s into action and, undaunted by tremendously superior numbers, intercepted and struck with such force that four Japanese fighters were shot down and the bombers were turned back without releasing a single bomb. His remarkable flying skill, inspiring leadership, and indomitable fighting spirit were distinctive factors in the defense of strategic American positions on Guadalcanal."

Joe Foss would eventually go back to active duty in the South Pacific as commander of VMF-115, but his celebrity status precluded further combat flying, so his official score remained at 26.

After the war, Foss returned to South Dakota as his home state's premier war hero, and was promptly elected to the state house of representatives. He was also instrumental in organizing the South Dakota Air National Guard, and he served as a colonel in the U.S. Air Force during the Korean War. In 1952, he became the chief of staff of the South Dakota Air National Guard with the rank of brigadier general. He later served as a director of the U.S. Air Force Academy.

In 1954, Foss was elected governor of South Dakota, and he was subsequently reelected to a second term. He also served as a commissioner of the American Football League (AFL) and he hosted two weekly television programs, *American Sportsman* and *The Outdoorsman: Joe Foss*.

He continued his interest in aviation, serving for six years as the director of public relations for Royal Dutch Airlines (KLM). In 1980, he was awarded the Outstanding American Award by the Los Angeles Philanthropic Foundation.

Boyington: The Black Sheep

One of the best-loved archetypes among warriors is that of the swashbuckling hero who breaks all the rules off the battlefield while being both brave and effective in battle. Among the aces of World War II, none exemplified this ideal better than Gregory "Pappy" Boyington. In the air, he was an extraordinary pilot and a skilled squadron leader with an almost uncanny knack for aerial combat. On the ground, however, he drank heavily and, indeed, broke all the rules. He had an almost unnatural proclivity for getting into fistfights.

Pappy Boyington was the "Bad Boy" fighter pilot who became highest-scoring ace to fly with the U.S. Marine Corps, but he scored only 22 of his 28 total victories while flying with a Marine unit. This left Joe Foss, who scored

26 victories as a Marine aviator, with the record for the most victories while flying as a Marine.

Boyington's image is that of a man who enjoyed success and the pursuit of the good life, but his own real life was nothing short of tragic. Afflicted with emphysema, alcoholism, and attention deficit disorder (ADD), Boyington lived a difficult life, was never able to make a career for himself after the war, and failed at nearly everything he attempted. Everything, that is, except flying fighter aircraft.

Born on December 4, 1912, in Coeur d'Alene, Idaho, Boyington grew up in the rugged mountains of the Idaho panhandle and eventually settled with his parents on an apple farm in Okanagan, Washington. Like many others of his generation, he joined the armed services during the depths of the Great Depression because there were simply no other opportunities available. He earned his wings in 1935 and, by 1941, was a U.S. Marine Corps instructor pilot at Naval Air Station Pensacola in Florida.

A divorced father of three with a well-chronicled mean streak, he was hovering on the edge of a dishonorable discharge for habitual disorderly conduct when he was suddenly offered a chance to change his life and to channel his wild side into combat flying. The United States had not yet entered World War II, but a former U.S. Army Air Corps fighter commander named Claire Chennault was putting together a clandestine air force—with the support of the United States State Department—to help the Nationalist Chinese side in the long-running Sino-Japanese War.

Many U.S. Navy and Marine aviators, as well as pilots from the Air Corps, were recruited to fly with Chennault's American Volunteer Group (AVG), and Boyington was one of them. Operating the shark-face-painted Curtiss P-40 Warhawks that earned them the name "Flying Tigers," the AVG flew combat missions against the Japanese from bases in Burma and southern China. This would continue for a year, lasting for seven months after the United States entered the war. During this time, Boyington became one of the AVG's aces, shooting down six Japanese aircraft. In July 1942, the AVG was officially incorporated into the U.S. Army Air Forces, but Boyington chose not to be inducted into the USAAF, but rather to return to the United States and to the Marine Corps.

It was not until January 1943, however, that he was finally able to get his Marine Corps commission reinstated and to have an opportunity to go overseas again. In May 1943, he became commander of Marine Fighter Squadron VMF-222 on Guadalcanal, but the unit saw little actual combat and Boyington became restless. After suffering a minor broken bone in a scuffle with some squadron mates, he was sent to New Zealand for recuperation.

When he returned to Espiritu Santo in the central Solomon Islands combat zone in September 1943, Boyington lacked a squadron assignment, so he set up a squadron of his own. Utilizing the unused designation VMF-214, he assembled his unit from unassigned Vought F4U Corsair fighters and unassigned pilots like himself. Some of the aviators—though not all—were facing disciplinary action for various minor infractions, and this tended to feed the folklore of VMF-214 being a band of misfits and outcasts, which they would always insist they were not. Nevertheless, they called themselves "The Black Sheep Squadron." Major Boyington was given the nickname "Pappy" because, at 31, he was almost ten years older than most of his pilots.

What followed for the ensuing 12 weeks was the stuff from which legends are made. Indeed, it was the stuff from which a Hollywood movie and a television series would be made. These were also the best weeks of Boyington's career. In less than four months, the Black Sheep of VMF-214 literally made that legend for themselves, shooting down 94 Japanese aircraft—mostly fighters—and damaging or destroying on the ground more than 100 others. Boyington himself would shoot down 19 of this total through the end of 1943, including 5 on one day.

As 1944 began, Boyington had 25 aerial victories (including the 6 scored with the American Volunteer Group) to his credit, one short of the 26 scored by Eddie Rickenbacker. There was a great deal of interest—including intense speculation by the media back in the United States—in when Boyington would match or exceed the "magic 26."

For Boyington, it naturally became something of an obsession. This was especially underscored by the fact that VMF-214's combat tour would end in a matter of days.

On January 3, 1944, Pappy Boyington and his Black Sheep took off on a mission to the Japanese base at Kahili on the island of New Britain. They were intercepted by an overwhelming number of Imperial Japanese Navy Air Force fighters, but Boyington managed to shoot down three, exceeding the Rickenbacker number, as well as that of Joe Foss, who had earlier achieved a total score of 26. However, the day was not to be one of triumph for Boyington. He was set upon by a Zero of the 253rd Kokutai piloted by Masajiro Kawato, an ace with 19 victories, and shot down.

It was not observed whether Boyington survived, and a massive search for him came up empty-handed. When he was not found, and nothing was heard through international channels regarding his capture, he was officially declared missing in action.

Assumed to be dead, and a fallen hero at that, Boyington

was posthumously awarded the Congressional Medal of Honor and the Navy Cross. The apparently posthumous citation for his Medal of Honor read: "For extraordinary heroism and valiant devotion to duty as commanding officer of Marine Fighting Squadron 214 in action against enemy Japanese forces in the Central Solomons area from 12 September 1943 to 3 January 1944. Consistently outnumbered throughout successive hazardous flights over heavily defended hostile territory, Major Boyington struck at the enemy with daring and courageous persistence, leading his squadron into combat with devastating results to Japanese shipping, shore installations, and aerial forces. Resolute in his efforts to inflict crippling damage on the enemy, Major Boyington led a formation of 24 fighters over Kahili on 17 October and, persistently circling the airdrome where 60 hostile aircraft were grounded, boldly challenged the Japanese to send up planes. Under his brilliant command, our fighters shot down 20 enemy craft in the ensuing action without the loss of a single ship. A superb airman and determined fighter against overwhelming odds, Major Boyington personally destroyed 26 [actually 22] of the many Japanese planes shot down by his squadron and, by his forceful leadership, developed the combat readiness in his command which was a distinctive factor in the Allied aerial achievements in this vitally strategic area."

The incorrigible "Bad Boy" ace, who had become a media celebrity at the end of 1943, had now become a dead hero.

As it turned out, however, Boyington survived the crash, and was picked up by a Japanese submarine and taken to New Britain. Over the next 20 months, he would be held captive, mainly in Ofuna, Japan. He and a number of others were held as "special prisoners," rather than as prisoners of war, meaning that they did not receive full rations, and their names were not part of the prisoner-of-war rosters supplied to the Red Cross, and ultimately to the families of prisoners.

Boyington survived the war and was repatriated shortly after the occupation of Japan in September 1945. As a colorful Medal of Honor hero and 28-victory air ace who had just "returned from the dead," he became the object of intense media attention as soon as he arrived in the United States.

The Marine Corps used Boyington—now promoted to lieutenant colonel—in a campaign to sell bonds, but on the last night of a nationwide speaking tour, he appeared in public very drunk and very incorrigible. Having embarrassed himself and the Marine Corps, much of the glory of his triumphal return quickly faded.

Discharged as a colonel in 1947, Boyington spent most of the next decade battling alcoholism and drifting from job to job, which included being a draft-beer salesman and a referee for wrestling matches. His life began to turn around by the late 1950s, though, as he got a job flying for a charter airline out of Burbank, California. He also completed his autobiography, *Ba Baa, Black Sheep,* which was published in 1957.

This popular book became the basis for a made-for-television movie of the same name that was first aired in 1976, and that evolved into a weekly series that continued on the NBC network until 1978. These programs, which starred Robert Conrad as Boyington, glorified the "misfit" aspect of VMF-214, and were derided as inaccurate in nearly every respect except that the fictitious Black Sheep flew F4U Corsairs, as had the real Black Sheep. But they did serve to keep the Pappy Boyington legend alive in the minds of the public.

Gregory "Pappy" Boyington finally pieced his life together and lived out his last years in Fresno, California, where he died on January 11, 1988. He is buried at Arlington National Cemetery near Washington, D.C.

Hanson: Top Corsair Ace

Robert M. Hanson scored more victories in the Vought F4U Corsair than any other pilot and he was the second-highest-scoring U.S. Marine Corps ace, with 25 victories. Of course, if Pappy Boyington's American Volunteer Group victories are counted, then Hanson would be in third place, but he scored all 25 with the Marines and Boyington scored only 22. Amazingly, all of Hanson's kills were scored between August 1943 and February 1944, and 20 of his 25 were scored in a single 13-day period. Hanson was also the youngest Marine Corsair pilot to receive the Medal of Honor.

Robert Hanson was born on February 4, 1920, at Lucknow in India, the son of American missionaries, and became the heavyweight wrestling champion of India's United Provinces during the mid-1930s. He later set out to tour Europe by bicycle, and as the story goes, the teenager was bicycling through Austria in 1938 when it was absorbed into Nazi Germany.

Joining the U.S. Marine Corps after the United States entered World War II, Hanson earned his wings and was assigned to VMF-215 in 1943. By the time that he reached the Southwest Pacific, the American forces had developed an unstoppable momentum, gradually retaking the islands that the Imperial Japanese forces had previously occupied and fortified. Advancing up the Solomons chain since February in a series of amphibious operations, the U.S. Navy and Marine Corps had moved from Guadalcanal toward

the Japanese naval base at Rabaul. Beginning with the un-
opposed landing in the Russells, these forces leapfrogged
through the islands, establishing bases and airfields as they
went. Moving into Segi of the New Georgia Group in June,
through Rendova, Onaivisi, Wickham Anchorage, Kiri-
wini, and Treasury islands by October. They reached Bougainville in November, where landings on Cape Torokina
were supported by Marine air strikes.

One of Hanson's initial tasks was helping to cover the
Bougainville landings. On November 1, 1943, he shot
down a pair of A6M Zeros, plus a Nakajima B5N "Kate"
attack bomber. These victories, scored over Empress Augusta Bay, would make Bob Hanson an ace. During the
1943 and 1944 period, VMF-215 would be home to many
other aces, including Harold Spears, who eventually scored
15 victories, and Donald Aldrich, who ended the war with
20.

By the end of 1943, Hanson had achieved a momentum
analogous to that of the Marine Corps as a whole during
1943. He very quickly became known as the Marine
Corps' master of multiples. On January 14, 1944, he
downed five A6M Zeros, and ten days later, he destroyed
another four. On January 26, he scored three for the day,
all Zeros. On January 30, the multiple contained a pair of
Zeros and a Nakajima Ki-44 Shoki.

On February 3, a day before Hanson would have turned
24, VMF-215 conducted a strafing run and hunt for targets
of opportunity over Japanese-held New Ireland. For Hanson, one of the targets was a lighthouse at Cape St. George
that the Japanese used as an antiaircraft platform. His fellow VMF-215 aviators observed Hanson's F4U taking hits
and starting to disintegrate. He seemed to still be alive just
before the Corsair hit the water, but it came apart in an

explosion of debris. They circled and saw no sign of life in the shark-infested water.

Hanson's Medal of Honor citation read: "For conspicuous gallantry and intrepidity at the risk of his life and above and beyond the call of duty as fighter pilot attached to Marine Fighting Squadron 215 in action against enemy Japanese forces at Bougainville Island, 1 November 1943; and New Britain Island, 24 January 1944. Undeterred by fierce opposition, and fearless in the face of overwhelming odds, 1st Lieutenant Hanson fought the Japanese boldly and with daring aggressiveness. On 1 November, while flying cover for our landing operations at Empress Augusta Bay, he dauntlessly attacked six enemy torpedo bombers, forcing them to jettison their bombs and destroying one Japanese plane during the action. Cut off from his division while deep in enemy territory during a high cover flight over Simpson Harbor on 24 January, 1st Lieutenant Hanson waged a lone and gallant battle against hostile interceptors as they were orbiting to attack our bombers and, striking with devastating fury, brought down four Zeroes and probably a fifth. Handling his plane superbly in both pursuit and attack measures, he was a master of individual air combat, accounting for a total of 25 Japanese aircraft in this theater of war. His great personal valor and invincible fighting spirit were in keeping with the highest traditions of the U.S. Naval Service."

3

GERMANY

OF ALL THE COUNTRIES THAT fought in World War II, none was better prepared militarily—on the ground and in the air—than Germany. The Germans had designed weapons for the "Blitzkrieg" (lightning war), a fast, aggressive type of warfare that coordinated air and ground forces to overwhelm an enemy with fast movement and ease of maneuver. This devastated all opponents that Germany faced on land or in the air in the first two years of the war. Britain was an exception, because the overwater crossing the English Channel had never been properly planned.

The German air force, the Luftwaffe, had a better than four-to-one superiority over every foe that it would meet during 1939 and 1940, and in most cases, it was able to bring a ten-to-one superiority to bear. With the possible exception of the Royal Air Force (which was outnumbered), the Luftwaffe was the best air superiority and ground attack force in the world in the early years of World War II. When the Soviet Union was invaded in 1941, the Luftwaffe was so superior to the Soviet air force, the Voenno-Vozdushnie Sily, that it was able to destroy a sizable proportion of Soviet frontline airpower within a few weeks. On the first day, over 300 Soviet aircraft were shot down, and nearly 1,500 were destroyed on the ground. By the end of the first week, 5,000 Soviet aircraft had been erased—more than in the entire air forces of most countries—but Luftwaffe losses were fewer than 200.

With the exception of certain British aircraft, the Luftwaffe also had far better equipment than any enemy that it would face between 1939 and 1942. In terms of training, only Britain's Royal Air Force had pilots that were on a par with those of the Luftwaffe during the first three years of the war, but these were much fewer in number. Part of the reason for this was that the Luftwaffe had been created from scratch between 1935 and 1939. Under the Treaty of Versailles that ended World War I, Germany had not been allowed to have an air force. The new Luftwaffe had been designed from the ground up for the Blitzkrieg under the direction of Hermann Göring, a World War I ace with high standing in the Nazi Party, and Erhardt Milch, a brilliant planner and tactician.

During the Spanish Civil War of 1936–1939, Germany supported the Nationalists militarily and the Luftwaffe sent its Condor Legion, an organization of "volunteers." This allowed Germany's air arm to test both weapons and tactics against the types of aircraft that they expected to face in the future war. It also gave many Luftwaffe pilots the air-to-air combat experience that they would need.

Having described it as a well-oiled war machine, it can certainly be added that Germany's military might have had serious shortcomings in its overconfidence and shortsightedness. Adolf Hitler had insisted on preparing for just 18 months of war. For all of their preparedness, the Germans failed to have a mechanism in place to replace pilots and aircraft that would be lost beyond that time. When the war lasted longer than expected, pilot training and increased aircraft production had to be organized and expanded under wartime conditions and the well-oiled machine became sloppy. By 1944 and 1945, the thoroughly trained pilots were being replaced by the hastily trained novices. The Luftwaffe planners never developed long-range strategic bombers, as the British and Americans did, and this proved to be decisive.

Germany also had a technological edge. German engineers and aircraft designers designed the most advanced weapons and aircraft in the world during World War II. However, because Hitler wanted to wage a war that he arrogantly thought he could win in 18 months, Luftwaffe planners were never able to develop a method to adequately test and mass-produce the leading-edge "secret weapons" that had been developed. Until nearly the end of the war, when it was much too late, the Reichluftfahrt-ministerium (the German Air Ministry) refused to give adequate funding or priority to the advanced aircraft projects that would have given German pilots the technological edge. The projects and machines existed, but most would never get close to becoming operational. The Luftwaffe was, however, the only air force in the world to have turbojet aircraft in squadron service and air-to-air combat during World War II.

Luftwaffe Aces

The first German ace of World War II was Hannes Gentzen, a Bf-109D pilot who shot down two Polish fighters and a bomber on September 3, 1939, and four attack bombers the following day. During the Battle of France, he would add ten victories flying Bf-110s, before being killed in a crash on May 26, 1940. At the time, he was the highest-scoring ace—of any nation—in World War II, but he would soon have his record eclipsed by Luftwaffe aces who scored by the dozen, and who eventually pushed their scores beyond 100.

To say that the German aces of World War II outscored the aces of any other air arm is a huge understatement. The Luftwaffe had over 100 aces who outscored the top ace of every other nation involved in the war. While other nations assigned "ace" status with a fifth victory, the Luftwaffe maintained the World War I practice of considering a pilot to be an ace only after he had scored *ten* victories. In the Luftwaffe, the word for ace was "experte."

During World War I, the highest scoring ace of any nation had also been a German, Baron Manfred von Richthofen, the legendary "Red Baron." His score of 80 victories was exceeded in World War II by one Finnish ace, at least two (but by no more than four) Japanese aces—and *158* Luftwaffe aces.

With the exception of two Japanese aces with possible uncounted victories, no aces of any country other than Germany exceeded 100 aerial victories. In the Luftwaffe, there were 105 aces that exceeded 100 confirmed victories and 15 that exceeded 200 confirmed. Two men exceeded 300— Erich Hartmann with 352, and Gerhard Barkhorn with 301.

The reason for the success of the Luftwaffe aces lies with their training and their experience. They were very well trained, they flew with reliable equipment, and they continued to fly—literally for years. Such long-term experience made excellent fighter pilots into extraordinary fighter pilots. Of course, it should be added that the years claimed the lives of a number of good and excellent pilots, while they turned mediocre fighter pilots into dead fighter pilots.

It is also worth noting that unlike von Richthofen, few

of the high-scoring Luftwaffe aces were killed by being shot down by enemy fighters. Most of those that did not survive the war died in accidents. It can also be said that all of the really high-scoring Luftwaffe aces flew on the Eastern Front, where they faced large numbers of Voenno-Vozdushnie Sily pilots, who were poorly trained and poorly equipped until the last 18 months of the war.

In addition to Hartmann and Barkhorn, the top Luftwaffe aces were Günther Rall with 275, Otto Kittel with 267, Walter Nowotny with 258, Wilhelm Batz with 237, Erich Rudorffer with 222, Heinrich "Pritzl" Bär with 220, Hermann Graf with 212, Heinrich Ehrler with 209, Theodore Weissenburger with 208, Hans Philip with 206, Walter Schuck with 206, Anton Hafner with 204, and Helmut Lipfert with 203. These Luftwaffe records are all world records that have stood through World War II and dozens of succeeding conflicts, and will probably stand indefinitely.

Werner Mölders was the leading Luftwaffe ace of the Spanish Civil War and of the Battle of France, with 14 and 25 victories respectively. He was also the first ace to exceed von Richthofen's 80 and the first to exceed 100 confirmed victories. At the time of his death in 1941, he was still one of the Luftwaffe's top aces. The Luftwaffe would be the only air force to include jet aces during World War II. The leading jet ace was Kurt Welter, with 29. He was followed by Heinrich Bär and Franz Scahll with 16 and 14, respectively. There was a three-way tie for fourth with 12 victories each for Hermann Buchner, Georg-Peter Eder, and Erich Rudorffer.

The Luftwaffe's top night fighter ace was Heinz-Wolfgang Schnaufer, with 121 victories scored in the dark. Emil Lang has the record for the most kills in one day, with 18, while Erich Rudorffer holds the record, 13, for the most victories on a single mission.

While most of these records, as we said, were established on the Eastern Front against the Voenno-Vozdushnie Sily, one man holds all of the records for combat against the better-trained and better-equipped Royal Air Force. Hans-Joachim Marseille was the highest-scoring ace—of any nation—outside the Eastern Front, with 158 victories—all scored before September 30, 1942, when he was killed in an accident. Of these 158, 154 were against fighters rather than slower bombers or transports. Throughout the remainder of the war, no ace on any front—other than Luftwaffe pilots flying on the Eastern Front—would exceed his record. Had he lived, he would probably have been the leading ace of World War II. Indeed, at the time of Marseille's death—which was relatively early in the war—only a half-dozen Eastern Front aces had equaled his score.

Luftwaffe Fighter Organization

At the core of Luftwaffe organization was the "geschwader," which was the equivalent to the "wing" in American organization or a "group" in British organization. It was a mobile and homogeneous unit contained within a "luftflotte" (air fleet), but it generally operated autonomously. A fighter wing was a "jagdgeschwader" (JG), literally translated as a "hunting wing." This contained three to four "groups," known as "gruppen" or "jagdgruppen" (the singular is "gruppe"). The gruppen, in turn, contained three or four squadrons, "staffeln" or "jagdstaffeln" (the singular is "staffel"). Operationally, Luftwaffe fighters flew in a four-ship formation called a "schwarm" (meaning "swarm"). The schwarm, in turn, was made up of two "rotte" of two aircraft each, a leader and his wingman.

German Decorations

Germany awarded decorations on a more regular and less subjective basis than most other countries. The penultimate decoration for heroism was the Iron Cross (Eisernes Kreuz) of which there was a first and second class. The ultimate decoration was the Knight's Cross of the Iron Cross (Ritterkreuz des Eisernes Kreuz). There were four stages to the awarding of the Knight's Cross. The basic Knight's Cross was awarded to a holder of an Iron Cross, and with each successive display of distinguishing heroism, an attachment was made to it. First there was the Oak Leaves (Eichenlaub), followed by Swords (Schwertern). The ultimate version of this decoration was the Knight's Cross with Diamonds (Ritterkreuz des Eisernes Kreuz mit Brillianten).

Late in World War II, an even higher decoration was conceived, the Knight's Cross of the Iron Cross with *Golden* Oak Leaves, Swords, and Diamonds (Ritterkreuz des Eisernes Kreuz mit Goldener Eichenlaub, Schwertern, und Brillianten). It was intended to be awarded to the greatest heroes after Germany won the war, which, of course, never happened. Only one such decoration was actually awarded, and this was to Hans Ulrich Rudel, the legendary ground attack pilot who destroyed hundreds of Soviet tanks on the Eastern Front.

There were only 27 Knight's Crosses of the Iron Cross awarded with Oak Leaves, Swords, *and* Diamonds. Of those, only 18 recipients survived World War II. Of the 27, nine were Luftwaffe aces. These men were Adolf Galland (104 victories), Gordon Gollob (150 victories), Hermann Graf (212 victories), Helmut Lent (110 victories, 102 at night), Hans-Joachim Marseille (158 victories), Werner Mölders (115 victories, including 14 in Spain), Walter Nowotny (258 victories), and Heinz Schnaufer (121 victories, all at night).

German Fighter Aircraft

During World War II, virtually all of victories by the aces of the Luftwaffe were scored in one or the other of two aircraft, the Messerschmitt Bf-109 (aka Me-109) or the Focke Wulf Fw-190. Lesser numbers were scored by the Messerschmitt Bf-110 (aka Me-110) "Zerstorer" (Destroyer), a twin-engine aircraft that saw service primarily in the ground attack role and as a nightfighter. In the final months of the war, important contributions to fighter tactics and technology were made by the Messerschmitt Me-262 jet fighter. This plane, however, came too late to make a major impact on air combat actions.

Built in larger numbers than any other warplane in history, the Bf-109 was Germany's standard fighter through all of World War II. It was also probably the best piston-engined air superiority fighter in the world for a longer time than any other, although this period probably ended midway through the war.

The development of this remarkable aircraft began in the middle 1930s as Germany was rearming and the Luftwaffe was looking for a high-performance fighter. The Bf-109 was designed by Willy Messerschmitt and Walter Rethel at Bayerische Flugzeugwerke (BFW), in competition with designers from other important German planemakers, such as Heinkel and Focke Wulf. Powered by a 650-hp Rolls-Royce Kestrel V engine, the Bf-109 prototype was first flown in October 1935, its remarkable speed and agility beating out the Heinkel He-112 and the Focke Wulf Fw-159.

Bayerische Flugzeugwerke was given a contract for production-model Bf-109Bs powered by German-made 610-hp Junkers Jumo 210A engines. These rolled off the assembly line in early 1937 and were sent to Spain a few months later, flown with German Condor Legion "volunteers" in the Spanish Civil War. Its unqualified success in Spain won the Bf-109 an international reputation.

By July 1938, when Bayerische Flugzeugwerke was reorganized as Messerschmitt AG, the Luftwaffe's jagdstaffeln (fighter squadrons) had taken delivery of about 300 Bf-109s, with the Daimler-Benz-powered Bf-109D now becoming available and Switzerland in line as the first export customer. (Though after 1938, the Bf-109 was technically the Me-109, contemporary literature lists it both ways and it is conventional to list it with the original design prefix.) The first truly mass-produced model was the Bf-109E, which entered Luftwaffe service early in 1939. It had a wingspan of 32 feet 4.5 inches, and a length of 28 feet 4 inches. It weighed 4,431 pounds fully loaded and fueled. It was powered by a 1,050-hp, air-cooled V-12 Daimler-Benz DB 601 engine that was adopted in favor of the less-reliable DB 600 used in the Bf-109D. This gave the Bf-109E a top speed of 342 mph. It had a service ceiling of 34,450 feet and a range of 410 miles. Armament consisted of two 20mm wing-mounted cannons, one 20mm cannon firing through the propeller spinner, and a pair of 7.9mm MG17 machine guns firing through the propeller arc.

When Germany launched the September 1, 1939, invasion of Poland that began World War II, there were 1,000 Bf-109s in Luftwaffe service. The Luftwaffe's Bf-109s easily overwhelmed the Polish air force, and saw little other action in the war's first winter other than intercepting a few British bombing raids. In May 1940, with the invasion of France, the Luftwaffe had fewer than 1,500 Bf-109s, but these were more than a match for the French defenders. Turning to the Battle of Britain in August 1940, the Bf-109s faced their most potent adversaries, particularly in terms of the Royal Air Force pilots. In a dogfight between a Bf-109 and a Spitfire Mk.I or Hawker Hurricane, the outcome often lay with the skill—or luck—of the pilot. Of more than 1,100 aircraft lost by the Royal Air Force in the Battle of Britain, however, the vast majority were shot down by Bf-109s.

The Bf-109F type was introduced late in 1940, and these were a part of over 400 Bf-109s available for the invasion of the Soviet Union in June 1941. While the Messerschmitts were clearly superior to the Soviet fighters, attrition alone took its toll on the Bf-109, and production was stepped up.

In 1942, the Luftwaffe began to take delivery of the widely produced Bf-109G, known as "Gustav." It had a wingspan of 32 feet 6.5 inches and a length of 29 feet, and weighed 6,834 pounds fully loaded and fueled. It was powered by a 1,475-hp, air-cooled V-12 Daimler-Benz DB 605 engine that gave the Bf-109G a top speed of 406 mph, which was respectable but inferior to the P-51Ds and later "mark" Spitfires with which it would tangle. It had a service ceiling of 39,370 feet and a range of 528 miles. Armament consisted of one 20mm cannon firing through the propeller spinner and a pair of 7.9mm MG17 machine guns firing through the propeller arc. Some later Gustavs were equipped with provisions for wing-mounted Wfr.Gr.21 mortars and rocket launchers.

Production of the Bf-109G reached a peak of 725 aircraft a month in July 1943 and Gustavs continued in production until well into 1944, when they were replaced on assembly lines by the Bf-109K. The Bf-109Gs were used as interceptors for Reich air defense and they served on every front where the Luftwaffe was active: from the Channel coast to North Africa, and from Italy to the Eastern Front. Other Bf-109Gs were exported to neutral Switzerland, as well as to Axis air forces such as those of Italy, Croatia, Slovakia, Spain, Romania, and the Royal Bulgarian air force. Hungary not only used Bf-109G, but a large number were manufactured there.

The Bf-109G series was produced in larger numbers than all of the other Bf-109s combined.

The last production type was the Bf-109K, which entered service in September 1944. It was similar to the Bf-109G and was powered by a 2,030-hp DB 605ASCM engine. Both the Bf-109G and Bf-109K took part in the last major Luftwaffe offensive action, Operation Bodenplatte, which inflicted severe damage on the Anglo-American Allies on the Western Front in January 1945. The Allies were able to recover, but German production was no longer able to recoup from any losses, and by February, the Luftwaffe was down to fewer than 1,000 Bf-109s.

Amazingly, a handful of Bf-109s were still being produced in 1945, and they were still in combat in the war's final weeks. An incredible 35,000 Bf-109s were manufactured between 1934 and 1945, and they continued to be produced by Hispano in Spain for a number of years. Bf-109s remained in service in Switzerland until December 1949, and in Spain until the 1960s.

Many people consider the Focke Wulf Fw-190 the best German piston-engine fighter of World War II, although many aces who scored high numbers with the Bf-109G considered the latter to be equal or superior. Erich Hartmann, the Luftwaffe's highest-scoring ace flew only Bf-109s in combat.

The Fw-190 project originated in 1937, conceived by the Reichluftfahrtministerium (German Air Ministry) as a complement to the Bf-109 program. Designed by the great aircraft designer Kurt Tank, the Fw-109 was originally equipped with an air-cooled BMW-139 radial engine rated at 1,550 hp. This engine was soon replaced in early test aircraft by the newer BMW-801 engine, rated at 1,660 hp. The prototype first flew in June 1939, and the first production series Fw-190A-1 aircraft entered squadron service in July 1941.

The new aircraft soon received their baptism of fire against the Royal Air Force, where they proved to be on par with or superior to the Supermarine Spitfire Mk.V. The only shortcoming was in armament, and this was soon corrected. Originally used as an interceptor and air superiority fighter, the Fw-190A series would also be used as a fighter bomber. Of the entire Fw-190 family, 13,367 of the 20,000 built would serve as interceptors or air superiority fighters, while the rest were used as fighter-bombers.

The definitive member of the family was the Fw-190D "Dora," which made its appearance in 1944. It was equipped with the Junkers Jumo 213A engine, which delivered 2,240 hp and a top speed of 453 mph. The Dora had a wingspan of 34 feet 6 inches, a length of 33 feet 6 inches, and weighed 10,684 pounds. Its speed was rated as 425 mph at 21,710 feet, but it had a service ceiling of 39,473 feet. Its range was 521 miles. Armament varied, but was typically two 20mm cannons, two machine guns, and 1,103 pounds of bombs in fighter-bomber configuration.

The dedicated fighter-bomber variants were the Fw-190F and Fw-190G, which were conceived in 1943. The

Fw-190F was derived from the original Fw-190A series, and was equipped with bomb racks and attachment points for air-to-surface rockets. The Fw-190G was similar to the Fw-190F, but with increased fuel and payload capacity.

The Fw-190D air superiority fighter, in turn, evolved into the Ta-152H series, the "Ta" prefix added in honor of designer Kurt Tank and the "H" suffix standing for "hohenjager" (high-altitude fighter). The Ta-152H had a pressurized cockpit and an increased wingspan for high-altitude work. Armament included one engine-mounted 30mm MK108 cannon and two 20mm MG151 cannons in the wings. Production-series aircraft first appeared in November 1944, but no gruppen were ever fully equipped. A few did, however, operate with a combination of Ta-152Hs and Fw-190Ds. The Ta-152H proved itself an excellent high-altitude interceptor, and it was probably the only piston-engine Axis fighter to seriously challenge the P-51D Mustang. However, it arrived too late in the war to make a significant difference.

Also arriving too late, the world's first operational jet fighter, the Messerschmitt Me-262, was the best operational fighter of World War II. It was an aircraft whose full potential and effectiveness was never realized, not because of opposition from enemy aircraft, but because of opposition and indecisiveness on the part of Germany's own leadership. In the final weeks of the war, Adolf Hitler is recorded to have babbled incessantly about imaginary secret weapons, but few who heard him realized that two years earlier, he had squandered and even sabotaged a powerful secret weapon that might have somewhat altered Germany's fate.

The turbojet engine was invented by Frank Whittle in Britain in 1928, but the first aircraft to fly purely under jet power was the German Heinkel He-178, which first flew in August 1939, powered by an HeS3B engine designed by Hans-Joachim Pabst von Ohain. The German Air Ministry took an early interest in jet propulsion and financed the development of the Heinkel He-280 and the Messerschmitt Me-262 twin-jet fighters even before practical jet engines existed to power them. The He-280 flew in April 1941, powered by two of Ohain's experimental turbojets, which were later replaced by a pair of Junkers Jumo 004 turbojets. The Me-262 made its first flight in July 1942, powered by a pair of BMW 003 turbojets. The He-280 never evolved past the experimental stage, but the Me-262 would have an interesting service career.

The slow development of the Me-262 in the year after its first flight was due in part to developmental problems with the engines, but also to a general ambivalence on the part of the German Air Ministry. The bureaucrats in Berlin saw it as new technology that was of less priority than production of established aircraft. Fighter pilots—including General Adolf Galland, the head of fighter operations for the Luftwaffe—were delighted with its speed and performance, and wanted it in production as soon as possible. They realized what the bureaucrats did not: that Allied fighters were steadily improving, and that instead of continuing to catch up or stay even, the Luftwaffe should—and could—leap into the lead. Men like Galland also knew that Allied bombing was a growing threat to Germany, and that jet interceptors could be far more effective than piston-engine interceptors.

The Me-262 program was further complicated by the fact that Hitler himself wanted the Me-262 completed as a fighter-bomber rather than as an interceptor or air superiority fighter. His obsession with offensive operations would critically delay one of the best defensive weapons then in development. It meant that when the first production Me-262As were finally ready in April 1944, they were further delayed in order to be fitted with bomb racks.

The Me-262A had a wingspan of 40 feet 11.5 inches and a length of 34 feet 9.5 inches. It weighed 14,101 pounds fully loaded and fueled. It was powered by two Junkers Jumo 004B-1 turbojet engines, each delivering 1,980 pounds of thrust, giving it a top speed in excess of the rated maximum of 540 mph. The highest speed achieved by the Me-262 was 624 mph, recorded in July 1944. It had a service ceiling of 37,565 feet and a range of 652 miles. Its armament consisted of four nose-mounted 30mm cannons, and interceptors carried eight R4M missiles.

The Me-262B was a two-seat night fighter variant equipped with Neptun V radar and its distinctive nose-mounted "deer antlers" antennae.

Kommando Nowotny, the first fully operational Me-262 unit, was set up in September 1944 under leading Luftwaffe ace Major Walter Nowotny, and it claimed 22 kills by the end of the month. However, most of the operational Me-262s were lost because of their pilots' unfamiliarity with jets and their having had limited training time to learn about takeoffs, landings, and handling characteristics peculiar to jets. In air-to-air combat, though, the Me-262s were truly superior because of their speed. They could not turn as tight as a piston-engined fighter, but they could maintain speed in a turn much better.

In October, Me-262s began service as fighter-bombers, being used against the Allies' bridgeheads across the Rhine. They were quite effective, as they were too fast for fighters or conventional antiaircraft guns.

A full-fledged jet fighter wing, Jagdgeschwader 7, was set up near Berlin in November, and this unit was to achieve an impressive record of 427 victories, 75 percent of them being Allied heavy bombers. Through the winter, a number of additional jet fighter units were established, and the toll they took on Allied airmen was equally devastating.

In March 1945, General Galland set up the ultimate jet fighter unit, Jagdverband 44, staffing it with a group of Luftwaffe aces that included ten pilots who'd earned the Knight's Cross. They were flying the Me-262A-1a/U1 variant, which was especially well armed with six cannons including two 20mm MG151s, two 30mm MK103s, and two 30mm MK108s—in addition to the rockets. Though JV 44 scored 50 victories in a month of operations, it was far too late. With their airfields captured or destroyed, German pilots resorted to flying from sections of four-lane highway near Munich, and they kept going until they were taken into custody by United States ground forces less than a week before Germany capitulated.

The Allies thoroughly analyzed the Me-262, and innovations designed into it by Willy Messerschmitt's designers found their way into postwar American jets. For example, Boeing and North American Aviation, among others, had jet projects on the drawing boards in 1945 that were changed from straight-to swept-wing configuration largely because of what was learned from the world's first operational jet fighter.

Hartmann: There Is Only One Number One

Erich Alfred Hartmann was the leading ace of all time. Flying exclusively with JG 52 on the Eastern Front, he scored 352 aerial victories, including seven USAAF P-51s that he downed in operations over Romania. He flew 1,425 missions between October 1942 and May 1945, and he was one of the select nine Luftwaffe aces to be awarded the

Knight's Cross with Oak Leaves, Swords, and Diamonds.

In Germany, he came to be known as "the Blond Knight," but to the Soviet pilots he was "the Black Devil," because the cowling of the Messerschmitt Bf-109s that he flew were painted with a sinister-looking black, tulip-shaped pattern. His radio call sign was "Karaya 1" ("Sweetheart 1") because he had a red heart with his girlfriend's name painted on the side of his Bf-109. To his friends and comrades, though, he was simply "Bubi," an affectionate term implying that he was just a baby-faced boy.

Despite the heroics for which he was awarded his decorations, Hartmann's greatest triumph was probably his surviving the Soviet gulag archipelago, where he was held, in violation of international law, for more than ten years after the war ended. He is remembered for never have been broken, despite the cruelty that he suffered, and for being an inspiration to fellow prisoners.

Erich Hartmann was born on April 19, 1922, in Weissach, near Stuttgart, in the German state of Württemberg. His father, Dr. Alfred Erich Hartmann, had served as a physician during World War I. By 1925, because of the deterioration of economic conditions in Germany, Dr. Hartmann decided to accept a job in Changsa, China. The family remained there until 1929, when a rash of violence against Europeans forced Dr. Hartmann to send his family home. Erich, his younger brother, and their mother returned to Germany by train, traveling across the Soviet Union, a place where Erich was destined to spend much more of his life than he could have imagined in 1929. Later in the year, Dr. Hartmann also came home to stay.

Back in Germany, Erich's mother, Elisabeth Wilhelmine Machtholf Hartmann, became an accomplished glider pilot, eventually making the transition to powered aircraft.

By the time he was 14, Erich, too, was flying. He graduated from the gymnasium (high school) at Korntal in April 1940, and had dreams of following in his father's footsteps as a doctor, but war—and compulsory military service—intervened. Eventually, his brother Alfred became a doctor and took up their father's practice, but Erich would follow another track.

Erich's other dream was flying. Early in World War II, the air aces of the Luftwaffe, such as Werner Mölders and Adolf Galland, were the heroes of the German media, and they inspired excitement in impressionable teenagers like Erich Hartmann, who already held a pilot's license. He joined the Luftwaffe in October 1940, and was assigned to the 10th Flying Regiment at Neukuhren in East Prussia near Königsberg.

Hartmann spent the better part of his first two years in the Luftwaffe learning how to fly high-performance fighter aircraft and gaining an intimate understanding of the Messerschmitt Bf-109, the aircraft that would serve him so well in the years to come. The exhaustive training that he received in 1940–1942 was in stark contrast to the brief time that would be available to pilots who were mustered into the Luftwaffe during the later years of World War II. Hartmann was finally sent to a frontline unit in October 1942.

Assigned to JG 52, based deep inside the Soviet Union, on the southern part of the Eastern Front, Hartmann flew with such great aces as Günther Rall (275 victories) and Walter Krupinski (197 victories). One of his first assignments was as Krupinski's wingman. Another JG 52 experte was Gerhard Barkhorn, who scored 301 victories to become the only experte, other than Hartmann, to exceed 300. In all, JG 52 would be the highest-scoring unit in history, credited with the confirmed destruction of more than 10,000 Voenno-Vozdushnie Sily aircraft in less than four years of war.

Hartmann's first aerial victory, an Ilyushin Il-2 Sturmovik, came on November 5, 1942, but he did not score his second until January. His inclination, like that of every other novice fighter pilot, was to shoot at his enemies from too far away. Krupinski would spend several months yelling, "Get in closer, Bubi!"

When Bubi finally did learn to get in close, he became lethal. His second victory on January 27, 1943, was followed by a third on February 9 and a fourth the next day. He scored his fifth on March 24, enough to make him an ace in any air force but the Luftwaffe, but by the end of April, he had exceeded ten. In May, he became commander of JG 52's 7 Staffel.

By this time, Hartmann had developed his four-step method of aerial combat: see, decide, attack, reverse. In other words, when the enemy was spotted, the hunter would decide whether to pounce, and if so, the attack came quickly and was followed by breaking off before the enemy formation knew what had hit them. As Hartmann would later instruct novice pilots, "Once committed to an attack, fly in at full speed. After scoring crippling or disabling hits, I would clear myself and then repeat the process. I never pursued the enemy, once he had eluded me. Better to break off and set up again for a new assault."

The baby-faced boy who took two months to score his second victory quickly became an accomplished hunter. He scored four on July 5, seven on July 7, and four more on July 8. During August, he scored 46 aerial victories, including five on August 4 and seven on August 7. On August 17, he matched Baron von Richthofen's score of 80 from World War I. Most of his kills were Lavochkin La-5s, Yakovlev Yak-1s, or Yakovlev Yak-7s.

On August 20, however, after bringing his score to 90, Hartmann went down behind Soviet lines. He had been hit by ground fire while he was chasing an Il-2 that was attacking German ground forces. He was captured by the enemy almost immediately but he feigned injury until he had an opportunity to make a break. He eluded capture and managed to walk to German lines.

Back in the air, Hartmann continued to run up his score. On October 29, he scored his 150th victory, making him second only to Krupinski, who had scored his 150th on the first day of the month. Of course, Krupinski had been in action since 1939. Hartmann had scored all but two of his kills in eight months. For this, he was awarded the Knight's Cross. Hartmann had developed an intuitive aggressiveness in combat. No longer timid, he knew that the only way to score a certain kill was to be aggressive and not shoot until he could not miss. "The key to the approach was simple," he later said. "Get in as close to the enemy as possible. Your windscreen had to be black with his image."

Despite the cold and bad weather, Hartmann scored 50 victories during January and February 1944. To this, he would add 10 in one day on March 2. His total was now 202. For this, he was sent home to Germany to have the Oak Leaves attached to his Knight's Cross in a ceremony at Berchtesgaden.

By the time Hartmann returned to JG 52 in late March, German forces were being pushed back, and the geschwader had to relocate itself farther and farther to the west on a weekly basis. The weather was wet and the airfields were muddy and crowded with equipment. By now, Hartmann was starting to face the reality of combat with pilots who truly knew their stuff. The opposition still contained novices, but it wasn't like the situation in 1941–1942. The

Voenno-Vozdushnie Sily pilots were aggressive, and like the Luftwaffe aces, they were hunters. "If I was taken by surprise," Hartmann wrote of reacting to Soviet attackers, "I would do one or the other automatically, depending on conditions. If I had time, and saw my attacker coming in, I would wait to see how close he would come before opening up. If he began firing at long range, I could always turn into him. If he held his fire, I got ready for a real battle. If your attacker held his fire until he was really close, you knew you were in with someone who had a great deal of experience."

In April and May, JG 52 started operating from bases within Romania. It was in late June that Hartmann would score his victories against the Americans. Units of JG 52 were assigned as part of the air defense net for the huge oil refinery complex in and around Ploesti, Romania, that was an important target for the B-17 and B-24 heavy bombers of the USAAF Fifteenth Air Force, based in Italy. During the course of these actions, Hartmann tangled with the North American P-51 Mustang, arguably the best piston-engine fighter of World War II. He shot down seven. In July, after recording his 239th victory, Erich Hartmann was awarded the Swords for his Knight's Cross, becoming one of 75 persons to receive the award.

Back with JG 52, Hartmann finally surpassed Gerd Barkhorn on August 22 to become the highest-scoring experte in the Luftwaffe. Two days later, he shot down 11 Soviet aircraft in one day. This brought his total to 301, making him the first experte to exceed 300. For this, he would become the 17th man to have Germany's ultimate decoration, the Diamonds, attached to his Knight's Cross.

The awarding of his Diamonds, by Adolf Hitler himself, took place at the Führer's "Wolf's Lair" headquarters in East Prussia. Only a few weeks had elapsed since Hitler had been severely wounded, nearly killed, in the bomb attack on the Wolf's Lair. It was a surreal environment. Damage was still evident and Hitler was obviously still traumatized by the assassination attempt. Security was so tight as to border on paranoid. Hartmann was ordered to surrender his sidearm, but he refused, saying that he did not wish to receive the Diamonds from a leader who did not trust him. He kept his pistol during the ceremony and a subsequent chat with Hitler, who did not notice, or seem to care.

Having exceeded 300 victories, Hartmann was given an extended leave, during which time he married his childhood sweetheart, Ursula "Usch" Paetsch, on September 9. Gerd Barkhorn was his best man. After a brief honeymoon, Hartmann returned to JG 52, where he succeeded in raising his victory total to 331 by November 24. He then was given a well-earned Christmas leave, the last he would have for 11 years.

In the early months of 1945, General Adolf Galland, the Luftwaffe's former commander of fighter units, put a great deal of pressure on Hartmann to join his "Jagdverband 44." Galland was personally assembling all the top Luftwaffe aces to fly in a special super-geschwader that would be equipped with the new Messerschmitt Me-262 jet fighter. During March, Hartmann took leave from JG 52 to fly the jet. However, when it finally came time to officially join JV 44, Hartmann told Galland that he felt he had a moral obligation to continue to fly with his comrades in JG 52. It seemed to him the right thing to do at the time, but it proved to be the most regretted decision of his life.

Hartmann had scored 14 victories with JG 52 in February, and he scored five more in April to bring his total to 351. However, by now the Eastern Front was collapsing and German forces were spending all of their time withdrawing. By early May, Germany was in full retreat, and JG 52 was at its last base, Deutsche Brod in Czechoslovakia.

On May 8, Hartmann took off on a reconnaissance patrol directed at identifying how close the Soviet ground forces were to the field JG 52 was using. In the course of this mission, he encountered a large number of Soviet fighters. He attacked quickly and shot down a Yak-7, his 352nd and last victory. After he broke off, he noticed a formation of USAAF fighters arrive on the scene. He then watched the surreal spectacle of Americans attacking the Soviet aircraft, each side thinking the others were Germans.

Hartmann landed back at Deutsche Brod and was informed that the war was over. He and his superior Hermann Graf—a "Diamonds" awardee and an experte with 212 victories—had been ordered to fly to Dortmund to surrender to British forces, but they chose to remain with the rest of JG 52, which would attempt to travel overland and surrender to American ground forces before the Soviet armies caught up with them. This was another huge mistake.

The men from JG 52 managed to surrender to an American unit, but because they were in an area that Soviet forces were scheduled to occupy, they had to be turned over to the Soviets. Had they gone to Dortmund as ordered, Hartmann and Graf would probably have been back with their families within two months. Instead, the passage of those two months found them deep in the Soviet Union, at a forced labor camp near Gryazovets. By this time, they realized that they would not soon be released.

The large number of German prisoners incarcerated at Gryazovets were starved, kept in primitive conditions, and tormented psychologically. Weeks gave way to months, and the prisoners endured the harsh winter under barbaric conditions. Hartmann's wife did not find out that he survived the war until January 1946, and he did not find out until May 1946 that his son had been born on May 21, 1945, while he was in a cattle car crossing the steppes.

The prisoners were in the custody of the dreaded NKVD, the Narodny Kommisariat Vnutrennikh Del (People's Commissariat for Internal Affairs), the brutal internal security police that Josef Stalin used to keep his iron finger on the pulse of the Soviet Union. One of the projects that the NKVD undertook was to try to get the former German officers to come over to the Soviet cause. The idea was that they would become pawns that the Soviet Union could use to help them run their sector of occupied Germany. Many would succumb to the pressure, but Hartmann, who was apolitical, never did.

Being the so-called Black Devil, however, Hartmann was singled out for especially harsh treatment. The NKVD starved him, and they intercepted and held his mail. In 1947, he was transferred to Kuteynikovo, a mile from where he had been stationed with JG 52 in 1943. It was here that he endured the first of the many months he would spend in solitary confinement. It was also in 1947 that Hartmann was declared to be not a prisoner of war but a war criminal, and sentenced to 25 years of hard labor.

When Hartmann was transferred to Shakhty to begin working in a coal mine, he refused, because under the Geneva Convention, officers are not required to work. This touched off a prisoner revolt in which Hartmann himself prevented the Germans from killing the Soviet guards. He then stared down a force of Soviet troops that came to restore order. Instead of going to the coal mine, Hartmann went back into solitary confinement at Novochgerkassk.

Hartmann almost never received his mail. He did not

know until 1948 that the son he had never seen died in 1947 at age two. He did not know about his father's death in 1952 for over a year. Months gave way to years. Except for about a year at Diaterka prison camp in 1953–1954, Hartmann would remain in Novochgerkassk until October 1955. Hermann Graf, who signed a "confession" to being a war criminal, was released in 1950.

Hartmann's release came as part of an effort toward mending relations between the Soviet Union and the new Federal Republic of Germany, known as West Germany. Stalin had died in 1953, and West German Chancellor Konrad Adenauer asked for the release of German prisoners as one of the conditions of a new trade relationship that the Soviet Union wanted. Suddenly, Hartmann was on a train to Germany to be reunited with friends and family after more than a decade in captivity.

Meanwhile, many of his former Luftwaffe comrades, including Barkhorn, Krupinski, and Rall, had joined the new West German air force, the Bundesluftwaffe. They invited him to join as well, and since the only trade he had ever known was flying aircraft, he did so. Hartmann resumed flying in 1956 at Landsberg, and he also trained at the facility that the Bundesluftwaffe established in Arizona, which has much better flying weather than Germany. Hartmann's wife, Ursula, recalled the Arizona experience as one of the most pleasant of her life with Bubi Hartmann.

Back in West Germany, Hartmann was assigned as commander of the newly formed geschwader, JG 51, which was equipped with the new Lockheed F-104 Starfighter that was to prove so problematic for the Bundesluftwaffe in the early 1960s. Though he did an exceptional job of turning JG 71 into a first-rate unit, Hartmann's lack of political skills caused him to be overlooked for promotions in the peacetime military, and he resigned to take a job with Germany's civilian aviation authority. He died in 1993.

Mölders: First to Top the Red Baron

Like Hans-Joachim Marseille, Werner Mölders died early in his career after having achieved an amazing record. Having been the highest-scoring German ace in the Spanish Civil War, he became the first to exceed von Richthofen and the first ace to top 100. Mölders was born at Gelsenkirchen on March 18, 1913, and grew up in Brandenburg, where his father was posted with the 35th Fuesilier Regiment. In April 1931, he joined the army and was assigned to an infantry regiment in East Prussia. Two years later, after becoming an officer, he joined the Luftwaffe at Cottbus.

Mölders began his combat career in 1938, as one of the Luftwaffe pilots who joined the German Condor Legion to fight on the side of Francisco Franco's Nationalists during the Spanish Civil War. In Spain, he flew both Heinkel He-51 biplanes and Messerschmitt Bf-109Cs, scoring 14 victories to become a leading scorer in the unit. His last two victories, a pair of Polikarpov I-16s, came on October 15, 1938.

When World War II began, Mölders was assigned to JG 53 on the Western Front and had scored four kills by the end of 1939. He quickly racked up an impressive roster of kills during the Battle of France and was the top-scoring ace of the war—with 25—when he was shot down on June 5, 1940. After two weeks as a prisoner of war, France capitulated and he was assigned to JG 51 for the Battle of Britain. During this pivotal campaign, Mölders vied with Helmut Wick for highest-scoring ace. Mölders would reach 40 (excluding his 14 scored in Spain) on September

20, followed by Adolf Galland four days later and Wick on October 6. Early on November 28, Wick downed a Spitfire, his 55th victory, to surpass Mölders. However, late in the day, Wick went into dogfight with John Dundas, a 13.5-victory ace with the Royal Air Force No.609 Squadron over the Isle of Wight. Dundas managed to down Wick's Messerschmitt Bf-109, but was himself downed by Wick's wingman.

By this time, Mölders had received the Oak Leaves for his Knight's Cross. He was also already being credited as a tactical genius and had developed the types of tactics that many younger pilots would use to become great aces. Indeed, he was known for setting up a kill, and then letting a newer man take the shot and get the score. One of his most important contributions to Luftwaffe tactics was the development of the two-ship "rotte" formation as a basic fighting unit.

In 1940, Mölders earned the nickname "Vati," meaning "Daddy," for being the "father" of German fighter tactics, for being a mentor to newer pilots, and for his relatively advanced age. He was 27.

Early in 1941, JG 51 made the transition to the Bf-109F, and on February 26, Mölders scored his 60th victory of World War II. In May, JG 51 moved east in preparation for Operation Barbarossa, the invasion of the Soviet Union. Mölders scored four victories on June 22, the first day of the operation, and surpassed von Richthofen's 80 a few days later. For this, the Swords were attached to his Knight's Cross. By July 15, his score stood at 99 for World War II. On that date, he scored his final two victories, exceeding 100 for World War II and raising his final score for both wars to 115.

On July 16, Mölders became the first man to be awarded Diamonds for his Knight's Cross, and he was promoted to become the youngest colonel (oberst) in the Luftwaffe. However, the Luftwaffe high command forbade him to fly further combat missions. The Propaganda Ministry did not want to lose the man who topped the Red Baron to a stray Soviet bullet.

On August 7, Mölders was promoted to the temporary rank of general in order for him to become inspekteur general der jagdflieger (inspector general of fighters), with duties at the Reichluftfahrtministerium overseeing the management of all fighter units within the Luftwaffe. In November 1941, he was on an inspection tour of JG 77 on the Eastern Front, when he was summoned to Berlin for the funeral of Ernst Udet.

Udet had been the second-highest-scoring German ace of World War I, with 62 victories. He had gone on to a career as an aerobatic pilot and had even flown in several motion pictures. When the Luftwaffe reformed, he joined and was assigned as inspector general of ground attack aircraft, in which capacity he helped develop the Junkers Ju-87 Stuka dive-bomber. On November 17, 1941, he committed suicide under questionable circumstances after a disagreement with Hermann Göring.

Since no transport aircraft was available, Mölders decided to fly to Berlin in a Heinkel He-111 bomber on November 22. The aircraft suffered an engine failure near Breslau (now Wroclaw, Poland) en route to Berlin, and on final approach into Breslau-Hundsfeld Airfield, the second engine failed. Mölders, who was on the flight deck, was killed in the crash, but his aide survived. In his honor, his old unit, JG 51, added his name to their designation, officially renaming the geschwader "JG 51 Mölders."

Recently, it has come to light that Mölders found out about the super-secret Nazi T-4 project and was so enraged that he threatened to return his Knight's Cross with Diamonds if it was not stopped. T-4 was the code name for the Reich Work Group on Sanatoriums and Nursing Homes (Reichsarbeitsgemeinschaft Heil und Pflegeanstalten). It was a grisly project that used mentally disabled people as guinea pigs for gruesome—and typically fatal—medical experiments. T-4 was also responsible for developing the means for killing large numbers of people under controlled circumstances, such as in concentration camps. The organization operated from the Reichschancellory in Berlin, specifically located at Tiergarten 4, hence the name T-4. Early in 1941, T-4 agreed to permit Shutzstaffel (SS) boss Heinrich Himmler to use its personnel and facilities to rid the concentration camps of "excess prisoners," such as those most seriously ill physically and mentally. This was called "prisoner euthanasia."

As people outside the inner circle started to find out about the project, there was a groundswell of condemnation. It was denounced by the clergy and by many in government, including Mölders. Himmler, meanwhile, was more upset that the secret had gotten out than about its hideous purport. He is reported to have said, "If Operation T-4 had been entrusted to the SS, things would have happened differently, because when the Führer entrusts us with a job, we know how to deal with it correctly."

It is not known whether Mölders's death was part of the process of "dealing with it correctly," but Himmler would not have shied away from such a "job."

On November 28, Mölders was interred near Udet at the Invalidenfriedhof in Berlin, close to the tomb of Manfred von Richthofen. The site was disrupted during the building of the Berlin Wall, and again during construction of other installations in 1975. The area was repaired in 1992 after the Wall came down.

The Luftwaffe was disbanded after World War II, but

restored in 1955. Under the new Bundesluftwaffe, JG 74 was formed in 1961, and in 1973 was given the name "Geschwader Mölders," which was transferred from the old JG 51. Based at Neuburg, north of Munich, JG 74 was originally equipped with North American F-86K Sabres and later Lockheed F-104G Starfighters. In 1974, the McDonnell Douglas F-4F Phantom II began to replace the Starfighter, and JG 74 would remain a Phantom unit until after the turn of the century.

Galland: The General Was an Ace

When one looks at the careers of World War II fighter aces, few stand out, both during the war and after, as much as that of Adolf Galland—the dashing young hero with the movie-star presence, jet-black hair, and pencil-thin mustache. One of the leading aces of the Battle of Britain, Galland became a geschwader commander, and was second only to Mölders in being a recipient of the Knight's Cross with Diamonds. Galland also succeeded him as inspekteur general der jagdflieger (inspector general of fighters). After holding that post longer than anyone, he went back into combat as commander of Jagdverband (JV) 44, the Luftwaffe's last all-jet geschwader. He then became an ace again, a jet ace. After the war, he wrote his memoirs— entitled *The First and the Last*—and became one of the leading spokesmen for German fighter pilots at reunions and air shows.

Adolf Galland was born on March 19, 1912, at Westerholt in Westfalia, the second of Adolf and Anne Galland's four sons. An avid glider pilot, he established a local soaring record of more than two hours aloft in February 1932. In February 1934, having joined the army, he was assigned to an infantry regiment in Dresden for basic training, but in March 1935, he transferred to the Luftwaffe's JG 1 in Doberitz.

In May 1937, Galland arrived in Spain as part of the Condor Legion and was placed in command of Jagdstaffel 88, which was known as the "Mickey Mouse Squadron" because of the insignia that the cigar-smoking Galland designed—a cigar-smoking Mickey Mouse holding an ax and a pistol. Unlike his friend Werner Mölders, Galland did not become an ace in the Spanish Civil War, although his staffel contained all the Condor Legion aces. For his work as a commander, he was awarded the Spanish Cross in Gold with Diamonds on June 6, 1939. It had been awarded only 12 times in Spanish history. One of his unique innovations was to base his unit aboard a train. The aircraft were mobile and could land in fields anywhere. With Galland's plan, the train brought the base to wherever the aircraft landed after a mission, rather than compelling them to fly back to a fixed base.

When World War II began in September 1939, Galland flew ground attack missions against Polish ground forces in a Henschel Hs-123, and was awarded the Iron Cross on October 1, 1939. He was then reassigned as a fighter pilot, flying Messerschmitt Bf-109s with JG 27, which went into action in the Battle of France in May 1940. He claimed his long-awaited first aerial victories on May 12, downing two Royal Air Force Hawker Hurricanes in two missions.

Prior to the Battle of Britain, Galland was reassigned to JG 26. This geschwader was known informally as the "Abbeville Boys" because they were based at Abbeville, which is in the Pas de Calais region of northern France, just across the Channel from Britain. This placed him in the thick of the action, and he shot down two aircraft on his first day with the unit. For his 17th victory, scored on

August 22, 1940, Galland was awarded the Knight's Cross and made kommodore of JG 26.

Galland was a colorful character, the kind of swaggering knight of the air that one would expect to encounter only in the movies. He was often seen in the company of glamorous women—after all, he was only a couple of hours' drive from Paris. He served gourmet food in his officers' mess, he liked good wine—as well as fine cigars. He even had a cigar lighter installed in the cockpit of his Messerschmitt Bf-109.

Galland's days with the Abbeville Boys were among the greatest moments of his life, filled with virtually nothing but combat and parties, the two activities that he enjoyed most. One of the wildest tales from Abbeville folklore concerns the day that he combined both, by accident. He was flying solo, en route to a party hosted by General Theo Osterkamp (ultimately a 32-victory ace)—carrying lobster and champagne in his Bf-109. Suddenly, he was jumped by three Spitfires. Galland succeeded in outmaneuvering the attackers and shooting down all three. Coincidentally, the entire exchange was overheard on the two-way radio at the party. When he landed at the site of the festivities, the lobster and champagne were shaken but undamaged, and Galland was neither damaged nor shaken.

Through the end of 1940, Galland scored 52 victories, half of his eventual tally. More combat and additional victories would come the way of JG 26 during early 1941, but the urgency of the Battle of Britain had subsided. Both sides knew that there would be no cross-Channel invasion in 1941—in either direction.

It was not all glory for Galland, however. On June 21, 1941, he was shot down twice. In the morning, the Abbeville Boys attacked a force of Royal Air Force bombers, but were jumped by Spitfires, and Galland's Bf-109 was badly damaged. He managed to limp back to base and crash-land. After lunch, he took off again, but was not so lucky. He was bounced by Spitfires after scoring against one, and barely managed to force his way through a jammed canopy before his Messerschmitt crashed. As the story goes, Galland was smoking a cigar on the operating table as doctors were sewing and patching him up. In one day, Galland had been responsible for downing four aircraft—two British and two piloted by himself.

One of the most interesting stories in World War II fighter ace folklore concerns the friendship between Galland and the legless British ace, Douglas Bader (see the British Commonwealth section). Like Galland, Bader was a colorful character with a media following and a relatively high score of enemy aircraft. On August 9, 1941, he was shot down by JG 26 over northern France. When Galland found out, he invited him to dinner. One of Bader's artificial legs was lost and the other damaged when his parachute brought him down. Galland made a request through the International Red Cross for replacements and guaranteed safe passage for a Royal Air Force aircraft to parachute them to the JG 26 base. As it turned out, the plane that dropped the prostheses also bombed the base.

Bader got the legs and was sent to a series of prisoner-of-war camps from which he subsequently made a series of unsuccessful escape attempts. The two met again after the war and remained friends until Bader's death in 1982.

Meanwhile, on August 7, Werner Mölders had been promoted to temporary rank of inspekteur general der jagdflieger, to manage fighter units within the Luftwaffe. When he died in a plane crash on November 22 en route to Ernst Udet's funeral, Galland was named to succeed him. As the story goes, Herman Göring pulled Galland aside at the funeral and gave him the job on the spot.

On January 28, 1942, when Galland arrived in Berlin to assume his new duties, he was awarded the Diamonds for his Knight's Cross by Adolf Hitler himself. One of his first tasks at his new desk job was to organize and plan the air cover for the German navy's famous "Channel Dash," in which the battle cruisers *Scharnhorst* and *Gneisenau*, and the heavy cruiser *Prinz Eugen* slipped through the English Channel from France to Germany. Between February 11 and 13, the three ships made their way, covered by a rotation of various fighter wings that provided an "air umbrella" to protect them from British air attacks. It was successful. Not a single major hit was made on the warships.

By the end of 1942, the 30-year-old Galland had been promoted to general major (the equivalent of an American brigadier general), and in November 1944, he became a general leutnant (the equivalent of an American major general)—but through it all, he missed flying fighters in combat.

It was during 1942 that Galland first inspected the Messerschmitt Me-262 jet fighter, which was still in development. He immediately recognized its potential. In 1943, after he'd had a chance to fly the aircraft, he said that piloting it was like "being pushed by an angel."

In his official capacity, Galland recommended to Göring and Hitler that the Me-262 go into production as soon as possible. He advocated devoting all production resources for fighters—except those building Fw-190s—to jets. He also recommended the deployment of a massive jet fighter force. Any fighter pilot who flew the Me-262 recognized that such a force would completely reshape the nature of aerial warfare in Germany's favor.

When Hitler saw the Me-262, he was impressed, but insisted that it become a bomber. This was a task for which it was utterly unsuited, but it would take until late 1944 to get him to change his mind. Galland was convinced that a force of Me-262s deployed to France in June 1944 could have stopped the Normandy Invasion by removing its air cover. Certainly, when Me-262s attacked the Allied bomber formations, they were deadly and unstoppable— while in the air.

In July 1944, a month after the invasion, Galland finally decided to prove to Hitler what the Me-262 could do as a fighter. He chose Walter Nowotny, a Knight's Cross holder with over 200 victories, to head a demonstration unit, based at Achmer, that would be called Kommando Nowotny. In combat, especially against bombers, the Me-262 proved to be a potent weapon, although it was found to be vulnerable to Allied fighters during takeoffs and landings. On November 8, Galland happened to be at Achmer when Nowotny himself was shot down by a USAAF P-51 while on final approach after a mission.

By the end of 1944, a deep chasm had opened between the Luftwaffe's flying officers and its desk-bound officers at the Reichluftfahrtministerium—and Galland was caught in the middle. Luftwaffe chief Göring was ignoring the tactical recommendations made by Galland and the Luftwaffe field commanders, and was ordering operations that were not only ineffective but were costing lives unnecessarily. The lack of initiative in getting the Me-262s into production was only the tip of the iceberg. Göring had lost the confidence of the flying officers, who demanded more effective leadership.

It all came to a head in January 1945. The leading commanders came to Galland, who set up a meeting with Göring. The leader of the revolt was Günther Josten, a geschwader kommodore and an experte with 178 victories. Also present was Johannes Steinhoff, a commander and an experte who would ultimately claim 176 victories, and well as Günther Lutzow, a Luftwaffe officer and the son of the great World War I admiral. The meeting was not pleasant. Göring was unreceptive and flatly refused to modify policies that the officers felt were damaging to Germany. The officers finally demanded that he resign. He became enraged and demoted everyone present, including Galland, who was not.

Hitler overruled Göring on Galland's demotion. He would be allowed to keep his rank, but he lost his job as inspekteur general. His new job, however, was much more to his liking. Galland was tasked with finally creating an all-jet jagdgeschwader. It would be designated "Jagdverband 44," the only such unit ever created, although if Galland had had his way, there would have been ten of them 18 months earlier. He brought in Johannes Steinhoff, who in turn recruited Heinrich Bär, Gerhard Barkhorn, Walter Krupinski, Erich Hohagen, Günther Lutzow, Wilhelm Herget, and Erich Rudorffer—all Knight's Cross holders with high scores in conventional aircraft. Erich Hartmann was invited, but chose to continue with JG 52 on the Eastern Front.

Though JV 44 did not get into action until March 1945—less than two months before the war ended—the impact was dramatic. By now, the new Me-262A-1a/U1 was available, with a withering complement of guns, including two 20mm MG151s, two 30mm MK103s, and two 30mm MK108s. Using high-velocity air-to-air rockets as well as guns, the Me-262s were extremely effective. It was as though the technology of the future had suddenly arrived aboard a time machine, but it was too late to affect the outcome of the war. Nevertheless, JV 44 ran up a very impressive tally. Many of the pilots—including Galland,

Steinhoff, Bär, and Rudorffer—became aces all over again in the jets.

Galland's last mission came on April 26. He had shot down a pair of USAAF Martin B-26 Marauders, his 103rd and 104th victories, but as he banked to turn back into the bomber formation, fire from anther Marauder poured into his cockpit, wounding him and damaging the Me-262. As he limped back to his base, he found that it was under attack by a large number of P-47s. As he struggled up from a missed approach, he was bounced by a Thunderbolt piloted by James Finnegan. Galland survived, but was badly injured. The war would end before he could recuperate. Bär took over JV 44 for the last ten days of the war.

Because of his role as inspekteur general, Galland was arrested by the Allies on May 14, 1945, and he remained as a prisoner of war until 1947. When he was released, he was forbidden to be a pilot in occupied Germany, so he held various odd jobs before being invited to Argentina to help build that country's postwar air force. President Juan Perón, an ardent nationalist who was often compared to Hitler and Mussolini, was anxious to build a powerful military, and he was able to find many capable advisors among the ranks of Germany's former military officers.

Adolf Galland established Argentina's air- force training and operations school, and he helped to develop its tactical training program. Many of the tactical doctrines he instilled were used successfully by Argentina in the 1982 Falklands War. Galland also played an important role in the development of the Pulqui, Argentina's first indigenously produced fighter aircraft. Most important for him, he was able to fly again.

In 1954, Galland married Countess Sylvina von Donhoff, and early in 1955, he left Argentina to relocate back to Germany. Later that year, the Defense Ministry rejected his application to serve as head of the newly constituted West German Bundesluftwaffe in favor of General Josef Kammhuber, who had headed the Luftwaffe's night fighter operations during World War II.

Over the ensuing years, Galland operated a successful aerospace consulting business in Bonn and was an active participant at fighter pilot reunions in Germany, as well as in Britain and the United States. He died on February 9, 1996, of a heart ailment at the age of 83.

Barkhorn: The Luftwaffe's Penultimate Ace

The only experte other than Erich Hartmann to score more than 300 victories, Gerhard "Gerd" Barkhorn flew most of his missions with Hartmann's unit, JG 52, on the Eastern Front. In April 1945, he was one of the pilots tapped by Adolf Galland and Johannes Steinhoff to fly Me-262 jet fighters with the all-jet geschwader, Jagdverband 44.

Barkhorn was born in Königsberg in East Prussia on March 20, 1919, and joined the Luftwaffe in 1939. In August 1940, during the Battle of Britain, he was assigned to JG 52—which was then based in France—but he did not score any kills during the campaign. In preparation for Operation Barbarossa, the invasion of the Soviet Union, JG 52 was transferred to the Eastern Front. On July 2, 1941, ten days after the invasion, Barkhorn scored his first victory.

On August 23, 1942, with 59 victories to his credit, Barkhorn was awarded the Knight's Cross. By the middle of December, he had pushed his score to 100, and on January 12, 1943, he received the Oak Leaves to mark his 120th kill. In June, he became a commander of II Staffel within JG 52, and on November 30, he reached 200 victories. By this time, Barkhorn had become one of the most effective fighter pilots on the Eastern Front. With his 250th kill on February 13, 1944, he joined a pantheon that only five Luftwaffe aces would reach, and on March 2, he became the 52nd man to have the Swords added to his Knight's Cross.

In January 1945, having surpassed 300, Barkhorn was transferred to JG 6 on the Western Front, although soon afterward he was picked to transition into the Me-262. On April 21, just six days after he joined JV 44, Barkhorn was badly injured in the crash of his Me-262. He would not recover in time to fly again, and the Luftwaffe's penultimate ace would add no jet fighter victories to the tally of 301 that he'd scored in piston-engine aircraft.

In 1955, when the postwar Federal Republic of Germany created the new Bundesluftwaffe, Barkhorn would be one of the former Luftwaffe aces called upon to serve as a general officer. Gerhard Barkhorn died in 1983.

Rall: Germany's Number-Three Ace

Günther Rall was the third-highest-scoring experte in the Luftwaffe, with 272 Eastern Front victories and three scored in the West. He was born in Gaggenau in the Schwarzwald on March 10, 1918, but he grew up in Stuttgart. He earned his Luftwaffe wings in 1938 and became a fighter pilot in 1939. His first combat assignment was flying Bf-109Es with JG 52 during the Battle of France in May 1940, and his first two victories were scored on May 12, 1940.

During the Battle of Britain, because of high attrition, Rall moved up the ranks quickly, and he was named top command 8 Staffel of JG 52. At the end of 1940, JG 52 was transferred to Romania, whence it took part in the Balkan actions during the spring of 1941. In April, Rall flew opposite the Royal Air Force's leading ace, Marmaduke "Pat" Pattle, in the air war over Greece.

After the occupation of Greece and Crete, JG 52 was reequipped with the new Messerschmitt Bf-109F in anticipation of Operation Barbarossa. After the invasion of the Soviet Union on June 22, JG 52 operated on the southern sector of the Eastern Front. They later moved through the Caucasus and saw action over Dniepropetrovsk and Stalingrad.

Rall was injured on November 28, when he crash-landed on the snowy steppes near Taganrog. He had been shot down by a Voenno-Vozdushnie Sily fighter after being blinded by the explosion of a second Soviet fighter that he had just destroyed. Although his Bf-109F disintegrated before hitting the snow, Rall survived and was pulled from the wreckage by a German tank crew.

His back was broken in three places and he was paralyzed on his right side. The prognosis was not good, and doctors were sure that if he lived, he would never fly again. However, the doctors were wrong. By August 1942, Rall was back in action. On November 26, just short of the first anniversary of the crash that almost killed him, Günther Rall was in Berlin to have the Oak Leaves added to his Knight's Cross in honor of his 100th aerial victory.

In April 1943, Rall was placed in command of III Gruppe of JG 52, still on the Eastern Front, and on August 29, he scored his 200th victory. Adolf Hitler added the Swords to his Knight's Cross on September 12. By now, Rall was on a roll. During October alone, he scored 40 victories.

By 1944, the USAAF Eighth Air Force was causing serious damage to German industry, and air defense (Reichsverteidigung) was becoming a very important priority for the Luftwaffe. The best pilots were needed to protect the Fatherland itself. In March 1944, Günther Rall was transferred from JG 52 to JG 11 in Germany to fly the Messerschmitt Bf-109G-5 on intercept missions against the American heavy bombers.

One of the challenges for the Luftwaffe interceptors was fighting their way through the defensive screen of fighter escorts that the USAAF put up to protect the bombers. On May 12, one of these fighters, a 5th Fighter Group P-47 Thunderbolt, attacked Rall's Messerschmitt and succeeded in shooting off his left thumb. Despite his disability, Rall continued to fly, and in March 1945, with World War II in its final weeks, he was assigned to a command job with JG 300. He ended the war with 275 victories in 621 missions, an enviable record of a victory for every 2.26 sorties.

Rall joined the Bundesluftwaffe as a pilot in 1956, being given his final wartime rank of major. Never granted an opportunity to fly the Me-262 jet fighters during World War II, he was now able the feel what Adolf Galland had characterized as "the angel's push." He flew both Republic F-84s and Lockheed F-104 Starfighters before getting bumped upstairs. He would serve as the commanding general of the Bundesluftwaffe in 1970 and 1971 and as inspekteur general from 1971 until his retirement in 1974.

Kittel: The Number-One Focke Wulf Ace

The fourth-highest-scoring experte in the Luftwaffe, Otto Kittel was the leading ace to fly the Focke Wulf Fw-190 series aircraft, considered the Luftwaffe's best piston-engine fighter. Of his 267 victories, 220 were achieved in the Fw-190, and most of these in the powerful Fw-190D "Dora," with its Junkers Jumo 213 engine.

Kittel was born in Kronsdorf in the German-speaking Sudetenland region of Czechoslovakia, on February 21,

1917. He was among the generation of young aviation-minded men who joined the Luftwaffe in 1939 on the eve of World War II. In 1941, after completing his fighter pilot training, Kittel was assigned to JG 54, which was known as "Grunherz," because its insignia was a green heart. This unit was being readied for action on the northern (Baltic) part of the Eastern Front for Operation Barbarossa, the German invasion of the Soviet Union. When Barbarossa was launched on June 22, 1941, Kittel was in action as one of the Bf-109 pilots providing air cover, and he scored his first two victories that day.

The Soviet Voenno-Vozdushnie Sily took a tremendous beating from the Luftwaffe in the early days of Operation Barbarossa. Nearly 5,000 of its aircraft were destroyed in the first week alone. Most of these Soviet aircraft were, admittedly, obsolete, but there were some golden threads in the mohair shirt of the Voenno-Vozdushnie Sily. The most effective ground attack aircraft in the Voenno-Vozdushnie Sily arsenal was the Ilyushin Il-2 Sturmovik (Stormbird). Some would argue that it was probably the best ground attack aircraft of the war. Its strength was in its durability. It was also hard to shoot down because it couldn't be attacked from the rear, which was usually the best way to kill an enemy aircraft. Unlike many other Soviet aircraft, it was heavily armored against rear attack and it had a rear-firing gunner.

Otto Kittel first met the Stormbird on June 30, 1941. Like most Luftwaffe pilots, he was frustrated by this unstoppable monster that came in low and fast to chew up the German columns with 20mm cannon fire. He would make it his goal to find a way to stop the Stormbird. After some experimentation, Kittel discovered that the Il-2 could be shot down by hitting it on the underside of the engine, where there was no armor and the rear gunner was unable to return fire. This method was tricky because the Il-2 pilots flew so low, but Kittel mastered the technique and became known as the best Sturmovik killer on the Eastern Front.

Whatever the situation on the ground, which did not go exactly as the German high command wished, the Luftwaffe was the master of Soviet skies through 1942. For Kittel, things went slower than for many. He finally reached a score of 30 in 1942, and on February 19, 1943, he scored his 39th victory, which is notable, because it was the 4,000th for JG 54 Grunherz.

With the introduction of the Fw-190A, the Grunherz totals would grow, and on October 29, 1943, Kittel was awarded the Knight's Cross after scoring 123 victories. The Focke Wulf Fw-190D would be introduced in 1944, and Oak Leaves would be added to Kittel's Knight's Cross on April 11, when his score reached 152.

By November 25, when the Swords were added, Kittel had arrived among the top five aces with 230 victories. By this time, however, it had become clear that the war was lost. The Luftwaffe could still outscore the Voenno-Vozdushnie Sily, but they were no longer fighting over the Soviet Union. The German armies had collapsed into retreat and the war had come home to the nation that had started it. The losses were not being replaced and the pilots were tired.

On February 14, 1945, Otto Kittel took off for the last time. Flying an Fw-190A-8, he intercepted and attacked eight Sturmoviks. He managed to damage one of the Il-2s seriously, but it disappeared over the horizon, showing no indication of having crashed, although it probably did. If it did, it would have been Kittel's number 268. As he tried to turn, Kittel was jumped by the remaining Stormbirds. The Focke Wulf shuddered from the impact of the 20mm cannon shells and burst into flames. The plane was too low for Kittel to get out before it exploded into the snowy landscape.

Nowotny: The Austrian Expert

The Luftwaffe's fifth-highest-scoring experte, and the first officer from any nation to command a jet fighter unit, Walter Nowotny was born on December 7, 1920, in Gmund. At that time, as it is today, Gmund was located in Austria. However, in 1938, when Nowotny was 17 years old, Austria was absorbed into the German Reich in the Anschluss, and Nowotny became a German. The following year, he joined the Luftwaffe and applied for training as a fighter pilot.

In the spring of 1941, he was posted to JG 54 Grunherz, which would be assigned to the northern (Baltic) part of the Eastern Front for Operation Barbarossa on June 22, 1941. Nowotny's first aerial victories came on July 19. Off to an auspicious beginning, he downed three Soviet aircraft that day. However, his luck quickly unraveled when his Messerschmitt Bf-109 was shot down by a Polikarpov I-153 over the Riga Bay off Latvia. After three days and nights adrift in the Baltic, Nowotny finally reached the shore and was picked up by German troops. As the story goes, the superstitious Nowotny was so glad to have survived that he flew all his subsequent missions wearing the same pair of pants that he had on during this ordeal.

Through the course of his first winter on the Eastern Front, Nowotny racked up 48 victories, a good showing, but nothing like what was to come. The second phase of his career as a fighter pilot began on August 4, 1942. On that day, JG 54 was on a bomber escort mission over Leningrad, when Soviet fighters jumped the bombers. No sooner had Nowotny nailed one of the enemy fighters than he had a second in his sights. The sky was so filled with Polikarpovs that this happened again and again, until Nowotny had claimed six. As he banked to turn for home, it happened again and he scored his seventh for the day. Nowotny was awarded the Knight's Cross on September 14, 1942, and on October 25, he was given command of 9 Staffel of JG 54.

Nowotny would reach 100 victories on March 25, 1943, and nine days later, he shot down 10 enemy aircraft in one day. Shortly after, he was placed in command of I Gruppe of Grunherz. His successes as a fighter pilot became legendary. During March, he scored 41, only to top this record with 49 in August. The August total included 9 on August 13 and 7 on August 21, to bring his tally to 157.

On the first day of September, Nowotny had his second run of ten in one day, and on September 4, the Oak Leaves were added to his Knight's Cross to honor him for 189 victories. Five days later, he would score his 200th kill. October began with Nowotny downing 32 Soviet aircraft in ten days, and on October 14, he became the first of only five aces in history to reach a total of 250 victories. Five days later, he became the eighth German to have the Diamonds added to his Knight's Cross.

Despite his Diamonds and his national-hero status, Nowotny continued to fly and fight with JG 54 through the blizzards of November. On November 15, however, as he scored his 255th Eastern Front victory, the Luftwaffe decided to bring him in from the cold. He was of more value at home as a living hero than on the Eastern Front, where he might get killed. Nowotny returned to Germany, a celebrity, who would help the German propaganda mill to inspire the populace with confidence.

In February 1944, after a round of public appearances,

Nowotny was assigned to command Schulegeschwader (literally "school wing") 101, a training unit located at Pau in France. While he was in France, the first Messerschmitt Me-262 jet fighters were finally reaching the Luftwaffe, and were being worked through their initial teething troubles. Most new aircraft go through such a stage when they are introduced, but the Me-262 represented such a leap into the stratosphere of unfamiliar technology that such problems were magnified. Despite their promise, the jets were plagued with difficulties. The Junkers Jumo engines were temperamental and fragile, and the Me-262s were vulnerable during takeoffs and landings. Finally, it was decided that the best way to shape the Me-262s into an effective force was to get them into an operational unit commanded by an experienced fighter pilot and geschwader commander. The Luftwaffe's inspekteur general der jagdflieger (inspector general of fighters), Adolf Galland, called Nowotny.

While a provisional Me-262 test unit already existed at Hesepe, Walter Nowotny was tasked with pulling together a jet fighter unit. On September 26, 1944, he formed his "Kommando Nowotny." The next day, it officially began operations at Achmer, near Osnabrück and not far from Hesepe, in the heart of the Ruhr industrial region. This is where the Eighth Air Force bombers were coming, and it was the place where interceptors were needed most. The idea was for Kommando Nowotny to become the prototype for the next generation of air defense.

On November 7, 1944, Adolf Galland came to Achmer to inspect the new air defense unit and its jet fighters. It would be an inauspicious day. Because of numerous and varied mechanical problems, only two of the jets managed to get off. Nowotny himself was grounded with a plugged fuel line. Each of the two that flew would claim an Allied fighter, but it was not what Galland—or Nowotny—were looking for.

The following day, Galland observed six Me-262s—led by Nowotny—take off to intercept an Eighth Air Force bomber stream. Several USAAF bombers and fighters were reported shot down, and Nowotny reported that he was coming back with one of his two engines out. Galland watched him coming in on his final approach, but suddenly, the jet was bounced by a P-51D Mustang, which was later determined to have been piloted by R. W. Stevens of the 364th Fighter Group. Stevens broke off after his first pass and Nowotny reported that he was on fire. Nowotny's Me-262 hit the ground, bounced up, came down, and disappeared in a fireball. Walter Nowotny was killed in action on November 8, 1944. His final score was 255 Eastern Front victories won in Messerschmitt Bf-109s and Focke-Wulf Fw-190As, plus three Boeing B-17s claimed while flying his Messerschmitt Me-262.

Rudorffer: Thirteen on One Mission

The Luftwaffe's seventh-highest-scoring experte of World War II, Erich Rudorffer was also a master of multiple kills and he achieved the record of 13 victories—in 17 minutes—on a single mission. The fighter pilot folklore also tells of the day in 1940 when Rudorffer took pity on a Royal Air Force Hurricane pilot and saved his life.

Erich Rudorffer was born in Zwickau in Saxony on November 1, 1917. He joined the Luftwaffe at the relatively mature age of 23 and was assigned to JG 2 early in 1940. He participated in the Battle of France and scored his first victory against the Armée de l'Air on May 14, 1940. By the time that France surrendered in June, Rudorffer's score stood at nine.

The incident involving the Hurricane occurred in August, when Rudorffer shot up the British aircraft, but rather than delivering the coup de grâce and forcing the pilot to bail out in the bitterly cold, uncertain waters of the English Channel, he flew with him until the damaged Hurricane crossed the English coastline. Two weeks later, a Royal Air Force pilot returned the favor when Rudorffer's Bf-109 was damaged over the Channel.

Rudorffer received his Knight's Cross on May 1, 1941, having scored 19 victories, and he remained in Europe until November 1942, when JG 2 was relocated to North Africa. Here, Rudorffer was promoted to command the geschwader's II Gruppe. It was while JG 2 was located in Tunisia that he began to achieve his mastery of multiple-kill dogfights.

Early in 1943, he scored 26 victories against the Royal Air Force over Tunisia, 15 of them in the space of 52 minutes on two missions. On February 9, he downed 8 in 32 minutes, and on February 15, he claimed 7 in just 20 minutes.

In June, after spending three months in France flying patrols over the English Channel, Rudorffer received the assignment to the Eastern Front that was inevitable for high-scoring Luftwaffe pilots in 1943. He was given the task of organizing IV Gruppe for JG 54, the geschwader known as "Grunherz" because of its green, heart-shaped insignia. He was in Königsberg in East Prussia working on this project when word came through on the last day of July that Heinrich Jung, the commander of II Gruppe, was missing in action. Erich Rudorffer was named as his replacement.

The master of the multiples was now in action against the Voenno-Vozdushnie Sily. On August 24, now flying the potent Focke Wulf Fw-190, he would claim five Soviet aircraft before lunch, and another three in the afternoon. Rudorffer was setting impossible records on an almost weekly basis. On October 11, for example, he is recorded to have scored seven kills in the course of seven minutes. On November 6, he entered his name on page one of the record books when he downed 13 enemies in 17 minutes.

He had scored more in a single mission than anyone before or since. The only records that come close are Emil "Bully" Lang's 18 victories in one day, scored on the Eastern Front, and Hans-Joachim Marseille's 17 victories in one day, which was scored against the Royal Air Force in North Africa.

By April 1944, when he received the Oak Leaves for his Knight's Cross, Rudorffer's score was up to 113. Still the multiple victories came. On October 28, he aborted a landing in order to chase a Soviet attack bomber force. He claimed nine of the heavily armored Ilyushin Il-2s, disrupted their attack, landed for lunch, and claimed two more in the afternoon.

In January 1945, with Germany's ultimate fate sealed, Rudorffer was awarded the Swords for his 210th victory, and reassigned to JG 7 to be brought up to speed on the Me-262 jet fighter. He would go on to score 12 of his 222 victories in the remarkable aircraft, tying him for fourth place among World War II jet aces.

After the war, Erich Rudorffer would go on to serve with the civilian aviation agency of the German Federal Republic.

Bär: The Top Me-262 Jet Ace

The man destined to be the highest scoring Me-262 jet ace in World War II, Heinrich Bär, was born on March 25, 1913, in Sommerfeld, near Leipzig. "Heinz," or "Pritzl," as he was called, grew up anxious to fly and made his first flights in a glider at an early age. He joined the Luftwaffe in 1937 and had been assigned as a Bf-109 pilot to JG 51 by the time World War II began September 1939. He scored his first victory on September 25 over Weissenberg, Germany. It was an American-made Curtiss Hawk Model 75 fighter belonging to the French Armée de l'Air.

In 1940, Bär's geschwader shifted to the Western Front, where, beginning in May, he flew Messerschmitt Bf-109Es in both the Battle of France and the Battle of Britain. In the latter, he was the Luftwaffe's top-scoring nonofficer, with a total of 17 victories. It would be a year and another ten victories before Bär was commissioned as an officer, but on July 2, 1941, his commission as a leutnant was accompanied by a Knight's Cross.

Almost immediately, Bär became commander of IV Gruppe of JG 51, which was reassigned to the Eastern Front on July 27, 1941, a bit over a month after Germany invaded the Soviet Union. His unit was reequipped with Bf-109Fs and attached to JG 53, which was known as "Pik As" ("Ace of Spades") because of its insignia. On August 14, Bär scored his 56th victory and was subsequently awarded the Oak Leaves for his Knight's Cross. The Swords, and a promotion to captain, would come on February 16, 1942, after his 90th victory. On May 1, Bär was transferred to the Mediterranean Theater, where he was made commander of I Gruppe of JG 77, based in Sicily. Over the course of the next year, he flew Bf-109Fs and Bf-109Gs on missions over North Africa and throughout the Mediterranean region, adding 45 victories to his total. However, as the story goes, the stress of combat and the blow of watching the Axis defeated in Africa and Sicily, pushed Bär into a nervous breakdown. Relieved of his command and demoted, he was sent back to Germany.

By the spring of 1944, the strategic bombing campaign being waged by the USAAF Eighth Air Force was in full swing, with raids hitting Germany's industrial heartland almost daily. Defense of the Reich now became a principal concern for the Luftwaffe, and pilots were needed to fly intercept missions. Bär was called back to duty to fly Fw-190As with JG 1. He proved that once again, he had the "right stuff," and on April 22, 1944, he scored his 200th victory, one of 21 USAAF heavy bombers that he would shoot down over Germany.

In June, Bär was promoted again, and given a geschwader, JG 3, to command. On January 1, 1945, he led JG 3 in Operation Bodenplatte (Base Plate), the massive Luftwaffe attack on the Western Front that was launched in support of the German Ardennes offensive that had resulted in the Battle of the Bulge. It was over Eindhoven in the Netherlands during this operation that Bär scored his last victories in a piston-engine aircraft—a pair of Royal Air Force Hawker Tempests.

In January, after the collapse of the Ardennes offensive, Bär was reassigned to Reich defense duties, this time with jet fighters. He became commander of a training geschwader at Lechfeld, designated EJG 2 (Ergaenzungs-Jagdgeschwader 2), which was created for the purpose of training pilots to fly the Messerschmitt Me-262 jet. He was taught to fly the new aircraft by Fritz Wendel, the Messerschmitt chief test pilot. In February, while he was flight-testing the Me-262, Bär set a speed record of 645 mph and an altitude record of over 48,000 feet.

One gruppe of EJG 2 became operational, and Bär flew his first combat mission in the Me-262 on March 2. He scored his first victory—a USAAF P-51D Mustang—over Ingolstadt on March 13, and quickly increased his score to 13. On April 23, 1945, Bär transferred to Adolf Galland's

Jagdverband 44 at Munich, the first operational all-jet geschwader. With this unit, he would score his last three victories—three P-47 Thunderbolts. His 220th kill—his 16th in a jet—came on April 28. When General Galland was injured on April 26, Bär became JV 44's last commander, serving until the unit surrendered to American troops on May 3.

Bär was the highest scoring Me-262 ace of World War II, but Kurt Welter was the highest-scoring jet ace. He was a night fighter (nachtjager) pilot with 60 total victories (50 at night). He scored 29 of his 60 in various jet aircraft, including the Arado Ar-234B-2n (a converted bomber), the Me-262A-1a, and the two-seat Me-262B-1a, which was developed specifically to be a night fighter. Welter flew with his own "Kommando Welter" and with Nachtjagd-geschwader 11.

After the war, Pritzl Bär, like Adolf Galland, became an aerospace consultant and, eventually, a private pilot. On April 22, 1957, he was performing aerobatics in his light plane to mark the 13th anniversary of his 200th aerial victory when he crashed to his death. The number 13 had always been considered his lucky number. Throughout World War II, he always flew an aircraft marked with "Lucky 13."

Steinhoff: The Man Without a Face

Johannes "Macky" Steinhoff scored 176 victories during World War II, including six in jets, but he was also highly regarded as a tactician and a leader. He is best remembered, however, for overcoming the disfigurement of his face, which was destroyed by fire, to rise to the highest position in the postwar Bundesluftwaffe.

Steinhoff was born on September 15, 1913, in Bottendorf, and he joined the German navy, the Kriegsmarine, in 1934. Two years later, however, he transferred to the Luftwaffe. When World War II began in September 1939, Steinhoff was assigned to JG 26. He scored his first two aerial victories—a pair of Vickers Wellington bombers—on December 18, during the Battle of the German Bight, a daylight offensive against German ports. This offensive was so costly to the Royal Air Force Bomber Command in terms of the number of bombers lost that they would switch to flying nighttime raids almost exclusively through the end of the war.

In February 1940, Steinhoff was transferred to JG 52, the geschwader with which he would serve through the Battle of Britain in August-September. JG 52 was moved to the Eastern Front in June 1941 in advance of the invasion of the Soviet Union on June 22. By August 30, when he was awarded his Knight's Cross, Steinhoff had raised his total score to 35. He was promoted to command II Gruppe of JG 52 in February 1942, and on September 2, the Oak Leaves were attached to his Knight's Cross. By this time, his score stood at 101.

On October 28, 1942, Steinhoff, now with 150 victories, was assigned to the staff of JG 77 in North Africa. In 1943, after the withdrawal of Luftwaffe forces to Italy, he was promoted to command JG 77. On July 28, 1944, after being relocated to France, Steinhoff received the Swords to his Knight's Cross to mark his 167th victory. In December, he was assigned to JG 7, which was starting to receive its first Me-262 jet fighters.

By the end of 1944, Steinhoff had become part of a political intrigue that was trying to force Hermann Göring to use the Luftwaffe more effectively. Isolated behind his desk, Göring was ignoring the tactical recommendations made by flying officers and was running the Luftwaffe in a way that was costing lives unnecessarily. In January 1945, Steinhoff was one of the leading Luftwaffe commanders who demanded that Göring resign. The Luftwaffe chief screamed and threatened, but in the end it was a virtual stalemate. Göring would not modify his flawed policies, but neither would he carry out his threat to execute those who had "conspired" against him.

General Adolf Galland lost his job as inspekteur general, but he did get the opportunity to set up the Luftwaffe's all-jet "jagdgeschwader of experts," Jagdverband 44. Johannes Steinhoff was one of the first pilots asked to join, and he scored the first of his six aerial victories in a Messerschmitt Me-262 in February.

On April 18, 1945, Steinhoff was one of six jet pilots taking off to meet USAAF bombers when he hit a crater on the runway and collapsed the aircraft's landing gear. The Messerschmitt bounced down the runway at takeoff speed until the highly volatile jet fuel exploded in a fireball. This, in turn, ignited the air-to-air rockets, turning the fireball into an exploding inferno. Somehow, Steinhoff struggled free of the cockpit and ran from the aircraft.

He had suffered severe disfiguring burns on every part of his body that was not covered. His face was effectively burned off. He survived, but years of skin grafts would never come close to repairing the damage.

Nevertheless, Steinhoff's indomitable spirit showed through, and he rebuilt his life in postwar Germany. He joined the government of the new Federal Republic of Germany (West Germany) in 1952, and was part of the organization that created a structure for the German Federal Armed Forces, which would eventually be integrated into NATO. The new Bundesluftwaffe was officially created on November 12, 1955, and its first commanding officer, or inspekteur general, was Josef Kammhuber, who had commanded Luftwaffe night fighter (nachtjager) units during World War II. He took office in June 1956, having been chosen over Adolf Galland, the only other serious candidate.

Among the officer corps of the Bundesluftwaffe were former Luftwaffe aces such as Gerhard Barkhorn, Günther Rall, Erich Hartmann—and Johannes Steinhoff. The new force was afflicted with many problems. Because of restrictions imposed by the Allies in 1945, Germany had not had an air force, or even a means of training civilian pilots. Indeed, former Luftwaffe pilots were specifically forbidden to fly. Aviation in Germany had suffered from the ten-year break and had to reconnect itself with international standards. Only a handful of German pilots had experience in jet fighters, but not since 1945. In 1955, a group of select pilots—including Steinhoff—began training on new jets in Britain and in the United States, and operations also started in January 1957 at Landsberg and Fürstenfeldbruck.

Steinhoff's career grew with the new Bundesluftwaffe, and with its relationship with NATO. In January 1965, now a general, he was named chief of staff and deputy commander allied air forces Central Europe. In 1966, he was named as commander of the force he helped create— or recreate—with the title inspekteur der Luftwaffe der Bundeswehr. He took over a force that was plagued by a series of crashes of the Bundesluftwaffe's newest fighter, the American-made Lockheed F-104 Starfighter. The deaths of many pilots had created a serious morale problem within the force, but also a serious scandal in the German government. Steinhoff is remembered for accepting the challenge of dealing with the crisis and reshaping procedures to correct the underlying problems.

In September 1970, he became the chairman of the military committee of NATO, a post he held until 1974. In

1978, General Steinhoff wrote the manifesto that would help shape NATO strategy regarding tactical nuclear weapons through the end of the Cold War: "I am in favor of retaining nuclear weapons as potential tools, but not permitting them to become battlefield weapons. I am not opposed to the strategic employment of these weapons; however, I am firmly opposed to their tactical use on our soil."

Johannes Steinhoff lived to see the Cold War end and the Berlin Wall come down; he died in February 1994.

On September 18, 1997, JG 73, based at Laage in Mecklenburg–Western Pomerania, took his name and was redesignated as "JG 73 Steinhoff." The former East German base was, at that time, home to 23 MiG-29 and 16 McDonnell Douglas F-4F Phantom fighter aircraft, but on October 9 of the same year, it was announced that it would be one of the geschwaders that would upgrade to the new Eurofighter Typhoon, scheduled for service early in the 21st century.

Schnaufer: The Spook of St. Trond

While many Luftwaffe aces overcame difficult situations to rack up scores in the hundreds, one man scored all of his victories in the most difficult environment of all—the dead of night. Just a few years before World War II, simply flying at night was impossible except over well-illuminated cities and highways, but eventually, instruments made navigation possible—even if it was impossible to see anything. It still took great skill to navigate in the dark.

During the war, the bomber pilots used navigation skills to find their targets, knowing that if they came by night, they would be invisible. Then came the night fighters. If it was hard to find a fixed location on the ground in the dark, it can be imagined how much harder it would be to find a fast-moving airplane that could be anywhere at any altitude. Mastery of the art of night fighting was one of the tactical and technological achievements in modern warfare to come out of World War II.

The master of this art, the top night fighter ace of all time, was Heinz-Wolfgang Schnaufer. He was born in Stuttgart on February 16, 1922, and was raised at Calw in the Schwarzwald. In Nazi Germany, the establishment was always on the lookout to recruit smart, healthy young men into their sociopolitical apparatus. In 1939, Schnaufer was picked to attend the National Political Educational Establishment at Potsdam, in suburban Berlin. While there, he expressed an interest in flying, and was one of a number of Hitler Youth who were diverted from politics to the Luftwaffe.

Having earned his wings in 1941, Schnaufer volunteered for the Luftwaffe's fledgling night fighter (nachtjager) program. The process of intercepting bombers at night was still experimental. Radar, which would ultimately prove to be the most practical way to track bombers at night, was still relatively crude and unreliable. Schnaufer was sent to Wunstorf for training, and teamed up with Fritz Rumpelhardt, who would fly with him for most of his missions as his radar operator.

In November 1941, Schnaufer and Rumpelhardt were assigned to fly in radar-equipped Messerschmitt Bf-110s with the first night fighter wing, Nachtjagergeschwader 1 (NJG 1). The unit was initially based at Stade, near Hamburg, but was later moved to St. Trond in Belgium in order to be in the typical path of bombers based in Britain and able to intercept them before they reached the German border.

Schnaufer and Rumpelhardt flew their first mission in February 1942, helping to cover the German navy's famous "Channel Dash," when they moved the battle cruisers *Scharnhorst* and *Gneisenau,* and the heavy cruiser *Prinz Eugen,* through the English Channel to Germany. Schnaufer and Rumpelhardt had their first contact with an enemy bomber in June 1942, when they claimed a Royal Air Force Handley-Page Halifax over Belgium. Unlike the fighter pilots who flew by day, however, the targets were hard to find and the scores came in spurts. The team managed only seven victories for the entire year of 1942.

In August 1943, with his score now at 17, Schnaufer was sent to Leeuwarden in the Netherlands to command 12 Staffel of IV Gruppe of NJG 1, and by year's end, he held a Knight's Cross and had a score of 43—all Royal Air Force bombers, and all scored by night. He remained in the Netherlands until March 1944, when he returned to St. Trond to assume command of IV Gruppe itself, a post that he held until November. In June 1944, Schnaufer was awarded Oak Leaves for his Knight's Cross when his tally reached 84 victories. A month later, after five more, he was awarded Swords. Rumpelhardt, meanwhile, was also awarded the Knight's Cross.

By September, the Allies had recaptured most of France and a large part of Belgium. Allied air superiority had extended through Belgium into Germany itself. Luftwaffe units were being withdrawn back inside the Reich, and NJG 1 relocated to the Ruhr area near Düsseldorf.

By now, the number of Allied bombers had increased tenfold since 1942. The night fighters had good hunting, but they worked frantically to stem the tide of destruction that streamed into Germany every night. On October 9, 1944, Schnaufer scored his 100th victory and was summoned to Berlin to receive his Diamonds from Adolf Hitler. A month later, he was given command of NJG 4 at Gütersloh.

As the numbers of bombers continued to increase, so, too, did the sophistication of detection methods. By early 1945, when the war was all but lost, the Luftwaffe was finally achieving a level of technological superiority that would have made it all but unbeatable had it been achieved two years earlier. For example, in February, Schnaufer equaled by night the achievements of day fighters on some of their best days. For Schnaufer, this meant a score of nine in a single 24-hour period. In the hours after midnight on February 21, he claimed a pair of bombers, went back to Gütersloh, slept, took off, and shot down seven more before midnight rolled around again.

In May, Schnaufer surrendered to British forces near the Danish border. The final score for this holder of the Knight's Cross with Diamonds was 121—excluding many probables that went unverified. He was barely 23 years old.

Late in 1945, he was released from a prisoner-of-war camp and the man the Royal Air Force called the "Spook of St. Trond" returned to the Schwarzwald and the family wine business.

Five years later, in July 1950, the prosperous merchant who flew hundreds of missions in complete darkness was on a business trip to Bordeaux when his sports car collided with a truck that had made an illegal turn at a blind corner. Heinz Schnaufer was killed—in broad daylight.

Marseille: The Best Fighter Pilot Ever?

Hans-Joachim Marseille's brilliant and deadly career as a fighter pilot was cut short by an accident that occurred on September 30, 1942, but in the months leading up to that date, he had become almost mythical—in the literal sense of the word. His ability to see the enemy and size up a situation before anyone else was remarkable. He was surrounded by accomplished pilots, many of them high-scoring aces, yet his marksmanship and his flying skills were beyond their comprehension. He was a man with an uncanny ability to score with impossible shots.

Watching him was like watching a magician. What he did was done in plain sight, but it was often impossible to tell just how he did it. He took virtually impossible, high-angle deflection shots and scored with short, split-second bursts of fire. Back on the ground after a mission during which he destroyed four or more enemy aircraft, ground crews were constantly amazed by how little ammunition Marseille had used.

Marseille's accomplishments became legendary throughout the Luftwaffe—and even with his foe, Britain's Royal Air Force (and its constituent Commonwealth air forces). The only aces in history that outscored him were the Luftwaffe pilots who fought on the Eastern Front, where the Voenno-Vozdushnie Sily was consistently less well trained and equipped. Marseille scored all of his victories against the Royal Air Force, and he also scored more victories against the Royal Air Force than any other Luftwaffe pilot. Of his 158 victories, 154 were against fighters, rather than slower bombers or transports.

During the last year of his career, Marseille not only scored in almost all of his combat actions, but he scored multiple victories in most of them. He would score multiple victories in every combat action in which he fought during 1942. He scored 17 victories in one day against the Royal Air Force as part of a four-day period in which he claimed 32 British aircraft, including several Spitfires. In the last month of his life, Marseille flew in nine combat actions—one with a jammed cannon—and scored 56 victories. His daily average for that month alone exceeded the score required to become an ace in most other air forces.

At the time that he was killed, only a half-dozen aces— all of them Luftwaffe pilots on the Eastern Front—were ahead of him. Erich Hartmann, the number one ace of all time, had not yet scored his *first*. Nor had any of the great American aces. Throughout the remainder of the war, no ace on any front—other than Luftwaffe pilots flying on the Eastern Front—would exceed his record. Had he lived, he would probably have been the leading ace of World War II.

Hans-Joachim Marseille was born on December 13, 1919, in the Charlottensburg district of Berlin, the son of Siegfried Marseille, who had been a pilot in World War I. The family was descended from French Huguenots who had emigrated to Germany in the seventeenth century seeking religious freedom, hence his French-sounding surname.

Marseille joined the infantry in October 1938, but he transferred to the Luftwaffe a month later. In November 1939, he was assigned to fighter pilot school in Vienna, and soon earned a reputation for his aerobatic skill. Marseille received his first operational assignment as a Bf-109 pilot with I Jagdgruppe of Lehrgeschwader 2 at Leeuwarden in the German-occupied Netherlands on August 10, 1940, during the Battle of Britain. He scored his first aerial victory over the English Channel on August 24, and his second in September. In the early days, his marksmanship left him disappointed, however. By December, he had scored seven victories and had been awarded the Iron Cross, but he was himself shot down four times. He knew he could do better.

Later in 1940, Marseille was transferred to JG 52, but he soon got into trouble. Because his flying skills came naturally, and because he seemed to have little regard for military regimentation, he quickly developed a reputation as an undisciplined daredevil. He dressed casually and always seemed to be grinning. His relaxed demeanor only deepened his reputation for being undisciplined. Even in the air, where he was especially skilled, he lacked self-discipline.

Johannes Steinhoff kicked Marseille out of JG 52 and sent him to JG 27 in February 1941. Steinhoff recalled that he had made this decision because of Marseille's "often irresponsible understanding of duty." However, Steinhoff added that Marseille had "irresistible charm."

JG 27 was assigned to the campaign in the Balkans on April 6, but Marseille flew primarily ground attack missions and scored no aerial victories. Meanwhile, in North Africa, Germany's combat role was growing and more and more units were being assigned to support Field Marshal Erwin Rommel's Deutsche Afrika Korps. Parts of JG 27 had been involved in an earlier deployment, but on April 21, after less than two weeks in the Balkans, Marseille's I Gruppe of JG 27 regrouped in Munich and went south to join the North African deployment. They would arrive at Gazala in Libya minus Marseille, who suffered engine trouble, crash-landed his Messerschmitt Bf-109E, and had to hitchhike. The brash young pilot had no qualms about asking to borrow General Hellmann's car and driver. The general, who respected Marseille's initiative, audacity, and commitment to duty, agreed to the request.

Despite his troubles, Marseille shot down a Royal Air Force Hawker Hurricane on April 23. It was his first victory in North Africa, but he took 30 hits in his own cockpit, forcing him into a crash landing—his second in three days. It was pointed out to him that he had lost more Luftwaffe aircraft in North Africa than he had shot down.

The typical mission for I Gruppe of JG 27 in North

Africa was escorting Luftwaffe attack bombers—mainly
Ju-87 Stuka dive-bombers—that were flying in support of
Deutsche Afrika Korps mechanized and armored ground
forces. The Royal Air Force, on the other hand, would
send out formations of fighters—usually at least a dozen
or more Hawker Hurricanes—to shoot down the attack
bombers. These would often be supported by more fighters
whose job it was to fight JG 27's Bf-109Es, which were
there to protect the dive-bombers. These actions were usually conducted in concert with ground operations, but there
were often fighter sweeps known as "frei jagd" (free hunting), in which fighters from the opposing sides hunted each
other and attacked each other's landing fields. On a typical
day, there would be a lot of aircraft in the sky.

On June 14, the British launched a major offensive in
which Marseille was shot down twice in three days without
scoring. Eduard "Edu" Neumann, commander of I Gruppe,
recognized Marseille's potential, but he also realized—and
he told Marseille—that the young pilot had best learn self-
discipline before he ran the Luftwaffe out of aircraft and
killed himself in the process. It was Edu Neumann's recognition of Marseille's potential, and ability to compel him
to channel that potential, that transformed Marseille from
a pretty good fighter pilot into being an extraordinary one.
On June 17, he downed a pair of Hurricanes over Halfaya
Pass. His score now stood at a relatively modest 18.

Things would change for Hans-Joachim Marseille in
September 1941. Maybe it was his pondering the admo-
nitions of Edu Neumann. Maybe it was pondering his own
mortality when he got lost flying over a sandstorm. Maybe
it was when JG 27 traded in its Bf-109Es for Bf-109Fs.
Maybe it was just the practice. Somehow, in September,
something just clicked.

On the morning of September 24, Marseille shot down

four British aircraft, three of them from within a defensive circle that guarantees that any attacker will come under the guns of at least one defender. To shoot down one—much less three—under such circumstances is a major accomplishment. Marseille did it by channeling his aggressiveness and molding it with skill. He attacked fast, maneuvered with gut-wrenchingly tight turns, and shot aggressively—getting in close to his quarry so that he could not miss. Hans-Joachim Marseille had found himself as a fighter pilot.

Marseille went on to down 12 Royal Air Force aircraft in 14 days, and on November 3, he was awarded the Ehrenpokal, a gold trophy authorized by Luftwaffe chief Hermann Göring. As the story goes, Göring had now asked JG 27 to inform him regularly of Marseille's accomplishments. Marseille spent most of November in Germany making the transition to the new Bf-109F-4, but on his return, he scored four kills in three missions between December 6 and December 10.

As the month wore on, JG 27 found itself in the difficult position of having to cover the Deutsche Afrika Korps as it retreated from a British offensive. The Luftwaffe could not be beaten in the air, but on the ground, it was a different story—that is, until January 21, when Rommel launched a massive counteroffensive.

In the meantime, Hans-Joachim Marseille was out of action for nearly a month, first in a hospital in Athens due to illness, and then back to Berlin to comfort his mother over the death of his sister, who had been murdered by a jealous lover. Little did his mother realize that she would lose two children to violent deaths in less than a year.

Marseille resumed combat again on February 8, 1942, when the British brought the fight to the skies over Gruppe I's own airfield. Marseille was coming in for a landing, returning from an escort mission, when he was jumped by seven Curtiss Tomahawks. Through a series of tight, low-speed maneuvers, he managed to outfly the enemy aircraft at very low altitude, picking off one after the other as the group overshot him or was forced to turn too wide. He downed four of the seven while JG 27 watched. The other three fled as other Bf-109s took off to give chase.

Four days later, he would claim another four. On February 15, he downed a pair of Hurricanes at close range, but a piece of debris damaged his radiator and his engine failed. As he was attempting to glide the stricken Bf-109 to friendly territory, Marseille noticed an enemy fighter far below. Unable to resist, he nosed down to gain speed, slipped in behind the British aircraft, and gave it a short burst. This would be one of the few victories in World War II that was scored by an unpowered aircraft.

On February 22, Hans-Joachim Marseille was awarded a Knight's Cross that many people felt was long overdue. It was awarded personally by Field Marshal Albert Kesselring, the Axis commander-in-chief for the entire Mediterranean region. During February alone, Marseille scored 18 victories, to bring his total to 52.

Marseille spent most of March and April back in Germany, but on April 25, his first mission upon returning, he downed two Curtiss Kittyhawks in the space of two minutes. During May, he would fly six missions and claim 14 enemy aircraft, including three on the last day of the month, in which he killed one in a steep dive and two more from below as he pulled out.

On June 3, Marseille added to this legend by downing six aircraft in just six minutes in a battle over the Free French fortress at Bir Hakeim. The battle was made even more remarkable by the fact that Marseille was vastly outnumbered, the enemy fighters were in a defensive circle, and Marseille's cannon jammed after his first kill. He scored five kills with just his pair of machine guns, and when he returned home, the armorers found most of the machine-gun ammunition unused. There were a number of witnesses who reported that had they not seen the battle they would not have believed it.

On June 6, Marseille had the Oak Leaves attached to his Knight's Cross. The Swords would be added just six days later. In those intervening days, less than a week, Marseille would have one of those streaks that helped build the legend. After claiming 6 in two days on June 10 and June 11, he shot down 4 on June 13, and an incredible 14 in three days through June 17. The latter date would be another day with six victories, and these were confirmed as having been scored in seven minutes. The last two were a pair of Supermarine Spitfires. Witnesses would report that he made several attacks in which he destroyed two enemy aircraft with a single short burst of gunfire.

His victories on June 17 made Marseille only the 11th pilot in history to surpass 101 victories. He was already at the point at which no ace except Luftwaffe Eastern Front pilots would ever top him. And his best days were yet to come. With this, he was summoned to Berlin, where he received a hero's welcome and had his Swords bestowed personally by Adolf Hitler on June 18.

Marseille remained in Germany this time for more than a month, receiving his medals and basking in the adulation of civilians who treated him like a late-twentieth-century pop star. The Berlin media referred to him now as the "Star of Africa." Aside from time spent with his fiancée, Hanneliese Kuppers, the highlight of his visit was not the lavish dinner party at Hermann Göring's Karinhalle compound, or his spartan lunch with the Führer. The high point came in a visit to Messerschmitt AG in Augsburg, the place where the aircraft type—the Bf-109 series—that he had flown to all his victories was manufactured. He toured the production line and met with Dr. Willy Messerschmitt. Finally, he was given an opportunity to test-fly the latest variant, the Bf-109G "Gustav." He was briefed about, but did not fly, the Messerschmitt Me-262 jet fighter.

Before leaving Germany, Marseille was awarded the Golden Pilot's Cross with Diamonds by Hermann Göring. Both men fully expected that Marseille would be back soon to have the Diamonds attached to his Knight's Cross.

Early in August, Marseille and Hanneliese traveled to Rome. In addition to a week of vacation with his fiancée, Marseille visited Benito Mussolini. On August 13, the Italian Duce awarded the German pilot Italy's highest decoration, the Medaglia d'Oro (Gold Cross).

Marseille returned to North Africa on August 22 and scored three victories on his first mission on August 31. Even after more than two months out of action, he was still amazing. However, his best was yet to come.

On September 1, 15 Bf-109s of JG 27's I Gruppe, along with aircraft of two other gruppen, took off on a mission to escort Stukas that were attacking massed British mechanized and armored forces. When the Royal Air Force aircraft attacked the dive-bombers, Marseille was the first to jump into their midst. He had claimed two when a Spitfire came at him from the six o'clock low position. Marseille nosed down and blasted the Spitfire as he dove past.

Moments later, six Spitfires attacked him and his wingman. The two Germans broke hard to the outside, let the British pilots overshoot, and twisted back for the kill. Marseille returned to base with four kills, having expended only 240 machine-gun rounds and 80 cannon shells.

He was soon off again on another escort mission. This

time, eight Tomahawks turned on Marseille and two other
I Gruppe men. Marseille attacked quickly, diving through
the enemy formation, claiming one on the way down and
another as he rolled out of his dive. As the remaining fighters attempted to run, the I Gruppe men gave chase, with
Marseille picking off four. Marseille then directed his
schwarm to climb to a higher altitude. No sooner had they
done this than Marseille spotted another British formation.
Adrenaline rushing, he dived into the enemy, claiming one
in the dive and another as he pulled up. Marseille landed
for lunch with eight victories to add to the earlier four,
and it was not yet noon.

After lunch, Edu Neumann ordered Marseille to sit out
the early-afternoon mission, and he lay down for a long
nap. He awoke in time to be briefed for the late-afternoon
mission that launched at 5:06. At 5:57, with Marseille leading his schwarm, the Germans made contact with the
Royal Air Force. The Star of Africa made his usual blinding, diving attack from above, popping short bursts at the
Hurricanes before they had time to react. Five went down
in flames.

His best day had netted Marseille 17 kills, the highest
ever scored against the Western Allies in one day by one
pilot. The following day, September 2, brought the news
that Hans-Joachim Marseille would be awarded the coveted Diamonds for his Knight's Cross. His Diamonds
would be the first awarded for action in North Africa. He
was ahead of even Field Marshal Rommel.

As if to prove that his 17 victories on September 1 were
not an anomaly, Marseille scored 5 on September 2 and 7
on September 3. The legend of the Star of Africa had
reached mythic proportions. Yet the story would continue,
with four victories on September 5, four victories on September 6, three victories on September 7, two victories on

September 11, seven victories on September 15, and seven more on September 26.

During September, Marseille was visited by Adolf Galland, and was invited to dine with Field Marshal Rommel. The field marshal, who was something of a folk hero himself, had been invited to make an appearance with Hitler and Göring at a big rally at the Sportspalast in Berlin on September 30. He asked Marseille to accompany him, but the Star of Africa declined. Marseille wanted to have a Christmas leave so that he could marry Hanneliese, and he was afraid that if he left again in September—after his July-August leave—his request for time off in December would be declined. Rommel was amused and delighted by the man who'd rather spend Christmas with his girlfriend than be on the dais with Hitler at a rally.

On September 30, Marseille and other elements from JG 27 took off on a routine patrol. For the first time, Marseille was flying the new Bf-109G into combat. The new aircraft had just arrived and soon JG 27 would make the full transition to its use. The patrol did not make contact with the enemy and was returning home when Marseille reported an engine fire. With his schwarm five minutes from German lines, he had smoke in the cockpit.

Gasping and choking, Marseille nursed the Bf-109G back to friendly territory. Once there, he announced that he had to get out. He rolled the aircraft over, popped the canopy, and as his comrades watched, he leaped into the slipstream. They watched him bounce slightly and then plummet away from the stricken Messerschmitt. They circled, waiting for his parachute to open. As they waited, it was obvious that something was wrong.

The Star of Africa fell to his death four miles south of Sidi el Aman at 11:26 on the morning of September 30, 1942.

The first on the scene was a doctor attached to a Deutsche Afrika Korps panzer regiment, but members of the JG 27 staff arrived soon after. It was soon determined that Marseille had struck his hip on the rudder of the Bf-109G. The fall had crushed his skull. The evidence indicated that the shock of the initial blow must have incapacitated the young pilot, as the parachute rip cord was untouched.

Hans-Joachim Marseille's father, General Siegfried Marseille, would be killed on the Eastern Front in 1943.

A monument was erected by Italian engineers on the site where Hans-Joachim Marseille fell, and he was interred with full military honors at Derna. His body was later moved to a memorial at Tobruk. A pyramid in his honor was dedicated in October 1989 at the German military cemetery at El Alamein in Egypt.

4

THE BRITISH COMMONWEALTH

WHEN WORLD WAR II BEGAN, Britain's Royal Air Force (RAF) was absolutely the most prepared of any of the Allied air arms, but it can be argued that Germany's Luftwaffe was the best prepared among all nations. Technically, the Royal Air Force was the oldest independent air force among any of the major combatants, having been formed in 1917 from old Royal Flying Corps. The air forces of Germany and the Soviet Union were not formed until well after World War I, and the air forces of Japan and the United States remained subsidiaries of their armies and navies through World War II. Within the Royal Air Force were Bomber Command, Coastal Command, and Fighter Command. The latter would be home to the aces of the British Commonwealth.

In World War I and World War II, the Royal Air Force was also the only air force that was the official "parent" to the air forces of several other nations. These included the Royal Canadian Air Force (RCAF), the South African Air Force (SAAF), the Royal Australian Air Force (RAAF), and the Royal New Zealand Air Force (RNZAF), whose aces are discussed in this section along with those of the Royal Air Force itself.

During both World War I and World War II, because of the sovereignty exercised by Britain over the nations of the British Commonwealth of Nations (formerly the British Empire), the air forces of these nations contributed pilots, aircrews, and aircraft to support Royal Air Force operations—even though during the first two years of World War II, Britain was the only major Commonwealth nation whose actual territory was located within the war zone.

Operationally, during the 1939–1941 period, all of the Commonwealth air forces and pilots that were in combat fought within the Royal Air Force command structure in Western Europe and the Mediterranean, with a large number of SAAF units in the Mediterranean and North Africa. After the war with Japan began at the end of 1941, many RAAF and RNZAF units and pilots returned to the Southwest Pacific Theater.

Britain is indeed indebted to its Commonwealth for supplying some of the top Royal Air Force aces. In World War I, only two of the top seven were English, and in World War II, the ratio was three in seven. It is strong testimony to the quality of pilots throughout the Commonwealth that the pantheon of the top seven pilots contained three Englishmen, two South Africans, a Canadian, and an Irishman.

Britain and France, unlike the other major powers involved in both wars, did not see the scores of their top World War I aces exceeded by their World War II aces. For the Royal Air Force, the top scorers in World War I had been Canadian William "Billy" Bishop, with 72; Englishman Edward "Mick" Mannock with an estimated 68; and Canadian Raymond Collishaw, with 62. Partially because of the practice of awarding full credit for shared victories during the earlier conflict, no Commonwealth aces would come close to matching these scores in World War II, although the Royal Air Force would boast over 1,200 aces, roughly twice the number of British Commonwealth aces in World War I.

Because of Britain's presence in the war zone, the Royal Air Force became an instrument of national survival in World War II. It is the only air force that is officially credited with saving its nation from defeat in World War II.

When the war began, the Royal Air Force was—after the air forces of Germany and Poland—the third to be mobilized. On September 1, 1939, the German Wehrmacht (armed forces) launched a full-scale attack on Poland. At this point, Britain and France issued ultimatums because their mutual assistance treaties with Poland called for them to finally take action to halt Hitler's aggression. On September 3, Britain and France declared that a state of war had existed for two days.

At this time, the German army and air force were the most well-trained, best-equipped, and overall superior military force in the world. Their coordinated air and ground offensive, known as the Blitzkrieg (lightning war), was the most rapid and efficient means of military attack the world had ever seen. The use of fast-moving tanks, mobile forces, dive-bombers, and paratroops all working together as one tight, well-disciplined force stunned the world, especially the Polish defenders. Germany was able to overwhelm Poland in just three weeks.

A British Expeditionary Force (BEF), including Royal Air Force units, was quickly deployed to France to meet an expected German invasion, but nothing happened. For the next several months, the war sank into a lull. Throughout the winter, Allied and German troops sat and stared at one another across the heavily fortified Franco-German border. So little was happening that the media called the situation the "sitzkrieg."

For the Royal Air Force, the first combat came in November, when E. J. "Kobber" Kain, a New Zealander flying with the Royal Air Force, shot down a pair of Dornier Do-17 bombers. He would claim three Messerschmitt Bf-109s during March 1940 to become the Royal Air Force's first ace of the war, but he was killed in an accident shortly thereafter.

Suddenly, on April 9, 1940, Germany attacked. Sitzkrieg became Blitzkrieg once again. German troops quickly occupied Denmark and Norway. On May 10, the Germans began a great offensive to the west that duplicated their advance on Belgium and France in 1914 at the beginning of World War I.

In the air, combat was the most intense that had yet been seen in war, rivaling anything that had occurred during World War I, especially in terms of the speed and armament of the aircraft. Of the air forces engaged, the Luftwaffe outscored the Royal Air Force, but the British managed to outscore the French Armée de l'Air.

After Kain, his mate from No.73 Squadron was the only ace prior to May 10, but within nine days, two men in No.85 Squadron—Geoffrey "Sammy" Allard and a South African, Albert Lewis—were aces twice over.

By May 28, Luxembourg, Belgium, and the Netherlands had surrendered and German forces were pouring into France. On June 14, Germany seized control of Paris, accomplishing in five weeks what it had been unable to do in four years of protracted fighting in World War I. France finally surrendered on June 22, leaving Britain to face the onslaught of Germany's Blitzkrieg alone. Only 20 miles of English Channel separated Germany's crack troops from an army that had abandoned all of its equipment in France when it barely managed to escape from the Germans at Dunkirk on the French coast at the end of May.

While Hitler's forces prepared for a cross-Channel invasion of Britain, the English people rallied around Prime Minister Winston Spencer Churchill, who had taken office on May 10 telling them he had "nothing to offer but blood, toil, tears and sweat." He defied Hitler by informing him that his troops would meet relentless opposition on the beaches, on the streets, and in every village. However, Luftwaffe commander Field Marshal Hermann Göring insisted that his bombers could easily subdue Britain, making the planned sea invasion a simple walkover.

Churchill had the British people brace for the worst. On June 18, he told them: "The Battle of France is over. I expect that the Battle of Britain is about to begin. Upon this battle depends the survival of Christian civilization. Upon it depends our British life, and the long continuity of our institutions and our Empire. The whole fury and might of the enemy must very soon be turned on us. Hitler knows that he will have to break us in this island or lose the war. Let us therefore brace ourselves to our duties, and so bear ourselves that, if the British Empire and its Commonwealth last for a thousand years, men will still say, 'This was their finest hour.' "

In August 1940, the Luftwaffe began a brutal, unremitting bombing assault on Britain's ports, factories, and cities. The only thing that stood in the way of an easy victory was the courageous, but vastly outnumbered, pilots of the Royal Air Force, specifically of Fighter Command, who met the Germans like gnats attacking crows. Despite the fact that the British had fewer than 1,000 fighters to face a Luftwaffe onslaught four times as large, the Royal Air

Force was able to destroy 12 bombers for each one of their own losses. Churchill called it the Royal Air Force's "finest hour."

Of the Royal Air Force Fighter Command pilots who met and turned back a vastly superior German Luftwaffe, Churchill said, "Never, in the field of human conflict, have so many, owed so much, to so few."

The British Commonwealth Aces

Among the early heroes of the Battle of Britain were men like Sammy Allard and Albert Lewis, as well as Alan Christopher Deere of No.54 Squadron and Robert Stanford Tuck of No.92 Squadron. James Henry "Ginger" Lacey of No.501 Squadron became a national hero on August 15, when he shot down the Heinkel He-111 that had bombed Buckingham Palace.

Many of "the few" were also shot down, but most of the time they managed to bail out, and since they were over friendly territory, they were back in action within days, if not hours. Frequently, the Royal Air Force pilots were shot down multiple times. By August, Al Deere had done this seven times—and each time he lived to tell the tale and to fly and fight again.

Although the Battle of Britain would technically drag on until the end of the year, the real turning point occurred on September 17 when Hitler made the decision to postpone the sea assault indefinitely. The highest-scoring Royal Air Force ace of the August-December Battle of Britain period was Eric Lock of No.41 Squadron. He got his first two kills on August 15, the same day that Ginger Lacey downed the bomber that had bombed Buckingham Palace. By October 20, his score stood at 19.5 and he downed a pair of Messerschmitt Bf-109s the same day that he was shot down and badly wounded. He would return to combat in June 1941 with No.611 Squadron and would end the war with 26 victories, making him the 13th-highest-scoring Royal Air Force ace and the seventh-highest-scoring English ace of World War II.

At the end of the pivotal year of 1940, the two Royal Air Force aces with the highest cumulative scores were Sammy Allard and Ginger Lacey, tied with 23, compared with the 21.5 that Eric Lock had at the time. Allard and Lacey would end the war with 25 and 28, respectively.

The Battle of Britain was the first major conflict in history to be decided solely by airpower, and it brought Hitler's remarkable string of successes to a halt. The Royal Air Force's turnback of Germany's Luftwaffe would later prove to be the point at which the tide of the war began to turn slowly in favor of the Allies.

The Battle of Britain was a major setback in Germany's effort toward world domination, but it did not stop Hitler's armies. Britain remained alone and isolated while the rest of the countries in continental Europe either allied themselves with Germany, became occupied territories, or waited in anticipation of a German attack.

The top-scoring ace in the Royal Air Force was the South African, Marmaduke Thomas St. John Pattle, who may have scored at least 51 victories. He was followed by Englishman James Edgar "Johnny" Johnson with 38. By 1941, Adolph Gysbert "Sailor" Malan, another South African, was the Royal Air Force's third-place ace with 34 victories when he was withdrawn from combat to be given a command role. He is also remembered as the Royal Air Force's leading aerial combat tactician.

Brendan Eamonn Fergus "Paddy" Finucane, the top-scoring Irishman in history, scored 32 victories with the Royal Air Force. Finucane flew with No.65 Squadron and

No.602 Squadron, as well as with No.452 (RCAF) Squadron, with whom he would score 19 of his victories. He was killed on July 15, 1942, an instant folk hero among the Irish, who sympathized with their former colonial master in its role in World War II.

George Frederick Beurling was the highest-scoring Canadian ace, scoring most of his 31 victories with the Royal Air Force before his reassignment to the RCAF.

Because of discrepancies in the crediting of shared victories, there is no definitive ordered list of British Commonwealth aces below the top five, but there were certainly about two dozen whose total count equaled or exceeded 20 no matter how the scores are calculated.

In the pantheon of Commonwealth aces, there were several in the second tier with a range of 28 to 29 victories. These were the Englishmen J.R.D. Braham, F. R. Carey, Neville Frederick Duke, Ginger Lacey, and Robert Stanford Tuck, as well as the highest-scoring Australian, Clive Robertson Caldwell. The highest-scoring New Zealander was Colin Falkland Gray, who had a total of 27.5 when he was killed in May 1940. The fact that he died before the Battle of Britain leaves room to speculate what he might have contributed if he had lived.

Royal Air Force Fighter Aircraft

During the Battle of Britain, when Prime Minister Churchill said that nobody had ever "owed so much to so few," the pilots of the Royal Air Force Fighter Command realized that the airplanes to which "the few" owed their success were the Hawker Hurricane and the Supermarine Spitfire. Indeed, the Spitfire would remain as the Royal Air Force's top air superiority fighter through the end of World War II. Today, it can be said that it is the most revered airplane in British history, and one of the greatest aircraft of World War II.

The legendary Hurricane was also one of the true icons of the Battle of Britain. It was the aircraft in which most of the Royal Air Force's highest-scoring aces secured most of their victories. Technically, it was the first fighter to mount eight forward firing guns, the first to exceed 300 mph in level flight with a full war load, and the first operational monoplane fighter of the Royal Air Force. The prototype first flew in 1935, and during the Battle of Britain, Hurricane pilots claimed 75 percent of all the victories. In succeeding years, it served in every theater of the war. The Hurricane Mk.I was armed with eight .303-caliber Browning machine guns, while the Hurricane Mk.IIC carried four 20mm Hispano-Suiza cannons and the Hurricane Mk.IID had two 40mm guns. As a fighter-bomber, the Hurricane could haul two 500-pound bombs and was the first plane to carry rockets.

The Hurricane was also widely used on His Majesty's aircraft carriers where Sea Hurricanes flew as convoy escorts. The Hurricane's prototypical two-bladed props were eventually replaced by three-bladed props, and its maximum speed was 339 mph, with a ceiling of 35,600 feet and a range of 460 miles.

The Spitfire, meanwhile, had its roots in the marvelous racing seaplanes designed by Reginald J. Mitchell and built by Supermarine for the Schneider Trophy races in the 1920s and 1930s. In the course of his work, Mitchell met and began to collaborate with Henry Royce of Rolls-Royce, and this association led to the Spitfire.

The project got under way in 1934 as the Royal Air Force was beginning to evaluate aircraft in order to modernize its fighter fleet. Mitchell designed the Spitfire like a racing plane, aerodynamically trim and optimized for speed. Meanwhile, Royce was developing the 12-cylinder Merlin in-line engine, which itself was destined to be one of the true classics of World War II machinery. The Spitfire was a brilliant combination of power and grace.

The Spitfire and Merlin came together in a prototype that first flew in March 1936. Performance was far beyond expectations, and the Royal Air Force was ecstatic. The first Spitfire Mk.Is joined Royal Air Force Fighter Command in June 1938, and by the time that World War II began in September 1939, nine squadrons were equipped, and there were over 3,000 Spitfires in the order books.

The Spitfire of the Battle of Britain was the Mk.I, with which 19 squadrons had been equipped by the autumn of 1940. It had a wingspan of 36 feet 10 inches and a length of 29 feet 11 inches. It weighed 5,332 pounds fully loaded and fueled. The Mk.I was powered by the 1,030-hp, liquid-cooled Rolls-Royce Merlin II engine that gave it a top speed of 355 mph. It had a service ceiling of 34,000 feet and a range of 500 miles. Armament consisted of eight wing-mounted .303-caliber Browning machine guns.

In 1941, Supermarine began deliveries of the Spitfire Mk.V, which was powered by the 1,440-hp, liquid-cooled Rolls-Royce Merlin 45 engine. It was armed with two 20mm cannons and four .303-caliber machine guns, an improvement over the original Spitfire armament that relied only on the .303 machine guns.

For the Royal Navy's aircraft carriers, the Merlin 45-powered equivalent to the Mk.V was the Seafire Mk.IIC. In July 1942, the Spitfire Mk.IX was developed, specifically to match the performance of the German Focke Wulf Fw.190. However, in 1942, the scope of the action had changed somewhat, and battles were more likely to take place over German-occupied territory than over Britain.

The Spitfire Mk.IX was eight inches longer than earlier

"marks" and weighed 7,500 pounds fully loaded and fueled. It was powered by a 1,515-hp, liquid-cooled Rolls-Royce Merlin 61 engine that gave it a top speed of 408 mph. It had a service ceiling of 44,000 feet and a range of 434 miles. Armament consisted of two 20mm cannons and four machine guns.

By 1944, with the Allies on the offensive, Supermarine delivered what was probably the most potent Spitfire to go into service during World War II. The Spitfire Mk.XIV was nearly three feet longer than the first Spitfires and weighed 8,500 pounds fully loaded and fueled. It was powered by a 2,050-hp, liquid-cooled Rolls-Royce Griffon 65 engine that drove a massive five-bladed propeller and gave it a top speed of 448 mph. It had a service ceiling of 44,500 feet and a range of 460 miles. As with the Mk.IX, armament consisted of two 20mm cannons and four machine guns.

The Spitfire was one of the few fighter aircraft in production before World War II that stayed in production after the war. Notable among these were the Mk.XIX photoreconnaissance aircraft, and the F.24, the last Spitfire. A total of over 20,000 Spitfires and Seafires of over 40 different "marks" were manufactured, making it the most-produced British aircraft in history. Though the Royal Air Force officially retired the Spitfire in 1954, its "Historic Flight" still maintains flying examples for demonstration purposes and as a tribute to the finest few of the finest hour.

Deere: A Hero of the Battle of Britain

One of the best remembered of "the few" is Alan Christopher Deere, who scored 22 confirmed victories, 10 probables, and 18 damaged—most of them during the Battle of Britain. He was born in Auckland, New Zealand, on

December 12, 1917, but later moved to Britain. Deere joined the Royal Air Force in October 1937 and was assigned as a fighter pilot to No.54 Squadron in September 1938. World War II began a year later, but the unit would see no action until May 1940.

Alan Deere scored his first aerial victory on May 23 while flying air cover for a rescue mission in northern France. In a precursor to the sorts of rescue missions helicopters would commonly perform a quarter century later in Vietnam, an attempt was being made to rescue a pilot downed behind enemy lines by using a trainer with short takeoff and landing capabilities. Deere and another pilot were flying above in Spitfires to provide air cover.

A flight of German Bf-109s arrived on the scene just as the trainer was taking off. Deere bounced one of the Messerschmitts as it made a low-level pass and blew it away. Deere managed to damage at least one Bf-109 as the other Spitfire shot down a pair. The rescue flight managed to get off and to reach the British coast without further incident.

Also on May 23, and very near to where Alan Deere was working, one of the largest rescue operations in history was under way. The evacuation of the 300,000-man British Expeditionary Force from defeated France could have turned into a disaster for Britain had the Germans used mechanized forces instead of the Luftwaffe to attack the troops waiting on the beach at Dunkirk. Overhead, Royal Air Force Squadrons flew top cover for the operation, battling the Luftwaffe for control of the Dunkirk skies. During this operation, code-named Dynamo, Al Deere hit his stride, claiming three Bf-109s and three Bf-110s between May 23 and May 29 to become an ace.

Early in June, King George VI himself came to Hornchurch to award Distinguished Flying Crosses to several Royal Air Force aces, including Al Deere and Robert Stanford Tuck. It had been a huge morale booster for Britain, but the Dunkirk operation was just a muted introduction to what the Royal Air Force would face in the coming months during the Battle of Britain.

For Deere, the weeks would be filled with constant combat, day in and day out, as the Luftwaffe threw their numerical superiority at the embattled "few." During the Battle of Britain, Deere reduced the size of the Luftwaffe by seven fighters and a bomber, for which he would have a Bar added to his Distinguished Flying Cross, the equivalent of a second Distinguished Flying Cross.

In January 1941, the Royal Air Force put Deere's expertise to work in the Fighter Command operations room as a controller. Eager to get back into the air, he was finally reassigned to an operational unit. He was posted to No.602 Squadron in Scotland on May 7 as a flight commander, and he became squadron commander on August 1. In the meanwhile, three days after he joined the unit, he was sent out to investigate a Messerschmitt Bf-110 that had penetrated Scottish airspace. The aircraft crashed before Deere's flight could intercept it. Assumed at the time to have been a routine reconnaissance flight, the aircraft was actually piloted by Germany's Deputy Fuhrer Rudolf Hess, who was on a clandestine mission to make contact with pro-German factions within Britain.

On the day that he took command of No.602 Squadron, Deere downed a Bf-109. It was his first victory since September 1940, but his days of intense combat were over. In January 1942, shortly after the United States entered World War II, he was sent across the Atlantic to brief American pilots on operational issues. Between May and August 1942, he commanded No.403 Squadron, but this would be his last operational tour, except of brief temporary duty with No.611 Squadron in February 1943. During this month, he saw action again and shot down a Focke Wulf Fw-190. In March, he was assigned as wing leader of the legendary Biggin Hill Wing.

Alan Deere ended the war with 22 confirmed victories, 10 probables, and 18 enemy aircraft damaged. His autobiography of his wartime experiences, *Nine Lives,* would be published in 1959. In addition to his British Distinguished Flying Cross with Bar, Deere earned the American Distinguished Flying Cross, the French Croix de Guerre, and a British Distinguished Service Order. When the war in Europe ended in May 1945, he was awarded an Order of the British Empire. Unlike many wartime aces, he remained in the Royal Air Force until 1977, retiring as Air Commodore Alan Deere.

Pattle: The Top Ace in the Royal Air Force

The Royal Air Force's leading ace of World War II was the South African Marmaduke Thomas St. John Pattle, best known by his nickname, "Pat." His final score is usually listed as "at least 40," because the actual tally is unknown, and may exceed 51. He is probably unique among World War II aces to have scored his first 10 victories in a biplane.

Pat Pattle was born in South Africa to English parents and joined the Royal Air Force in 1936. Posted in Egypt in 1938, he was among the pilots of No.80 Squadron who did battle with the Italians in Libya and Ethiopia during the early months of World War II. Unlike many of the other early Royal Air Force aces, Pattle earned his victories in the Mediterranean region rather than in the skies over Britain and France.

No.80 Squadron was not exactly equipped for modern combat, as they were flying the aging Gloster Gladiator

biplanes at a time when "the few" in Britain were flying
Hurricanes and Spitfires. Nevertheless, Pat Pattle managed
to score his first four victories in rather short order. He
was shot down himself in August 1940, but was soon back
in action.

Italy had invaded Albania in 1939, five months before
World War II began, and in November 1940, Benito Mussolini's armies used their foothold in the diminutive former
kingdom as a springboard for an invasion of Greece. Mussolini's plan had been to score a fast victory and to incorporate Greece into his idea of a "New Roman Empire" in
the Mediterranean region. When this invasion occurred,
Pattle's unit was among those air and ground forces Britain
was sending to Greece to help in a counterattack. The Italian invasion force became bogged down, and the Royal
Air Force managed to exact a terrific toll on the Regia
Aeronautica. By the end of the year, Pattle was an ace
twice over and had been awarded the Distinguished Flying
Cross.

It was not until February that No.80 Squadron finally
received its first Hawker Hurricanes. On February 28, finally flying the Hurricane, Pattle downed a pair each of
Fiat BR-20 bombers and CR-42 fighters in a single day.
His innate skill as a fighter pilot was clearly manifesting
itself. Five days later, he added three G-50 fighters to his
score during one sortie.

In March 1941, Pat Pattle was promoted to squadron
leader and placed in command of No.33 Squadron, which
had just been sent to Greece from North Africa, where it
had seen action against the Italians in Egypt and Libya.
Pattle had brought his score to 25.66 by the time that he
first tangled with the Luftwaffe.

By April, the stalemated and embarrassed Mussolini was
compelled to ask Hitler for help. On April 6, Germany

attacked Greece within the larger context of their spring 1941 drive into the Balkans. As air cover for the invasion, the Luftwaffe sent in the fighters of JG 52. Pat Pattle and No.33 Squadron met them on the first day, and Pattle shot down two Messerschmitt Bf-109Es.

It was here that the story of the Royal Air Force's highest-scoring ace fades from documented fact to the stuff of legend and folklore. This is because all of the records of No.33 Squadron from this day forward were lost. Based on anecdotal evidence and the accounts of men who were there, Pattle had an extraordinary run of successes, matching his Hurricane against the Messerschmitts of JG 52. Evidence generally confirms that he scored five kills on April 14 alone, and six on April 19, to bring his score to no fewer than 38.

Pattle's successes against the Luftwaffe are even more remarkable in light of the overall tactical situation. The Greek army, which had held the Italians at bay, was no match for the battle-hardened Germans. The Greeks—and the British ground troops that had come to their aid—were never able to put up more than token resistance. The Luftwaffe, meanwhile, took a terrible toll on retreating troops. The Royal Air Force units did the best they could, but they were outnumbered ten to one. On April 19, when Pattle scored his six-in-one-day, the Germans had Athens surrounded and were closing in for the kill.

The following morning, Pattle awoke sick with fever. In a normal situation, a flight surgeon would have grounded him, but this was a desperate day in a desperate campaign. A Luftwaffe bomber attack was incoming. He had to go up.

The ailing squadron leader led the lads of No.33 Squadron against the attack. He was observed as having killed two Messerschmitt Bf-110 Zerstorers, and he had scored a probable against a Bf-109, when another Hurricane pilot got in trouble. As he went to the aid of this pilot, Pattle was jumped by a cluster of Bf-110s who tore his Hurricane to shreds. Pat Pattle spiraled down into Eleusis Bay.

Three days later, the Greek government capitulated and the British troops scrambled to escape. As they did, any hope of nailing down an exact final score for the Royal Air Force's top-scoring ace was lost. The evidence combines to suggest a minimum of 51, with "at least 40" that are considered certain.

Johnson: The Top-Scoring Englishman

James Edgar "Johnny" Johnson is remembered not only as the highest-scoring Englishman in the Royal Air Force, but also as a pilot who survived the war with his aircraft being hit only once—by a single shell—in all his aerial combat career. Furthermore, he made it a practice to engage only the toughest of foes—high-performance air superiority fighters—rather than lumbering bombers and attack aircraft.

Johnson had joined the Royal Air Force Reserve prior to the war, and his unit, No.616 Squadron, was one of those called up in August 1939, when war seemed inevitable. However, he was hospitalized through much of the Battle of Britain and did not score the fifth victory required for ace status until early in 1942.

His leadership skills led Johnson to a series of promotions and he became commander of No.610 Squadron in time to lead it as part of the air cover for the ill-fated Dieppe raid on northern France in August 1942. During this fight, he scored two assists.

Typically, men in higher command are more insulated from combat than pilots of lesser rank, but Johnny Johnson's success as a fighter pilot really began to take off early in 1943, when he was promoted to head the Kenley Wing. Composed primarily of RCAF units, the Kenley Wing was equipped with the relatively new Spitfire Mk.IX.

First introduced in July 1942, this aircraft was essentially a Spitfire Mk.V upgraded with the powerful new Model 60 series Merlin engine that would be turbo-supercharged for high-altitude interception duty. It was developed as an interim fighter to replace the earlier marks until the Spitfire Mk.VIII—with strengthened fuselage as well as more powerful engine—was available. The Spitfire Mk.IX equipped many Fighter Command units based in Britain through the winter of 1942–1943, and was produced in much larger numbers than originally anticipated. When it finally entered squadron service in June 1943, the Spitfire Mk.VIII was used primarily overseas.

Between April and September, Wing Commander Johnson claimed 18 victories, all of them save one against the top German air superiority fighters such as the Focke Wolf Fw-190 and later-model Messerschmitt Bf-109s. The one exception was a Bf-110, Johnson's only multiengine victory.

Johnson was a careful and meticulous fighter pilot. As he said later, "In a dogfight when the odds are heavily on your side, there is a great temptation to lower your guard, to get in close, and hammer your enemy until he falls. Too many pilots concentrate on one target and forget to keep a sharp lookout for friend or foe; too many airplanes converge, in a dangerous funnellike movement, on the single quarry and the risk of midair collision is high."

By the autumn of 1943, Johnson's score stood at 25, enough to put him in the upper echelon of Allied aces, and he was reassigned to a staff job with the 83rd Group of the 2nd Tactical Air Force. By late spring 1944, however, he managed to get himself back into a flying command, this time with another Canadian unit, No.144 Wing. He scored three kills on the eve of the June 6 Normandy Invasion, and another ten over Europe during the Allied sweep across northern France.

In early 1945, Johnson was promoted to group captain, and given his last assignment of the war, as commander of No.125 Wing. By that time, it was being equipped with the Spitfire Mk.XIV, which was powered by the supercharged Model 61 Rolls-Royce Griffon engine with its distinctive, five-bladed Rotol propeller.

Johnny Johnson's final score officially stood at 38, making him the Royal Air Force's second-highest-scoring ace. After World War II, he would have a long career in the Royal Air Force, retiring as Air Vice Marshal James Edgar Johnson, but still "Johnny" to those who had been his comrades when they were "the few."

Malan: The Sailor Was an Airman

The Royal Air Force's number-three ace, like its number one, was a South African. Born in 1910, Adolph Gysbert Malan left home to join the British Merchant Marine and spent his formative years on the high seas. In 1935, having arrived in Britain, he joined the Royal Air Force, where his previous career earned him the enduring nickname "Sailor." During World War II, it was easily a more popular name than "Adolph."

Whatever his aptitude for sea life, Sailor Malan's skill as a pilot was considerable, and by the time that the war began, he was already commanding a flight within No.74 Squadron at Hornchurch. He first saw action in late May 1940, leading his Spitfire-equipped squadron into battle over the Dunkirk evacuation beaches during Operation Dynamo. For his part in the operation, he earned a Distinguished Flying Cross. In less than a week, his score stood at three victories, two shared kills, and a pair of probables.

He would earn a Bar to his Distinguished Flying Cross on the night of June 19, when he downed a pair of Heinkel He-111 bombers over southern England. This was only a prelude to what would come two months later when Hermann Göring launched the air offensive that became the Battle of Britain. By that time, Sailor Malan had been promoted to command No.74 Squadron. In the life-or-death battle for the future of Britain, Malan would find himself and his No.74 Squadron very much in the thick of things. By mid-August, his score stood at ten.

During a rest-and-recuperation leave, Malan wrote his famous "Ten Rules for Air Fighting," which would fast become required reading for a generation of combat pilots.

In September 1940, No.74 Squadron moved from Hornchurch to Biggin Hill, where it would be assigned high-altitude interceptor duties, and Malan resumed his command. At the beginning of 1941, he would be placed in charge of the entire Biggin Hill Wing, with the newly created rank of wing commander. By this time, his own score stood at 14 solo kills, plus 4 shared victories.

During the summer of 1941, he had an exceptional run of victories, raising his official score to 34, which was, at that time, the highest of any living ace in the Royal Air Force. Withdrawn from action and sent to the United States on a liaison mission that also included fellow ace Robert Stanford Tuck, he would not see combat again.

When Sailor Malan returned from America, he rose steadily through the ranks, eventually becoming Group Captain Malan. In 1944, he was placed in command of the Royal Air Force Advanced Gunnery School at Catfoss.

Malan remained in the Royal Air Force until 1946, when

he retired to return home to South Africa. After a successful career as a businessman, he became an energetic voice in opposition to apartheid. He would remain active until he became debilitated by Parkinson's disease. He died in 1963, at the relatively young age of 53.

Malan's 10 Rules for Air Fighting

1. Wait until you see the whites of his eyes. Fire short bursts of one or two seconds, and only when your sites are definitely "ON."

2. Whilst shooting, think of nothing else, brace the whole of your body, have both hands on the stick, concentrate on your ring site.

3. Always keep a sharp lookout. "Keep your finger out!"

4. Height gives you the initiative.

5. Always turn and face the attack.

6. Make your decisions promptly. It is better to act quickly even though your tactics are not the best.

7. Never fly straight and level for more than thirty seconds in the combat area.

8. When diving to attack, always leave a proportion of your formation above to act as top guard.

9. *Initiative, aggression, air discipline,* and *teamwork* are words that *mean* something in air fighting.

10. Go in quickly . . . Punch hard . . . Get out!

Tuck: The Caged Eagle

With 29 victories each, Robert Braham and Robert Stanford Tuck were tied as second-highest-scoring Englishmen in the Royal Air Force during World War II and for sixth place overall. Tuck was born on July 1, 1916, at Catford in Greater London, and like "Sailor" Malan, he left school in his teens to join the British Merchant Marine. Also like Malan, Tuck left his life at sea in 1935 to join the Royal Air Force for a life in the clouds.

Tuck was mustered in at Uxbridge and took his pilot training at Grantham in an Avro Tutor biplane in October. When he graduated in 1936, he was assigned to No.65 Squadron at Hornchurch. He would spend the next two years perfecting his skills with the Gloster Gladiator biplane. In January 1938, he was involved in a midair collision with two other aircraft, in which another pilot was killed and Tuck was injured. His biographers have interpreted the incident as a turning point in his career, curbing an impulsive streak and helping mold him as a combat pilot.

At the end of 1938, Tuck was among those pilots that were picked to transition into the new Supermarine Spitfire at Duxford.

When the war began in September, there was an urgency within the Royal Air Force to form new Spitfire squadrons, and in May 1940, Tuck was transferred to become deputy squadron leader for No.92 Squadron, based first at Croydon and later at Hornchurch along with No.54 Squadron, No.65 Squadron, and No.74 Squadron. These squadrons would be tasked to fly air cover for Operation Dynamo, the evacuation of the British Expeditionary Force from Dunkirk on May 23.

During the course of the morning, Tuck's formation was

bounced by Messerschmitt Bf-109Es. As the formation broke, Tuck chose one enemy fighter and promptly shot it down. After a quick refueling stop at Hornchurch, the Spitfires were back over Dunkirk. This time, it was No.92 Squadron's turn to do the bouncing, and the target was a flight of Messerschmitt Bf-110C Zerstorers. Tuck claimed one and pursued a second into a low-altitude gun duel in which the Zerstorer was forced into a crash landing. As the story goes, Tuck circled the downed flyer and waved. The German shot at him with a pistol, and with uncanny accuracy, almost hit the circling Englishman. Enraged, Tuck finished off the "unsporting" German with his machine guns.

Robert Stanford Tuck had scored three victories on his first day in action and No.92 Squadron had claimed 20 against a loss of only 5. One of these, however, was the squadron commander, and Tuck, as second in command—and top scorer in the squadron—got a battlefield promotion to squadron leader.

On May 24, he led No.92 Squadron back into action over Dunkirk. This time, they spotted a formation of about 20 Dornier Do-17 bombers. Tuck picked one off from the edge of the group and then plunged in for a second kill. In less than two days, Robert Sanford Tuck had gone from being a pilot with no combat experience to being an ace and a squadron leader.

On June 28, 1940, King George VI himself came down to Hornchurch to award decorations to the Royal Air Force heroes—including such men as Robert Tuck and Alan Deere—of Operation Dynamo. For Tuck, it was to be the Distinguished Flying Cross for his "initiative" and "personal example."

The beginning days of the Battle of Britain found No.92 Squadron assigned to the Royal Air Force Fighter Command's 11th Group in southeast England, where it was heavily engaged in stemming the tide of German bombers that were sweeping across the English Channel every day. During two days in mid-August, Tuck shot down three Ju-88 bombers, and on August 18, he took off in the midst of a raid on the Royal Air Force base at Northolt. He gave chase, shooting down one Ju-88 and getting shot down himself by another.

A week later, Tuck would be shot down again. On August 25, he was over the Channel, leading his last patrol as commander of No.92 Squadron, when he attacked a Dornier Do-215 bomber that was trying to sink a British ship. The Dornier's gunner managed to shoot up his engine, forcing him into a long, powerless glide that fortunately brought him across the English shoreline.

On September 11, 1940, Bob Tuck became squadron leader at No.257 Squadron, a Hawker Hurricane Mk.I unit based at Martlesham. While he did not like the Hurricane at first, he eventually took to it, finding it to be a "good gun platform" for the work of killing bombers, which was, after all, the primary business of the Royal Air Force in the autumn of 1940.

Tuck had gotten the reassignment because Fighter Command had decided that No.257 Squadron was a "problem" unit that was incapable of combat. He introduced a series of drills and mock dogfights in an effort to sharpen the skills of the pilots, and within a few days, he was able to report his new squadron ready to face the enemy. This was music to the ears of the powers that be at Fighter Command headquarters, because the Battle of Britain was taking its toll. Every plane and every pilot would be necessary to defeat the Luftwaffe onslaught.

On the afternoon of September 15, Bob Tuck led No.257 Squadron, along with No.17 Squadron and No.73

Squadron, to intercept a huge formation of German bombers—plus escorting fighters—who were flying against London. Word of the impending attack came too late for the interceptors to get an altitude advantage on the attackers before they reached London, so they were forced to climb into the strike force from below. Nevertheless, the interceptors managed to disrupt the attack, and Tuck scored one confirmed kill of a Bf-110 and claimed a Bf-109 as damaged.

By now, Robert Stanford Tuck had become the kind of fearless, yet effective young fighter pilot that the British media loved. He was often written up in the London newspapers. In October, when he shrugged off the honor of an added Bar to his Distinguished Flying Cross by saying simply that he had been "bloody lucky," the public loved it. On January 28, 1941, he was awarded the Distinguished Service Order for his work in turning the "problem" No.257 Squadron into a well-oiled fighting machine.

Early in 1941, No.257 Squadron began converting to the Hurricane Mk.IIC, with its 20mm cannons in place of .303-caliber machine guns. Tuck was a firm proponent of this extra firepower, which proved useful in March, when No.257 Squadron was tasked with intercepting German night bombers.

By June, No.257 Squadron was flying missions over the English Channel and the northern edges of the continent, repaying the aggressive Germans with a bit of aggressiveness of their own. On June 21, Tuck was on a solo flight over the Channel when he was jumped by three Bf-109s. He quickly claimed one of them and outmaneuvered a second at wave-top level before finally nailing him as well. He got into a shoot-out with the third that left both aircraft badly damaged. Finally, both opponents turned away. Tuck attempted to nurse his Hurricane home, but the aircraft gave out and Tuck was forced to abandon it over the water. Badly injured in both shoot-out and bailout, he would eventually be picked up, but he spent nearly a month recovering.

When Bob Tuck returned to duty, it was as a wing commander in the Duxford Wing, where he now had three squadrons to oversee. One was a Spitfire unit, No.12 Squadron, flying the Spitfire Mk.V, and it was with this unit that Tuck himself chose to fly. The other units were No.56 Squadron, equipped with the new Hawker Typhoon Mk.IA, and No.601 Squadron with its American-made P-39 Airacobras. This mix of aircraft would be a problem operationally, because each type had a different performance level and it was hard for them to operate together. Again, as it had been with No.257 Squadron earlier in the summer, Tuck was tasked with flying missions over the continent.

In October 1941, he was one of several leading Royal Air Force pilots sent to the United States on a liaison mission that predated the American entry into the war by two months. By December, when the United States actively entered World War II, Tuck was back in Britain, where he was given command of the five squadrons of the Biggin Hill Wing. Unlike the Duxford Wing, the Biggin Hill Wing had a unified family of aircraft, with four of the squadrons being equipped with Spitfires. These were No.72 Squadron, No.91 Squadron, No.124 Squadron, and No.401 (RCAF) Squadron. The odd squadron was No.264 Squadron, which was a night fighter squadron flying the somewhat elderly Boulton Paul Defiant Mk.II, a two-man fighter with a rear-firing turret as defensive armament.

Tuck's last mission came on January 28, 1942. It was a fighter sweep over northern France, in which the Biggin Hill Spitfires were assigned to destroy targets of opportunity. The 29-victory ace attacked a train that was parked on the outskirts of Boulogne, but when he emerged from the steam cloud that erupted from the exploding locomotive, he was hit by antiaircraft artillery fire. He managed to crash-land his Spitfire, but he was soon surrounded by German soldiers.

The news spread quickly that Robert Stanford Tuck was in custody. Within hours, he was summoned by the commander of Luftwaffe JG 26, Adolf Galland. Also an ace, Galland would later command all Luftwaffe fighter operations and would end the war with 111 victories. In a bizarre situation that is illustrative of the camaraderie that existed between aces—even while they were at war—Galland invited Tuck to dine with him, and they spent the evening talking about other Luftwaffe and Royal Air Force aces as though they were all part of the same fraternity.

On the morning of January 29, however, Tuck awoke as just another prisoner of war. Eventually, he found himself in Stalag Luft III, a prisoner-of-war camp at Sagan, near Berlin. For more than three years, the man who had been the toast of the London media would endure the gradually worsening conditions of captivity in a German camp.

Bob Tuck and his fellow pilots made numerous unsuccessful escape attempts. For years, they were working on a major tunnel project that would inspire numerous postwar movies, including *The Great Escape,* which was based on the March 24, 1944, breakout from Stalag Luft III that used the tunnel. A total of 76 men sneaked 400 feet through the tunnel to freedom, but the results were not so good. Only three men were able to elude capture. Of the others, 23 were recaptured and thrown back into imprisonment. The rest were shot and killed. But Robert Stanford Tuck was not among any of these groups. A few weeks before "the great escape," he and several other prisoners of war were transferred to another stalag.

Nearly a year later, Tuck and many other prisoners were moved again, but by now a pall of chaos had descended over the Reich and the Germans were not nearly as well organized as they had once been. Tuck and another man managed to elude roll call one morning after an overnight stop during the prisoner move, and they got away. Making their way through the snow and sleet for several weeks, they finally linked up with the vanguard of an advancing Soviet column on February 22, 1945. The Soviets sent them to the rear, and eventually they were put aboard a British ship at the Russian Black Sea port of Odessa on March 26.

Robert Stanford Tuck enjoyed a homecoming before the war had actually ended, but by the time that he had fully recuperated, there would be no more combat flying for him. He would go on to fly jet fighters—albeit never in combat—and would play a role in the postwar evolution of the Royal Air Force, remaining in the service until May 1949. As a civilian, Tuck moved to Kent, where he would spend his life as a farmer, until his death on May 5, 1987.

Bader: The Legless Ace Who Couldn't Be Caught

One of the most indomitable pilots to serve with the Royal Air Force during World War II, Douglas Robert Steuart Bader was a top ace in the Royal Air Force during the difficult days of the Battle of Britain and its aftermath, and he scored 23 victories despite the handicap of having no legs.

He joined the Royal Air Force in 1928 at the age of 18 and showed immediate promise as a pilot. Assigned to No.23 Squadron, he demonstrated so much skill that he became part of the squadron's aerobatic team. In 1931, No.23 Squadron converted from Gloster Gamecocks to Bristol Bulldogs, an aircraft that was much better suited to aerobatics. The aircraft's appellation might well have been a symbol for the aggressive Bader, whose skill led him to be a bit reckless. In December 1931, his luck ran out. In a crash, he lost the lower part of his left leg, and his right leg was cut off above the knee.

Despite these debilitating injuries, Bader got himself a set of crude artificial legs and had soon learned to walk without a cane. He also learned to drive and, at last, to fly again. When the Royal Air Force refused to assign him to flying duty, he quit the service in 1933 and went to work selling fuel at an airport. It was work that he detested, but at least it kept him near the aircraft.

By 1939, things had changed. With the winds of war blowing, the Royal Air Force needed pilots badly, and when Bader applied, he was promised a flying job if he would reenlist. In February 1940, he was assigned as a Spitfire pilot with No.19 Squadron at Duxford, but before long he was promoted to flight leader and transferred to No.222 Squadron at Hornchurch. It was with No.222 Squadron that Bader would get a taste of combat over France at the end of May 1940, during Operation Dynamo, the evacuation of the British Expeditionary Force from Dunkirk.

The following month, he was named to command No.242 (RCAF) Squadron, a Hawker Hurricane unit being formed at Coltishall as the first Canadian fighter squadron in the Royal Air Force. Leading No.242 Squadron into combat during the Battle of Britain in August and September, Bader decided to employ the tactic of a massed formation—such as Baron Manfred von Richthofen had used during World War I with his so-called Flying Circus—

rather than small cells of fighters. With Bader, however, the favored nickname would be "beehive." Unlike the Red Baron, Bader took his hives to the ceiling so that when attacking bombers, they could dive to build up a speed advantage.

Bader liked speed, on the ground as well as in the air. According to one story, during the time when he was becoming a hero of the Battle of Britain, there was a warrant out for his arrest for unpaid speeding tickets.

When Bader was given command of the Tangmere Wing in 1941, the "Bader Beehives" often contained up to 200 Spitfires. He had started with 60, but when his flight claimed 152 German bombers in a month, Fighter Command gave him all he wanted. The call sign of the Tangmere Wing was "Green Line," a reference to an English urban bus line, so another nickname of the unit was "Bader's Bus Company." Bader is also credited with the development of the "finger-four" formation in which the two leaders of a four-ship formation fly abreast, with their respective wingmen doing likewise.

By August 1941, Douglas Bader was hitting his stride as a fighter pilot and as a commander. He had raised his score to 22 and had been awarded both the Distinguished Flying Cross and the Distinguished Service Order. Then suddenly, the war ended abruptly for him. During a dogfight over northern France, his Spitfire was involved in a midair collision with a Bf-109. In the process of bailing out of the mortally crippled aircraft, his right artificial leg became entangled and was ripped from his body. He survived his parachute landing, and was captured.

Just as would be the case with Robert Stanford Tuck five months later, Bader was quickly recognized as a celebrated catch and invited to dine with Adolf Galland, the commander of Luftwaffe JG 26, at his officers' mess in

Abbeville. The Germans also retrieved Bader's prosthesis from the wreck of his Spitfire and returned it to him. It was smashed beyond recall, and his other was damaged, so Galland graciously made a request through the International Red Cross. The British were offered safe passage for an aircraft to drop replacement artificial legs. They complied, dropping the leg, and bombing Galland's base in the process.

Bader was fitted and sent to a German prison hospital, where he returned the favor by escaping, using the classic trick of tying bedsheets together.

A fugitive in France, Douglas Bader was eventually recaptured and thrown into a succession of stalags, from one of which he would escape again, only to be recaptured a second time. He escaped a third time and was recaptured yet again. After this, the Germans put him in Colditz, the infamous eighteenth-century castle prison that was located on a mountaintop with sheer cliffs all around.

When the war ended, Douglas Robert Steuart Bader was welcomed home as a returning hero. He was awarded Bars to both his Distinguished Flying Cross and the Distinguished Service Order, the equivalent of a second of each. In 1976, he became Sir Douglas Bader, having received a knighthood for his service to the United Kingdom. In later years, he met Adolf Galland again, under more congenial circumstances, and they became good friends.

Bader died in 1982, at the age of 72. Today, the Douglas Bader Sports Centre at St. Edward's in Oxford, his former school, is a living tribute to the legless air ace whom the Germans could not keep from escaping.

Beurling: The Highest-Scoring Canadian Ace

Many pilots from Canada distinguished themselves during World War II, flying for both the Royal Air Force and

Canada's own RCAF. George Frederick "Buzz" Beurling would fly for both, scoring 29.5 victories with the Royal Air Force and two with the RCAF for a total of 31.5, making him the "number-five man" among Commonwealth pilots and/or those flying with the Royal Air Force.

Beurling was born in 1921 at Verdun in Quebec, and took an early interest in aviation, devouring books about World War I aces and watching airplanes at the local airport. He took his first ride at age nine and made his first solo flight by age 17. He then quit school to work as a bush pilot, flying mail and supplies to mining camps in the far north of Canada.

At one point, Beurling won an aerobatic contest in Edmonton, Alberta, flying against a number of RCAF pilots. In commenting about his victory, he made some pointed remarks about the quality of RCAF flight training and pilots that would not be forgotten. In 1939, he applied to join the RCAF and was refused. They claimed that it was his deficiency in "academics," but Beurling knew the real reason.

World War II had begun and Beurling was itching to get into the action. He had been rejected by the RCAF, but when the Soviet Union invaded Finland at the end of November 1939, he decided to join the Finnish air force. However, the Finnish embassy asked for his parents' permission because he was just 18. They said no.

Undaunted, Beurling signed on as a hand on a ship bound for Glasgow, and once he arrived, he headed for the first Royal Air Force recruiting office he could find. They were ready to sign him on, based on his knowledge of aviation, but they needed his birth certificate, which he didn't have. In a scene that could have been from a movie, Beurling walked out, signed on to another ship, and made a round trip across the Atlantic—during which the vessel was hit by a torpedo from a German U-boat—to retrieve his birth certificate.

Once in the Royal Air Force, Beurling progressed quickly, and he had soon earned the nickname "Buzz" for his low-level—often unauthorized and unsanctioned—aerobatics. During his early months with the Royal Air Force, Beurling crossed paths with—and was trained by—James Henry "Ginger" Lacey, who would soon be one of the leading aces in the Royal Air Force, and who was the man who shot down the bomber that bombed Buckingham Palace. Lacey was impressed by Beurling's flying skills, and so were the RCAF squadron commanders who offered him an RCAF commission. Beurling refused, deciding that he'd rather remain an enlisted pilot in the Royal Air Force than become an officer in the RCAF. It was his turn to snub the RCAF.

Beurling scored his first victory in March 1942 while flying a Spitfire Mk.V with No.41 Squadron on a sweep over northern France. He was flying last place in a four-ship formation, when five German fighter pilots attacked, especially keen to pick off the man at the end of the queue. Beurling pulled up and let the Focke Wulf Fw-190s overshoot him. He then got one in his sights and picked him off. Two days later, again over France, Beurling saw a flight of Fw-190s and broke formation to attack them. He shot down the lead aircraft, but was sanctioned for breaking formation for a second time.

Displeased with the leadership at No.41 Squadron, Beurling volunteered for duty with No.249 Squadron, which was based on the British island garrison at Malta in the Mediterranean. Malta was being referred to as an unsinkable British "aircraft carrier" in the Mediterranean and the Germans and Italians wanted it out of commission. This was because the British used it as a base from which to attack the Mediterranean supply lines the Germans and Italians used to resupply their forces in North Africa. For General Erwin Rommel's Deutsche Afrika Korps, these supplies were the key to victory. The Luftwaffe and the Regia Aeronautica were tasked with eliminating Malta, and No.249 Squadron was about all that stood in their way. Being sent to Malta was not pleasant duty, but for George Beurling, it offered a welcome change.

Along with 16 new Spitfire Mk.Vs and 15 other pilots, Beurling was soon on the way aboard HMS *Eagle*. Because the Germans controlled the air over the continent, one of the only ways that the Royal Air Force could get aircraft to Malta was to send them aboard Royal Navy aircraft carriers. The only problems, beyond the danger of being torpedoed by the Germans, were that the Spitfire Mk.V was never designed for carrier operations, nor had the Royal Air Force pilots been properly trained for this kind of takeoff.

Beurling managed to get off HMS *Eagle* and fly the last 600 miles to Takali Field on Malta, when he was ordered to takeoff immediately to intercept a strike force of German bombers headed for the island. He would soon learn that flying an intercept mission was something to look forward to. Despite the danger, anything was better than being on alert for a mission at Takali, which meant sitting in an ovenlike cockpit under the blistering Mediterranean sun—and waiting.

On July 6, 1942, George Beurling and seven other Spitfire pilots intercepted three Regia Aeronautica bombers en route to Malta, escorted by an estimated 30 Macchi MC-200 fighters. Beurling led the assault, diving straight through the Macchi formations and pulling up to fire on a big Cant Z-1007 bomber. His first pass damaged a bomber, and he quickly shot down two of the Macchis. These were his first victories since coming to the Mediterranean.

With the first attack disrupted, the Spitfires returned to Takali to refuel, only to be sent up again. This time, it was a pair of German Junkers Ju-88s and about 20 Messerschmitt Bf-109s. A pair of Messerschmitts double-teamed Beurling, and he had to turn hard to get out of the way. This put him in firing position and he poured a burst into the Bf-109.

The young Canadian ace took his job seriously. He spent hours calculating range and deflection angles, making notes on what worked and what did not. In his spare time, he hunted fast-moving lizards with a pistol. As the story goes, he would shoot when their size approximated the size of an enemy fighter at 250 yards. He soon got to the point where he never took more than one shot to hit his target. The same soon became true of the enemy aircraft. He was a master of marksmanship and of hitting his foe with an absolute minimum of shells.

On his morning patrol on July 27, Beurling downed two Regia Aeronautica aircraft—including one flown by six-victory ace Furio Niclot—and one of two Luftwaffe Bf-109s that attacked him. On his afternoon outing, Beurling would claim one Bf-109 as a confirmed kill, and a second as damaged. For this day's success, he would be awarded the Distinguished Flying Cross.

In October, when the enemy made a major effort to defeat the defenders on Malta, Beurling actually welcomed the massed formations of bombers because this situation favored his hit-and-run tactics. He could come in hard and fast, kill at least one, and escape in the confusion. He had added five to his score when he flew his last mission out of Takali. He and seven others attacked a force of Ju-88s that were escorted by several dozen Messerschmitts. In the process of downing one of the bombers, he was badly wounded by a bomber gunner and a pair of Bf-109s that got on his tail. Amazingly, he managed to shoot down a third Messerschmitt as he dove to escape the first two.

At last, it seemed like every Messerschmitt in the sky had ganged up on him, riddling the Spitfire's cockpit with gunfire. His fighter nosed over and went down, its throttle jammed wide open. Somehow, he managed to get out, but he feared pulling his rip cord too soon and being shot at while he descended. He finally opened his parachute with seconds to spare. He was picked up by a British boat, but his Malta flying days were over.

He was to be sent back to Britain to recover from his wounds, but the transport carrying him crashed on landing at Gibraltar. He was one of only three survivors, but he was badly injured and suffering from shock. His additional injuries, especially a badly infected heel, would take a long time to mend, so he was sent home to Canada, not just a wounded pilot, but a returning national hero—a national hero who had not yet turned 22. The kid who was rejected by the RCAF was now a great air ace lunching with Prime Minister MacKenzie King.

Because of his injuries, the starvation diet on which he had subsisted on Malta, and the fatigue of daily combat for several months, Beurling spent the next several weeks in the hospital. This was followed by a several-month-long tour of Canada, making appearances at victory bond rallies, work he strongly disliked.

When he finally returned to England during the summer of 1943, George "Buzz" Beurling would be faced with many other things that he did not like. He was assigned to a Royal Air Force gunnery school, but he disliked this and badgered his superiors to allow him to get back into action. When the Royal Air Force refused, he did the unthinkable and requested a transfer to the RCAF. In September 1943,

Beurling was assigned to No.403 (RCAF) Squadron, based at Kenley. He was promoted to flight commander, but he did not like this either, because it interfered with the "lone wolf" tactics he had favored when he was on Malta and in England previously.

While he managed to shoot down three Fw-190s between September 1943 and April 1944, Beurling was depressed and he seemed to be sabotaging a career that had been at its peak when he came home from Malta. He refused to cooperate with others and deliberately disobeyed rules. On patrol, he broke formation and refused to attack except in the most difficult of circumstances.

With some of his dangerous stunts, it almost seemed like he was trying to commit suicide. He had become anything but the highly effective fighter pilot who had been a hero of the Malta campaign. Finally, he was grounded and written up for a court-martial. Instead, he was simply discharged and sent home.

This time, there would be no hero's welcome.

Woodward: Canada's Penultimate Ace

The second-highest-scoring Canadian ace of World War II was a study in contrasts and similarities with George "Buzz" Beurling. They both had what it took to be excellent combat pilots and they were both pragmatic men who put their missions ahead of red tape. However, while one alienated himself from the Royal Air Force establishment, the other made the system work for him. Vernon Crompton "Woody" Woodward commanded squadrons in North Africa and scored 21.8 victories. He flew with the Royal Air Force's number-three ace from the First World War, and he flew as wingman to the Royal Air Force's greatest ace of the Second World War on his last successful mission.

Woodward was born on Vancouver Island, north of Victoria, British Columbia, on December 22, 1916, and grew up in the woods of the Pacific Northwest, learning to be an extraordinary marksman. He also took an interest in aviation, and in 1938, he enlisted in the Royal Air Force because, unlike the RCAF, they were actively expanding and they wanted pilots—especially bomber pilots.

Woodward went through his initial flight training in Perth, Scotland, and because of his aptitude for aerobatic flying, he was steered toward fighters rather than bombers. From Perth, the Royal Air Force sent him south to No.6 Flying Training School at Little Rissington, north of Oxford, for intermediate and advanced training in Hawker Audaxes and Furies. He earned his wings in December 1938 and took advanced training at Warmwell in Dorset.

In June 1939, with the war just three months away, Woodward was assigned to No.33 Squadron, part of Egypt Group, based at Ismailia in Egypt and flying the aging Gloster Gladiators. There, his commander was none other than a fellow Canadian, Air Commodore Raymond Collishaw, the third-highest-scoring ace in the Royal Air Force during World War I.

For Britons at home, the Axis threat was obviously Germany, but in North Africa, it was Italy. To the west of Egypt lay Libya, an Italian colony since 1911, and to the south lay Italian Somaliland and recently conquered Italian Ethiopia. When World War II began in September 1939, Italy remained neutral, but Egypt Group went on alert.

On June 10, 1940, when Germany invaded France, Italy declared war on Britain and France, and the Italian forces in Libya went on the offensive. No.33 Squadron was in action immediately, and on June 14, while on patrol near the Libyan border, Woodward and another Gladiator pilot

attacked a Caproni Ca-310 bomber and Woodward got a
"probable" on a Fiat CR-32 fighter.

He scored his first confirmed victories over a pair of
CR-32s on June 20. In a battle four days later, No.33
Squadron Gladiators downed four out of five Fiats, with
Woodward claiming one of the four and a "probable" on
the fifth. He would become an ace the following day with
one confirmed and a shared kill.

In October, No.33 Squadron started to convert from
Gladiators to Hawker Hurricanes, a quantum leap in fighter
aircraft technology. From elderly biplanes, they had
switched to the aircraft that had outscored the Supermarine
Spitfire in the recent Battle of Britain. Woodward flew his
first Hurricane mission on October 11, 1940.

Through the autumn, the Italian forces managed to push
deep into Egypt, while the British withdrew to regroup. In
December, the British forces launched Operation Compass,
a major counteroffensive aimed at pushing the Italians in
Libya. As the attack got under way, No.33 Squadron was
overhead flying air cover. On December 9, Woodward's
flight attacked a large number of CR-42s. He shot down a
pair and damaged a third. Within three days, Operation
Compass was deemed a success, with 38,000 prisoners and
vast quantities of equipment and materiel captured as well.

On December 19, Woodward shot down two more CR-
42s, bringing his score for the month to five, plus two
damaged Savoia SM-79 bombers. By February, 1941 the
British Commonwealth forces had occupied a large slice
of Libya, including the city of Benghazi.

In October 1940, while his legions were on the offensive
in Egypt, Benito Mussolini launched his ill-fated invasion
of Greece. With British Commonwealth—mainly Australian and New Zealand—reinforcements, the Greeks
stopped the Italians and held them in a stalemate, until

Mussolini finally asked Adolf Hitler for help.

In February 1941, No.33 Squadron was sent to Greece, and in March, it was placed under the command of the legendary fighter ace Marmaduke St. John "Pat" Pattle. At this time, the Royal Air Force was still facing only the Italian Regia Aeronautica, as the Germans had not yet intervened. Nevertheless, the Italians were outnumbering the British two to one in most engagements. For some pilots, such as Woodward, this just meant more targets. On April 6, he shot down three Cant Z-1007 bombers in one day, despite withering defensive fire from the gunners aboard the bombers. One of an original five had been shot down after a raid, and Woodward scrambled to intercept the survivors.

When he landed, Woodward found out that Germany had just invaded Greece, and No.33 would now be facing the Luftwaffe. Instead of being outnumbered two to one, the Royal Air Force was now outnumbered ten to one. They had just 80 fighters to counter a force that numbered 800. Woodward first faced the Luftwaffe on April 13 and managed to down one of three Messerschmitt Bf-109s that attacked him while he was on a solo patrol. The following day, he and his wingman intercepted and downed three Ju-87 Stukas while they were dive-bombing an Anglo-Greek position.

Five days later, Woodward was part of a three-ship patrol with Pat Pattle when they were jumped by nine Messerschmitt Bf-109s. Pattle and Woodward managed to get behind them, with Pattle claiming two and Woodward a single. This was the day that Pattle would score his six-in-one-day. Meanwhile, however, the third Hurricane had been hit. Time was running out for the Royal Air Force— and for Pat Pattle.

The following day, April 20, the Germans launched their

huge air offensive against Athens. Pattle ordered everybody aloft, and he flew himself, despite a debilitating fever. Woodward managed to claim a Bf-110 that day, possibly one of those that shot down Pat Pattle. Woodward also claimed two Bf-110s and damaged a Ju-88.

Within days, the Commonwealth troops evacuated mainland Greece for the island of Crete. On May 20, with a powerful Luftwaffe flying air cover, the Germans invaded Crete. In the face of overwhelming enemy numbers, it was obvious that the only Commonwealth troops that would live to fight again would be those who managed to escape to the south side of the island to be picked up by the Royal Navy. Woodward took charge of the Royal Air Force contingent and started across the island. Moving by night, they crossed through German lines several times before finally being picked up by the Australian destroyer HMAS *Nizam*. From there, they were evacuated to Egypt.

Back where he had started the war, Woody Woodward picked up the Distinguished Flying Cross that he had been awarded while he was fighting for his life in Greece. The remnants of No.33 Squadron joined No.30 Squadron and went back into action in the desert, where the enemy now included Field Marshal Erwin Rommel's Deutsche Afrika Korps as well as the Italian armies. Woodward managed to down an Italian Fiat G-50 on almost his first outing with No.30 Squadron, but he was coming near the end of his tour.

Woodward's final score marked a technological turning point. On July 12, 1941, he was directed to intercept a Junkers Ju-88, not by a pilot or spotter who had actually seen it, but by a radar operator miles away in the Mediterranean aboard the HMS *Formidable*. Vectored by radar, as modern interceptors are, Woodward got a visual on the Ju-88 and sent it flaming into the desert sand.

Woodward's score now stood officially at 21.8, although it might be higher—No.33 Squadron's records were lost in the evacuation from Greece. In September 1941 he was reassigned to the Rhodesian Air Training Group at Salisbury, Southern Rhodesia (now Harare, Zimbabwe). Through June 1942 he flew as an instructor, training new pilots to fly and fight under the combat conditions that he had experienced so vividly during the first year of the war in the Mediterranean Theater.

Late in 1942, Woodward returned to an operational command as head of No.213 Squadron, based at Martuba near Alexandria, Egypt. By this time, the war had moved far to the west and the nature of the missions being flown from Egypt had changed considerably. Instead of flying life-and-death duels in skies dark with the enemy, the No.213 Squadron Hurricanes flew escort duty on missions where the Germans and Italians were never seen.

In August 1943, Woodward had a Bar attached to his Distinguished Flying Cross and was reassigned to the headquarters for Air Defence, Eastern Mediterranean, and then to the Royal Air Force Staff College at Haifa in Palestine. His final squadron command was the Middle East Communications Squadron, which was actually an executive transport unit tasked with ferrying visiting dignitaries, both military and civilian, throughout the region. After the war, Woodward remained in the Royal Air Force, and in 1946, he was assigned to the staff at the Central Fighter Establishment, back in Britain.

Woodward would have a variety of assignments in the postwar years, including several tours commanding flying squadrons. Between 1948 and 1950, he commanded No.19 Squadron, which was equipped with de Havilland Hornets, a long-range attack bomber with twin piston engines that was a successor to the great de Havilland Mosquito of the war years. In 1955, he was assigned to command No.122 Wing, a fighter unit based at Jever in West Germany that was equipped with Hawker Hunter jet fighters, which represented leading-edge technology for the time.

In the interim, Woodward was assigned to a project with Fighter Command that was tasked with developing a network of underground and hardened shelters for aircraft and communications facilities throughout Britain for use in time of nuclear war. He also served a tour with the Royal Air Force Flying College at Manby. Woodward's last command was No.39 Squadron at Luqa on the island of Malta. Equipped with English Electric Canberras configured for high-altitude photographic reconnaissance missions, No.39 Squadron conducted such missions around the periphery of Soviet satellite nations in southeastern Europe. In the event of a nuclear war, No.39 Squadron would have had the dubious distinction of flying poststrike reconnaissance missions over targets of nuclear strikes in the southern Soviet Union.

Woody Woodward retired from the Royal Air Force in 1963, and operated an air charter company until 1967, when he retired to his native British Columbia.

Caldwell: The Top-Scoring Australian Ace

When Britain was pulled into World War II in 1939, many Commonwealth pilots joined the Royal Air Force to fight the Germans, many not thinking that the war would soon spread closer to home. Clive Robertson Caldwell was one of these pilots. He was an ace in the European Theater, but when his native Australia became a battleground, he came home to defend Australia and to become an ace in the Pacific Theater as well.

Clive Robertson Caldwell was born at Lewisham in suburban Sydney on July 28, 1911. He had a civilian pilot's license when the war began in 1939, so he enlisted in the RAAF. He became an officer, but when he saw that he was going to be assigned as an instructor rather than as a combat pilot, he resigned and reenlisted as an enlisted aircrew trainee. The RAAF got the idea. His commission was reinstated in January 1941, and he was sent to the Middle East, where he was assigned to the Royal Air Force's No.250 Squadron, flying Curtiss Tomahawks in Syria and Cyprus.

As the Deutsche Afrika Korps replaced or supplemented the Italian forces in North Africa, the British were forced to rush reinforcements to blunt the Axis drive toward the Suez Canal. No.250 Squadron would be part of this reinforcement effort.

By the middle of 1941, when Caldwell had scored no victories over three dozen outings, he began to wonder whether he had the "right stuff" to be a fighter pilot. As he pondered the "how to" of being a successful pilot one day, he was watching his own aircraft's shadow flitting across the desert. He opened fire and watched the hits relative to the position of the moving shadow of the Curtiss Tomahawk. Gradually, he began to understand the physics of deflection shooting relative to speed and position.

During the last four days of June, he added 3.5 kills to his roster, including 2.5 on the final day of the month over the Mediterranean off Tobruk—two Ju-87 Stukas and a shared Bf-110. He became an ace on August 16, claiming a Regia Aeronautica G-50 over the Mediterranean.

Two weeks later, Caldwell was on patrol over Sidi Barrani when he was jumped by a pair of JG 27 Messerschmitt Bf-109Es. One was piloted by Werner Schroer, an ace with 114 kills against people just like Caldwell. Bullets and cannon shells riddled the Tomahawk's fuselage and cockpit, hitting Caldwell in the back, shoulder, and leg. The aircraft was also badly damaged. Nevertheless, Caldwell managed to return fire, downing Schroer's wingman as the great ace himself slipped away.

Out of action for a month, Caldwell proved that he still had that "right stuff" when he returned to the fray in September. On September 27, he downed a Bf-109 over Buqbuq, and he claimed another the following day in a fight over Bardia. On November 23, he shot down two Bf-109s in a single day, including one piloted by Wolfgang Lippert, the Knight's Cross holder who commanded II Gruppe of JG 27.

The best day of Caldwell's career as a fighter pilot came on December 5, when he plunged into a massed formation of Ju-87 dive-bombers over El Adem during the British Operation Crusader offensive. Caldwell attacked from the rear, claiming two of the Stukas. He then went after the leader and downed two more after that for five. This brought his total score to 14, plus two shared kills. The El Adem action also led to the nickname "Killer Caldwell" being assigned, much to the discomfort of the honoree, who did not feel it to be an accurate description.

After another pair of Bf-109 kills, Caldwell was awarded a Distinguished Flying Cross—with Bar—on December 26. In January 1942, he was promoted to squadron leader and assigned to lead No.112 "Shark" Squadron. Caldwell soon experienced the difficulties of command, as many of the "Sharks" proved to be inexperienced and vulnerable. In a battle with JG 27 Messerschmitt Bf-109s on February 21, Caldwell claimed one of the enemy, but No.112 Squadron lost three of its own. On March 13, two Sharks went down, but the following day, Caldwell claimed a pair of Regia Aeronautica Macchi C-202s over Tobruk—one of them a shared kill.

Caldwell's last victory in North Africa—another Messerschmitt Bf-109—came on April 23 during the great battle for the French Foreign Legionnaire fortress at Bir Hakeim.

Things were turning ugly down under, and his presence was required at home. The Japanese were on the offensive, and the northern cities of Australia were under attack. The Philippines, Hong Kong, and Singapore had fallen like dominoes and it was feared that Australia itself might be invaded. The RAAF wanted its best pilots at home.

Before he left North Africa, however, the Royal Air Force awarded Caldwell a Distinguished Service Order. Because of the Polish pilots in No.112 Squadron that he'd commanded and nurtured, the Polish government awarded him the Walecznych Cross (Cross of Valor).

Back in Australia, Caldwell was given command of RAAF No.1 Fighter Wing, which was based at Darwin, in the Northern Territory. He would get his first victories against the Imperial Japanese Navy Air Force on March 2, 1943, off Point Charles, when he claimed one of Japan's dreaded Mitsubishi A6M Zero fighters, as well as a Nakajima B6N bomber. On May 2, he would claim another pair of Zeros in a dogfight less than 60 miles from Darwin.

During June, Caldwell downed another pair of Zeros and a Mitsubishi G4M bomber. His final victory of the war came on August 20, when he claimed a Mitsubishi Ki-46 reconnaissance aircraft of 202 Sentai near Cape Fourcroy.

In April 1944, after an extended leave, Caldwell commanded RAAF No.80 Wing, with aircraft based at both Darwin and Morotai. By this time, Japanese aircraft were no longer a threat to Australia. Indeed, they had been virtually eliminated from the skies of the Southwest Pacific, and RAAF operations centered around ground attack missions against isolated Japanese troop concentrations. These units were no longer capable of offensive operations, and many people in the RAAF—Caldwell included—felt that attacking them was a waste of time.

By 1944, there was a seething dissatisfaction with the American-dominated command structure's relegation of the RAAF to mere nuisance work. The RAAF pilots who had proved themselves in the darkest days of the war wanted to be used in the offensive against Japan in the Philippines and farther north—where the "action" was.

This displeasure finally reached its boiling point with the Morotai Mutiny in April 1945. Eight frontline RAAF officers, including Caldwell, resigned in protest over the RAAF's allowing itself to become a second-class air force in the final battles for the defeat of Japan. In a major government crisis, much of the RAAF's top leadership, including Air Commodore A. H. Cobby—himself a World War I ace—were compelled to resign.

The action was anticlimactic. In April, the war was expected to last for another two years, with the final invasion of Japan's main island of Honshu not even scheduled until March 1946. However, Japan announced its surrender on August 15, 1945.

By this time, Clive Caldwell had been named to the headquarters staff of the RAAF 1st Tactical Air Force at Melbourne. He left the RAAF in 1946 and pursued a successful business career until his death in August 1994.

Gray: New Zealand's Top Ace

While Clive Caldwell, Australia's leading ace, went home to finish his wartime career fighting the Japanese, the top-scoring New Zealander would serve his entire wartime career with the Royal Air Force in Europe, ending World

War II with 27.5 victories. Colin Falkland Gray and his twin brother, Ken, were born in Christchurch on the South Island on November 9, 1914. Having moved to Britain, Clive became a fighter pilot in the Royal Air Force in 1939, a year after Ken became a bomber pilot. When World War II began, Ken Gray would be one of the pilots who flew the first tentative raids against the Reich. Two months later, he was awarded a Distinguished Flying Cross. Colin Gray, meanwhile, was posted to No.54 Squadron in November 1939 and saw very little action through the "sitzkrieg" period.

In May 1940, everything changed. Ken Gray was killed in an accident and Colin Gray faced his first combat. On May 26, during a bomber escort mission, Colin Gray's flight was bounced by German fighters. Gray managed to shoot down a Bf-109 before his Spitfire was hit. He managed to recover from a steep dive and nurse the damaged Spitfire back to Britain. Mrs. Gray would not lose two sons in one month.

Gray's second victory, another Messerschmitt Bf-109, came on July 13 over Calais. During the Battle of Britain, he saw a great deal of combat, and by the first week of September, he had raised his score to 14 kills and 14 probables. By then, Colin, like Ken, had pinned a Distinguished Flying Cross on his shirt. In January 1941, after a short assignment with No.43 Squadron, Gray became a flight commander with No.54 Squadron, replacing fellow New Zealander Alan Deere, who was one of the highest-scoring Battle of Britain aces.

In June, Gray was transferred to No.1 Squadron as a flight commander, and in August, he was given command of No.616 Squadron. By September 20, when he received a Bar on his Distinguished Flying Cross, he had raised his score to 17 victories.

Colin Gray spent most of 1942 behind a desk, but late in the year, he was reassigned to North Africa as commander of No.81 Squadron, the first squadron in the theater to be equipped with the new Spitfire Mk.IX. Gray quickly added five kills and four probables to his victory tally, and by the time the campaign ended in May 1943, he had added a Distinguished Service Order to his Distinguished Flying Cross.

With Operation Husky, the invasion of Sicily, in the planning stages, Gray was promoted to command the Malta-based No.322 Wing. During June, as Allied forces were getting into position for the coming fight for Sicily, Gray led patrols over the Axis-held island. During this period, he claimed a Bf-109 and a Macchi MC-202. On July 10, while flying air cover for the invasion forces, he downed a Bf-109. No.322 Wing relocated to Lentini on Sicily after the island was occupied by Allied troops, and continued to fly patrols from there. On July 25, Gray was leading such a patrol when they encountered a large number of German Ju-52 transports landing reinforcements at Cap Milazzo. In the ensuing fight, five German fighter escorts went down, along with 21 Ju-52s, two of which were destroyed by Colin Gray.

After the successful conquest of Sicily, Gray was reassigned to Britain to help train newer pilots. In July 1944, when the Germans began to launch their V-1 cruise missiles at Britain, the Royal Air Force turned to him to help coordinate intercept operations.

When World War II ended, Colin Gray remained with the Royal Air Force until March 1961. After his retirement, he returned to New Zealand, where he lived at Waikanae until his death on August 1, 1995.

Wade: The Yank in the Royal Air Force

The 1941 Henry King film, *A Yank in the RAF,* starring Tyrone Power and Betty Grable, wasn't about Lance Wade, but he would have made a better subject. With his dark eyes, Texas drawl, and black mustache, Wade had the same leading-man charisma as Tyrone Power, but he was the real thing, the American who felt strongly about defeating the "Jerries"—or at least strongly about feeling the rush of combat from the cockpit of a Spitfire.

Lance Wade was indeed the real thing. He would score 25 victories (some sources list 23) with the Royal Air Force, tying him for tenth among all American aces in history, and 12th among all Royal Air Force aces. He was born in Broaddus, Texas in 1915, and when World War II began, he decided that he wanted to be part of the action. He traveled to Canada to join the Royal Air Force in December 1940.

He was assigned to No.33 Squadron—Pat Pattle's old unit—in Egypt in September, where he would be flying the Hurricane Mk.I against the Italian Regia Aeronautica. He scored his first victories, a pair of Fiat CR-42s, on November 18, and the magic fifth on November 24. By September 13, Wade had scored 13 victories flying a Hurricane Mk.II since April, and he had been awarded the Distinguished Flying Cross.

With the United States now in the war, Wade could have chosen to transfer to the USAAF, but he remained in the Royal Air Force. He did, however, spend some time in the States during late 1942 on a liaison mission for the Royal Air Force. When he returned to combat in early 1943, he became a flight leader with the Royal Air Force's Desert Air Force No.145 Squadron, but was soon promoted to squadron leader.

Now flying a Spitfire Mk.V, Wade scored 8 victories in the Tunisia campaign to raise his score to 21 by April 1943, and had a Bar attached to his Distinguished Flying Cross. At the end of April, No.145 Squadron converted to Spitfire Mk.IXs and relocated to a base in Italy. By autumn, they had upgraded to Spitfire Mk.IXs, and Wade scored his first kills in the new machine, a pair of Focke Wulf 190s, on October 2. By now, he was the highest-scoring ace in the Desert Air Force, slightly ahead of his nearest rival, Neville Duke, also of No.145 Squadron.

The last claim in Wade's logbook would be three damaged Fw-190s, penciled in on November 3. After that, he was awarded a Distinguished Service Order, promoted to wing commander, and kicked upstairs to a desk job on the staff of the Royal Air Force Desert Air Force headquarters. On January 12, 1944, he was killed in a flying accident at Foggia, Italy.

Duke ended the war as the leading ace of the Desert Air Force, and the third-highest-scoring Allied ace in the Mediterranean, with 26.83 victories. Lance Wade would be fourth in the Mediterranean, behind Pat Pattle, George Beurling, and Duke. Wade was also the highest-scoring American ace ever to serve exclusively with a non-American air force.

Neville Duke went on to a distinguished career as one of Britain's most important test pilots. In 1953, at the Royal Air Force base at Tangmere, he flew the prototype of the Hawker Hunter jet fighter to a record speed of 727 mph.

5

JAPAN

THE INVOLVEMENT OF THE JAPANESE Empire in World War II was a direct outgrowth of its prewar foreign policy, which called for the empire's political and economic domination of the Far East. Japan's aggressiveness was a half century in the making when it launched an all-out war on China in 1937.

In the middle of the nineteenth century, Japan had still been a reclusive feudal monarchy whose social structure had changed little in centuries. It had been ruled since 660 B.C. by a succession of emperors who called themselves "tenshi"—"the sons of heaven." Being an island nation, Japan was geographically isolated from mainland Asia— and indeed from the rest of the world—completely removed from the mainstream of world history, and this was exactly how the emperors preferred it. Japanese society was very rigid and immigration was nonexistent. In fact, the edict of 1636 forbade Japanese from leaving their native country. Foreign merchants were strictly prohibited from conducting business in Japan, although after 1842 certain ports began to allow foreign ships to dock for water and supplies.

This condition of total isolation changed in 1853, when U.S. Navy Commodore Matthew Perry sailed into Edo Bay with a squadron of armed gunboats and a message from President Millard Fillmore: Japan should open its harbors to American trade or risk war. It was a demand that Fillmore's successor 88 years later would regret, but with this, Japan had finally joined the world community.

In 1868, the young Emperor Mutsuhito, also known as Meiji, initiated a program to modernize Japan by importing machines and machine tools from the leading edge of the industrial revolution. At the time of Perry's first landing in 1853, Japan was the technological level of Europe in 1553. Within a quarter century of the Meiji Reformation of 1868, however, it had industrialized to the same level as Europe and the United States. It was an effort that the world had never before witnessed. Japan would enter the twentieth century as *the* leading industrial power in Asia.

Meiji had transformed Japan from a closed society, where its citizens were forbidden to have contact with foreigners, to a nation that was anxious to have contact with, and to emulate, the outside world. In less than half a century, Japan progressed from medieval feudalism to a modern, industrial power. Meanwhile, in 1873, the emperor had established a national army, based on the Prussian model and equipped with up-to-date weapons. A navy, unnecessary while Japan was still an isolated kingdom, was also created. The Japanese had come full circle from total isolation to an eagerness to assert themselves as a world power.

From Europe, Japan had emulated elements of government, military organization, and the industrial revolution. Next, Japan copied the concept of building an empire. For a country whose foreign policy had always been *not* to have a foreign policy, asserting itself throughout Asia represented a bold, new step. Japan annexed the neighboring Riuku Islands in the 1870s and, in 1894, engaged China in a war for control of Korea and Manchuria. Although China's landmass, population, and resources greatly exceeded that of Japan, China proved to be ill-equipped for a major war. When Japan won the war in 1894, it succeeded in gaining a foothold on the Asian mainland.

Only the influence of the vast Russian Empire stood in the way of Japan's total domination of Manchuria and Korea. In February 1904, Japan attacked Russian ships and bases in the Far East. The Russo-Japanese War, the twentieth century's first major conflict, resulted in an embarrassing defeat for the Russians. For the first time since Genghis Khan, an Asian force had resoundingly defeated a major European power in a sustained series of battles. After the peace treaty was signed in 1905, Japan controlled all of Northeast Asia, becoming the first world power to emerge in that continent in modern times. This victory also established Japan as a major force to be reckoned with, both politically and militarily, in the world community.

Emperor Hirohito, who came to power in 1926, presided over a dramatic expansion of the Japanese Empire. Though he would later blame Japan's military government for its aggressiveness, Hirohito saw his domain expand to a geographic scope ten times that of the empire of Meiji. In 1931, Japan incorporated Manchuria into the empire, renaming it Manchukuo and setting up a puppet emperor. In 1937, Hirohito's forces moved on China itself. Shanghai, Beijing (then known as Peiping), and Nanking were battered into submission and occupied.

On September 27, 1940, Hirohito signed the Tripartite Pact, or Triple Alliance, with Germany and Italy, to form the Rome-Berlin-Tokyo Axis, and Japan occupied former French Indochina as a spoil of war. The Japanese were expanding their empire into Southeast Asia under the guise of the so-called Greater East Asia Co-Prosperity Sphere, by which Japan assumed a natural claim to occupy both Indochina and the Netherlands East Indies (now Indonesia). President Franklin Roosevelt, increasingly concerned about Japanese aggression, ended exports to the empire and began to consider further sanctions. Japan viewed these actions as a major impediment to their plans to dominate the Far East and decided to take action.

At 7:30 on Sunday morning, December 7, 1941, bombers launched from Japanese aircraft carriers struck at American military installations in Hawaii, particularly the naval base at Pearl Harbor. The attack was a complete surprise and an immense success for the attackers. When it ended, 3,000 Americans were dead, 100 aircraft had been destroyed, and the U.S. Navy's Pacific Fleet had been decimated. Eight out of the nine battleships that were anchored in Pearl Harbor had been put out of commission.

The following day, President Roosevelt, calling December 7 "a day of infamy," asked Congress for a declaration of war. On December 11, Germany and Italy declared war against the United States and Japan declared war on Britain.

In the months following the attack on Pearl Harbor, the military successes the Japanese achieved were reminiscent of the German Blitzkrieg of 1939 and 1940. Within a month of Pearl Harbor, they had captured Wake Island, Guam, Hong Kong, and the allegedly impregnable British fortress at Singapore. After landing in the Philippines, they seized control of the capital at Manila and cornered a doomed garrison of Americans on the Bataan peninsula. The Japanese Empire now encompassed most of the Pacific, including three of Alaska's Aleutian islands and nearly all of the Asian mainland's coastline, from Korea almost to India, and plans were being made to invade Australia.

Like the German juggernaut that had swept across Europe a year and half earlier, the Japanese seemed invincible, but there was a fatal flaw. The forces of Germany and Japan were well trained, well equipped, and highly motivated, but they had no depth. As in Germany, the pilot-training and aircraft-procurement methods were designed to create an exceptional force, not the means to perpetuate it indefinitely. Neither Hitler nor Hirohito had planned for a long war.

The men who went through—perhaps endured is a better word—Japanese military pilot training in the late 1930s would experience the most rigorous and exacting course in the world. The numbers of students who passed would be relatively few—just 100 annually—but their quality would be extremely high. Ironically, the demanding course, designed to weed out all but the "very, very best," weeded out the "very best" and left Japan critically short of the pilots that it would desperately need six years later.

When Japan drew the United States into the war in 1941, all of its pilots were among the best in the world, but they were—as a result of the brutal culling process—relatively few in number. By 1943, as the ranks of the pilots who did make the grade were thinned, the "very best" were not there to take their places, and Japan had to settle for hastily trained second- and third-rate replacements who were incapable of fighting the by-now-highly-trained Americans.

Japan's Air Forces

During World War II, Japan, like the United States but unlike Germany, Britain, and the Soviet Union, had no air force. As with the United States, all of the nation's military air assets were distributed between its army and navy. Within the United States military, the U.S. Army Air Forces would soon evolve organizationally into a de facto air force. However, both the Imperial Japanese Navy Air Force (IJNAF) and the Imperial Japanese Army Air Force (IJAAF) were much more closely linked to their parent services. Another difference was that the Imperial Japanese Navy Air Force was larger and saw more combat action than the Imperial Japanese Army Air Force during World War II. With the United States, it was just the opposite.

While most U.S. Navy combat aircraft (other than long-range patrol aircraft) were based on aircraft carriers, there were as many or more IJNAF fighter units based ashore than based on the IJNAF carrier fleet. This was especially true later in the war, as the carriers were being sunk faster than they were being replaced.

There was also a geographical division between the IJNAF and the IJAAF. The IJNAF was assigned to operations throughout the Pacific islands and New Guinea, which is where most of the air combat with United States and Australian forces took place. Both the IJNAF and IJAAF would be involved in the Philippines, but the IJAAF primarily had responsibility for operations in places, such as inside China, where aerial combat frequency was less than in the Pacific islands. Both the IJNAF and IJAAF would take part in operations defending Japan from American air attacks during the final months of the war.

The First Japanese Aces

The Spanish Civil War of 1936–1939 was a proving ground for the weapons, tactics, and pilots that European nations would use in World War II. The same was true for Japan with the Sino-Japanese War of 1937–1941 and the little known war that Japan and the Soviet Union fought in 1938–1939 in Mongolia. In fact, in 1941, the Sino-Japanese War *became* a theater of World War II. Many of Japan's leading World War II aces would get their start in China.

The Japanese land invasion of China in July 1937 was supported by a modest, though soon to be escalated, tactical air campaign. The Nationalist (Kuomintang) Chinese air force fought back, and achieved some early successes with their American-made Curtiss Hawks and Soviet-built Polikarpov I-15s. Stunned by the unexpected Chinese successes, the Japanese high command ordered the Imperial Japanese Navy Air Force carrier *Kaga* to sail for China with the crack 13th Kokutai (13th Air Group). Flying the Mitsubishi A5M (Type 96) fighters, which outclassed anything in the Chinese inventory, the IJNAF pilots were to succeed in achieving aerial superiority by the end of September.

Japan's first ace was IJNAF Ensign Kiyoto Koga of the 13th Kokutai, who scored his fifth and defining victory on October 6, 1937. He would score all of his 13 victories by December 9. Koga was killed in an accident on September 15, 1938, and thus did not serve during World War II. The second man to become an ace with the IJNAF 13th Kokutai was Kanichi Kashimura, who scored eight victories in the Sino-Japanese War through March 1938. He served in World War II, and had raised his score to 12 when he turned up missing on March 6, 1943, after combat with American units over the Russell Islands.

The top-scoring ace in Japanese history and the leading ace of any nation in the Sino-Japanese War *and* the Pacific Theater of World War II was Tetsuzo Iwamoto. He began his career as a fighter pilot in early 1938 when he was assigned to the 12th Kokutai to fly A5Ms against the Soviet-built Polikarpov I-16s of the Nationalist Chinese air force during the Japanese assault on Hankow. On February 25, he became the first Imperial Japanese Navy Air Force pilot to score five victories in a single day, and on April 29, he scored four in one day over Hankow. When Iwamoto returned to Japan in September 1938, he had flown 82 missions and he had scored 14 victories.

In addition to Kiyoto Koga, two other Japanese fighter pilots scored 13 victories in the Sino-Japanese War to tie for second place behind Iwamoto's 14. Like Koga and Iwamoto, both Toshio Kuroiwa and Watari Handa flew with the IJNAF. Kuroiwa and Handa first arrived in China in the *Kaga* deployment in the autumn of 1937. Kuroiwa went on to serve with the 12th Kokutai, scoring all of his victories in three months of 1938.

Handa scored his first victory on September 7, 1937, shortly after the *Kaga* reached China. On September 20, he scored three in one day. He had seven victories by the time he was rotated back to Japan. He returned to China in 1938 for a second tour of duty, this time with the 15th Kokutai ashore, and he added six more victories to his score through November.

The third-place Japanese ace in the Sino-Japanese War— after Iwamoto and the three-place tie—was Kuniyoshi Tanaka. He scored 12 victories in China, flying with the 13th Kokutai. He was the only one of the top five—other than Iwamoto, of course—to add additional victories (five) during World War II.

As would be the case in World War II, most of the aerial victories scored during the Sino-Japanese War were scored by IJNAF pilots. Sadaaki Akamatsu and Motonari Suho would each score 11, and Mamoto Matsumura would have a score of 10. Akamatsu would score an additional 16 during the coming conflict to bring his total to 27, while Suho and Matsumura added 5 and 3 respectively.

The lesser scores of the Imperial Japanese Army Air Force pilots was not so much a reflection on the pilots themselves, but a function of deployment. The IJAAF operated deep inland, in northern China, far from the coast and the major cities, where most of the combat action was taking place. The IJAAF aircraft were also inferior to the Mitsubishi A5M that was being flown by the IJNAF. Initially, the IJAAF went to war in China with the Kawasaki Ki-10 biplane as its leading fighter, but by 1938, units were equipped with the Nakajima Ki-27.

Nevertheless, the highest-scoring Imperial Japanese Army Air Force ace in the Sino-Japanese War, Captain Tateo Kato, scored his first four victories in a Ki-10 during a single mission in January 1938. The commander of the 1st Chutai (1st Army Air Group), Kato was an experienced veteran of nine years of flying. He scored all nine of his victories in just three missions, and added nine in World War II.

The second-highest-scoring Japanese Army ace of the Sino-Japanese War was Kousake Kawahara, who shot down his first Kuomintang aircraft on October 27, 1937. He added another four—plus a shared victory—before the fateful day of March 25, 1938. In a massive air battle over Shanghai, Kawahara shot down three enemy aircraft, to bring his score to 8.5, before he himself was killed by a Chinese defender.

The Sino-Japanese War provided the proving ground for the Imperial Japanese Navy Air Force aerial tactics that would allow them to rule the skies of the Pacific War in 1941–1942, but it was not the most intensive aerial combat environment that Japanese pilots would experience in the

years leading up to Pearl Harbor. This distinction belongs
to the all but forgotten border war that took place during
the summers of 1938 and 1939 between Imperial Japanese
Army Air Force soldiers in the Japanese puppet kingdom
of Manchukuo and Soviet forces based in Mongolia.

Japan had achieved unprecedented economic clout in
East Asia, but Japan's empire-building warlords were hun-
gry for a land empire on the Asian continent. Manchukuo
had been incorporated into the Japanese Empire in 1931,
and the invasion of China in 1937 had shown the disci-
plined and well-equipped Japanese army to be virtually
invincible. Against this backdrop, Japan became greedy for
more land in Soviet-controlled Mongolia. Japan had defeated Russia in 1904, and expected only success.

The Second Russo-Japanese War of 1938–1939, known
as the Khalkin Gol (Nomonhan) Incident, was anything but
a replay of the 1904 action. Deep inland on the continent,
the Imperial Japanese Navy was not a factor, as it had been
in 1904. The Imperial Japanese Army attack was blunted
by the Soviet army, and Japan was forced to withdraw.

However, during the final phase of this war, the IJAAF
would experience much more air combat in a few short
months than the IJNAF would throughout the entire Sino-
Japanese War. While their brothers on the ground were
being routed by the Soviets, the IJNAF pilots achieved air
superiority over the vast, dusty dry steppes of Central Asia.
The fixed-gear, enclosed-cockpit Nakajima Ki-27s, crude
by World War II standards, were nevertheless far better
than the Polikarpov I-15s that the Soviets were flying, and
the IJAAF successes were astounding.

There were over 50 IJAAF aces in Mongolia, and more
than a dozen who outscored all of the IJNAF pilots then
in action in China. The highest scorer among these was
Hiromichi Shinohara, who entered combat with the 11th

Sentai on May 27, 1939. Between that date and his death in the sights of a Soviet pilot exactly three months later, Shinohara downed 58 Soviet aircraft, more than quadruple Tetsuzo Iwamoto's score in China. The tremendous scores were the result of many factors in addition to the skill of the pilots. The flying weather was near perfect, and the terrain itself favored the easy construction of numerous airfields close to the action and the use of open ground as emergency fields. There were also a lot of planes in the air.

In his first action, Shinohara shot down 3 Soviet aircraft, and 30 days later, while his comrades watched from the ground, he shot down 11 enemy planes. In early July, he scored 14 further victories in two missions. On August 27, before his luck finally ran out, Shinohara managed to take out another 3 Soviet fighters.

Shinohara's amazing final total of 58 was more than double that of the second-leading Imperial Japanese Army Air Force ace in Mongolia, Mitsuyoshi Tarui of the 1st Sentai. Yet the 28 kills racked up by Tarui were double that of Iwamoto in China. Tarui would eventually add another 10 in World War II before his death in 1944. Two other important aces of the 1st Sentai were Hitoshi Asano and Isamu Hosano with 22 and 21 respectively.

Like Shinohara, the third- and fourth-top-scoring IJAAF aces in Mongolia flew with the 11th Sentai. Captain Kenji Shimada entered combat the same day as Shinohara and would score 27 victories in less than three months—including 5 in a day three times. Tomio Hanada scored 25 victories in a similar span of time. On one occasion, he rescued his squadron commander by landing his Nakajima behind Soviet lines. Both Shimada and Hanada were killed in Mongolia. The former was shot down on September 15, 1939, and the latter died in an accident on October 7.

Other top 11th Sentai aces were Shoji Kato with 23, Saburo Togo with 22, Zenzaburo Ohtsaka with 22, Goro Furugori with 20, Jozo Iwahashi with 20, and Bunji Yoshiyama with 20. Among these, only Furugori and Iwahashi would add additional victories (10 and 2 respectively) in World War II.

The 24th Sentai boasted two of the IJAAF's top Mongolia aces. Shogo Saito scored 25, and Chiyogi Saito claimed 21. Both would add to their scores during World War II, but only modestly—1 and 7 respectively.

The little-remembered side show in Mongolia accounted for some of the fiercest aerial combat among all the conflicts that simmered on the eve of World War II, but few of the veterans of Mongolia were around to use the lessons of their experiences.

Aces of the Imperial Japanese Army Air Force

The Imperial Japanese Army would see most of its action on the Asiatic mainland, while the Imperial Japanese Navy saw nearly all of its combat in the Pacific Theater and Southwest Pacific Theater. IJAAF aces would be eclipsed in prominence by their more well-known comrades in the islands. IJAAF aces would earn most of their victories over Burma and in China, where the pilots were much less likely to see combat. Another difference between the IJAAF and the IJNAF was that a larger number of IJAAF pilots were officers. It was rare to find an IJNAF combat pilot above the rank of ensign, but among the IJAAF, many were captains and majors among the sergeants and warrant officers.

During World War II, the highest-scoring Imperial Japanese Army Air Force ace was Master Sergeant Satoshi Anabuki, who is credited with 51 victories. Born in 1921,

Anabuki joined the Imperial Japanese Army Air Force late in 1941 and was assigned to the 50th Sentai (Fighter Group) flying a Nakajima Ki-27. He first saw action in the Philippines during the Japanese invasion in December 1941, where he claimed three American aircraft.

In 1942, the 50th Sentai was reassigned to action in Burma and reequipped with the fast and maneuverable Nakajima Ki-43 Hayabusa (Peregrine Falcon). Known by the Allied code name "Oscar," the Ki-43 was produced in larger numbers than any other Imperial Japanese Army Air Force fighter, and it was very effective until improved Allied aircraft reached the field in 1943.

It was in Burma, between June 1942 and October 1943, that Satoshi Anabuki shot down 13 American and 28 Royal Air Force aircraft. On January 26, 1943, he became possibly the first Japanese pilot in Southeast Asia to bring down a Consolidated B-24 Liberator strategic bomber. On October 8, 1943, Anabuki had his best day ever, shooting down three B-24s and a pair of P-38 fighters in a single action near Rangoon. Having exhausted his ammunition shooting down these five, Anabuki rammed the tail of a third B-24 and then crash-landed his Hayabusa. In the Japanese armed forces, decorations for heroism were almost never given to individuals and especially not to living individuals. The theory was that heroism was part of a team effort and that individual heroism—when it occurred— was defined by a person sacrificing his life. Nevertheless, Satoshi Anabuki's actions on October 8, 1943, were so outstanding that he was decorated.

In February 1944, Satoshi Anabuki was involved in a project to deliver a contingent of the exceptional new Nakajima Ki-84 Hayate (Storm) fighters from Japan to the Philippines. On one of these missions, he shot down six

Grumman F6F Hellcats that had attacked the delivery formation.

He is also credited with developing an air combat tactic known as the "Anabuki Run," which was widely used throughout the Imperial Japanese Army Air Force. In this move, a pilot who is attacked from behind pulls up, rolls his f.ghter into an inverted position, then dives vertically, opening fire at 300 feet.

After the fall of the Philippines, Anabuki returned to Japan to fly air defense missions, piloting the new Nakajima Ki-100 fighter. This plane, one of the best high-altitude interceptors flown during the war, was the last production aircraft the IJAAF put into service, but only a handful saw action. Anabuki's last victory came during an air defense mission in June 1945 when he shot down a Boeing B-29 Superfortress, a far more formidable foe than the B-24 Liberator of two years before.

Satoshi Anabuki's final score of 51 is generally accepted as a best-guess estimate, although some sources credit him with as few as 39.

The second-highest-scoring IJAAF ace was Isamu Sasaki, who, like Anabuki, flew with the 50th Sentai in Burma. He scored 32 victories in Southeast Asia before being rotated back to the homeland. Flying air defense interception missions, Sasaki succeeded in shooting down six B-29s to bring his score to 38.

The third-place IJAAF ace was Major Yasuhiko Kuroe, who commanded the 64th Sentai in Burma. A veteran with two kills in the action over Mongolia, Kuroe began his World War II career in Malaya, assigned to fly the Nakajima Ki-44 Shoki (Demon), an innovative fighter optimized for speed over maneuverability. Known to the Allies as "Tojo," the Ki-44 was a remarkable fighter in 1942, but was ultimately superseded by the Ki-84. Kuroe flew with the 64th Sentai from April 1942 through January 1944, scoring 20 victories during this period, including two P-51 Mustangs, two Royal Air Force Mosquitoes, and a B-24 Liberator.

Kuroe returned to Japan to fly against the B-29 onslaught in 1945 in the heavily armed, twin-engine Ki-102. He downed his first Superfortress in March 25, 1945, and his last two in May to end the war with 30 victories.

The fourth-place IJAAF ace was Goichi Sumino, who flew with Yasuhiko Kuroe in the 64th Sentai in Burma from March 1943. In fact, he scored all of his 27 victories with the 64th—as opposed to Kuroe's 20 with the 64th—to make him the Sentai's highest-scoring ace. Amazingly, he scored 25 of his kills before he turned 21 in February 1944. He was killed just four months later, when he tangled with a P-38 on June 4, 1944.

Tied for fifth place among IJAAF aces, with 20 victories, were Saburo Nakamura, another 64th Sentai pilot, and Teruhiko Kobayashi, who commanded the 244th Sentai. A former bomber pilot who made the transition to Ki-61 Hien (Swallow) interceptors in December 1944, Major Kobayashi scored most of his victories against bombers. The youngest Sentai commander in the IJAAF, he claimed a dozen B-29s through April 1945.

Aces of the Imperial Japanese Navy Air Force

Thanks to their being assigned to the Pacific Theater, where air combat was more intense than over the Asiatic mainland, the Imperial Japanese Navy Air Force aces generally scored higher than their countrymen in the Imperial Japanese Army Air Force. Indeed, Japan's top seven aces of all time flew for the IJNAF.

The top two Japanese aces—both navy men—were Hiroyoshi Nishizawa and Tetsuzo Iwamoto. With a generally accepted score of 87 victories, Nishizawa was Japan's top-scoring ace in World War II, while Iwamoto is credited with 80 in World War II, but an additional 14 in the Sino-Japanese War, for a total of 94. Some sources, however, credit Iwamoto with as many as 250 victories or as few as 66, and Nishizawa with as many as 202. Because of the wide discrepancies, there is still a debate over which man had the highest World War II score. There is little question, however, that Iwamoto and Nishizawa were the top two.

For a number of reasons, attributing precise scores to individual Japanese aces has never been an exact science. The official practice in the field credited victories to the group or squadron rather than to the actual pilot. Such individual scores were kept informally and are not always accurate. Furthermore, Japanese fighters were not equipped with gun cameras, so victories that were not directly witnessed—and in the heat of battle, pilots could not spare the time to "witness" another pilot's work—were often not credited. For all of the important Japanese aces, there is a wide spread of numbers that are mentioned in the literature as their possible final score.

The next five top-scoring IJNAF aces were Shoichi Sugita, generally credited with 70, Saburo Sakai with 64, Junichi Sasai with 60, and Hinomichi Shinohara with 58; Takeo Okumura is often credited with 54, although some sources give him as many as 98.

The leading fighter unit in Japanese history was the Tainan Kokutai (Tainan Air Group), which was named for its original base at Tainan on the island of Taiwan (then known as Formosa). The Tainan Kokutai achieved its notoriety during early to mid-1942—when the IJNAF ruled the skies over the Southwest Pacific—when it was based at Lae on the island of New Guinea. Tainan Kokutai in 1942 is especially notable in that four of Japan's top six aces—Nishizawa, Sakai, Sasai, and Okumura—were assigned to it at the same time.

The Tainan Kokutai brought some of the best fighter pilots in the Imperial Japanese Navy Air Force together in what was probably the most elite Japanese fighter group of the war. In addition to Nishizawa, Sakai, Sasai, and Okumura, there were such men as Toshio Ota, who would score 34; Shizuo Ishii, who would score 26; Toshiaki Honda, who would score 23; Masaaki Shimakawa, who would score 20; Kazushi Uto, who would score 19; Hiroshi Okano, who would score 19; and Takeo Tanimizu, who would score 18. Most of these victories would be scored in the Southwest Pacific during 1942.

The Legendary Zero

One of the key factors that allowed the IJNAF pilots to rule those tropical skies for at least a year was an incredible aircraft, the Mitsubishi A6M Reisen, best known as the "Zero." The most important aircraft to be produced in the first half century of the Japanese aviation industry, the A6M was also arguably the best combat aircraft in widespread service in Asia and the Pacific from 1940 through 1942.

Mitsubishi had been producing aircraft for the Imperial Japanese Navy since the early 1920s, and its first monoplane fighter, the open-cockpit A5M, had gone into service in 1937. In combat during the Sino-Japanese War, the A5M was a successful aircraft, but it lacked the range needed to escort bombers deep into the interior of China. Noting this, and considering their expansionist plans for the near future, the Imperial Japanese Navy issued its 12-

Shi requirement for a long-range air superiority fighter that could match the performance not only of the Chinese fighters, but of the then-current British and American fighters they expected to face as their war to control Asia expanded.

Mitsubishi sent A5M designer Jiro Horkoshi back to the drawing board. He accepted the challenge and went to work to develop an aircraft that pushed the limits of aeronautical technology. First flown in April 1939, the A6M was his masterpiece. The name "Zero" came from the developmental designation A6M Type 0, with the "0" being the last digit of the year it was expected to enter service, the Japanese year 2600 (1940 A.D.). In Japanese, it was known as Rei Shiki Sento Ki (Type Zero Fighter), or Reisen for short. The Allies (following the code-name practice of giving fighters male names and bombers female names) officially called the A6M "Zeke," but in practice, everybody called it "Zero."

From the moment that the first A6Ms went into action in China in July 1940, it was evident that it was the best air superiority fighter in Asian skies. The A6M2, the first operational variant, had a wingspan of 39 feet 4.25 inches and a length of 29 feet 9 inches. It weighed 6,164 pounds fully loaded and fueled. It was powered by a 950-hp, air-cooled, 14-cylinder Nakajima NK1C Sakae 12 engine that gave it a top speed of 332 mph, better than anything then in service on either side of the Pacific. It had a service ceiling of 32,810 feet and a range of 1,930 miles. Armament consisted of two machine guns and two 20mm cannons, and the A6M2 was configured to carry 250 pounds of bombs.

In the surprise Japanese attack against Pearl Harbor, the Zero itself was one of the biggest surprises. American intelligence knew of its existence, but drastically underestimated its performance.

The Zero was a lethal weapon in the early part of the war, greatly outclassing and outfighting the P-40 Warhawks that it met in the Philippines and the F4F Wildcats with which it did battle in the skies over Guadalcanal and the Southwest Pacific. In 1940, American military planners had discounted it as probably an inferior copy of an older American aircraft. In 1942, the Zero had come to be regarded as an almost mythical secret weapon.

In the Battle of Midway in June 1942, Americans faced the A6M3. The Zero was still superior, but the losses in aircraft carriers and pilots this began here would mark the beginning of the end, although that would not become fully evident for another year. The Zero's primacy would extend into 1943, with the introduction of the A6M5, which was probably the best of the widely produced and widely used Zero types. The A6M5 had a wingspan of 36 feet 1 inch and a length of 29 feet 11 inches. It weighed 6,025 pounds fully loaded and fueled.

The A6M5 was powered by an 1,130-hp, air-cooled, 14-cylinder Nakajima NK1F Sakae 21 engine that gave it a top speed of 351 mph, better than the A6M2, but not fully a match for the Grumman F6F Hellcat, Lockheed P-38 Lightning, and Vought F4U Corsair, which it would face in ever-growing numbers in 1943. The A6M5 had a service ceiling of 38,520 feet and a range of 1,194 miles, less than the A6M2, because range had been sacrificed for performance. The armament was the same as the A6M2. What it lacked were features then standard on American fighters, such as self-sealing fuel tanks and adequate rear cockpit armor. These were omitted to achieve maximum performance.

In one-on-one combat, an A6M5 in the hands of a good

pilot could outmaneuver its American opponents, but by late 1943, as mentioned earlier, a large number of good pilots had been lost, and the training system wasn't replacing them adequately. Conversely, the quality of American pilots was steadily improving.

By the end of 1944, the Imperial Japanese Navy had begun to resort to its kamikaze tactics, recklessly throwing away both pilots and Zeros in a desperate attempt to sink aircraft carriers. By early 1945, the Zero's era of air superiority was a distant memory. With the losses in carriers, pilots, and Zeros, the Japanese no longer met their foe in air battles reminiscent of 1942–1943.

Meanwhile, Mitsubishi had developed the A6M8, powered by a 1,560-hp Mitsubishi Kinsei engine, as well as the Zero's successor, the A7M Reppu, powered by a 2,070-hp 18-cylinder Mitsubishi Ha43-11 engine. The former would have been the ideal fighter for 1943, but it was not available until April 1945. The latter would have been a formidable fighter in 1945, but the B-29 attacks had so seriously disrupted industrial production and transportation that there was no place to build them and no way to get needed parts. When the war ended, eight prototypes had been manufactured and there were a few half-finished production models.

The A6M remained in production to the last, with a few Zeros coming off the assembly line even as the emperor pondered surrender. There were 10,499 Zeros produced between 1939 and 1945, making it the most-produced airplane in Japanese aviation history. Despite its dismal last chapter, the story of the Zero is one of a brilliantly designed airplane that was ideal for its times, and proved that fact well.

Nishizawa and Iwamoto: The Two at the Top

Of the leading pair in the pantheon of Japanese aces, Hiroyoshi Nishizawa and Tetsuzo Iwamoto, the latter was already an ace twice over before the war even started. He had scored his initial victories against the Chinese in the Sino-Japanese War, and he would go on to be the top-scoring Imperial Japanese Navy Air Force ace to serve aboard an Imperial Japanese Navy aircraft carrier. He was also the only one of the top Pacific Theater aces who flew on the opening day of World War II in the Pacific—December 7, 1941.

Tetsuzo Iwamoto's career as a fighter pilot began in early 1938 when he was assigned to the 12th Kokutai to fly Mitsubishi A5M fighters against the Soviet-built Polikarpov I-16s of the Kuomintang Chinese Air Force during the assault on Hankow. On February 25, he became the first Imperial Japanese Navy Air Force pilot to score five victories in a single day, and on April 29, he scored four in one day over Hankow. When Tetsuzo Iwamoto returned to Japan in September 1938, he had flown 82 missions and scored 14 victories.

During the coming years, Iwamoto became part of Japan's ambitious plan to create aircraft carrier battle groups for offensive operations in the Pacific. In 1941, having made the transition from the clumsy Mitsubishi A5M to the exceptional A6M, he was assigned to the Fifth Carrier Division, specifically to the Zuikaku Kokutai aboard the carrier *Zuikaku,* whose sister ship, *Shokaku*, was also part of the Fifth Carrier Division. The *Zuikaku* was commissioned on September 25, 1941, and underwent a shakedown cruise in the Kobe and Kure area, moving out to Oita and Saeki.

On November 26, *Zuikaku* was added to Vice Admiral Nagumo Chuichi's First Air Fleet, which departed from Hittokapu Bay in the Kurile Islands to be part of the four-carrier task force destined for the attack on Pearl Harbor. On December 7, the fighters of the Zuikaku Kokutai and Shokaku Kokutai escorted the bombers against the Pearl Harbor Naval Base and other targets, engaging the Americans who rose to intercept them.

After the Pearl Harbor raid, the Japanese task force withdrew quickly, returning to Japan on December 23. *Zuikaku* sailed for the island fortress of Truk on January 8, 1942, and moved south to provide air support for Japanese operations against Rabaul and Lae on January 21. During the first week of February, the *Zuikaku* was part of a strike force operating against American shipping in the Marshall Islands, after which it returned to the Yokosuka Naval Base in Japan by way of Truk.

After a layover in Japan through early March, it sailed for air attack operations in the Indian Ocean with First Air Fleet, Carrier Division 5. On April 5 and April 9, *Zuikaku* launched air strikes against the cities of Colombo and Trincomalee in the British colony of Ceylon (now Sri Lanka). In the latter attack, Tetsuzo Iwamoto added four Royal Air Force aircraft to his score.

On April 19, the *Zuikaku* began operations in the Coral Sea that would culminate in its being involved in the Battle of the Coral Sea on May 7 and 8, 1942. This battle was a milestone in the history of aircraft carrier operations in that it was the first battle in naval history conducted by air. The ships of the opposing combatants were not visible to one another. For his part, Tetsuzo Iwamoto claimed two American aircraft. Though losses were heavy and it was not a victory for either side, it was a moral victory for the U.S. Navy because it was the first major operation since the beginning of the war in which Japan did not win decisively.

Zuikaku's sister carrier, *Shokaku*, was badly damaged in the Battle of the Coral Sea, but the *Zuikaku* managed to slip away into a rainstorm. The Zuikaku Kokutai, however, took severe losses in terms of both pilots and aircraft, and the ship was forced to sail for Japan to take on replacements. As such, the *Zuikaku* missed the Battle of Midway, which was to be a major defeat for the Imperial Japanese Navy, a rout that cost it four of its carriers—*Akagi, Hiryu, Kaga,* and *Soryu*—along with nearly 300 aircraft and many of its best pilots. The losses represented more than a third of Japan's carrier strength. On July 14, 1942, *Zuikaku* would receive a new assignment as part of the Striking Force of the Third Fleet's Carrier Division 1, but she would be in drydock until August 12 and unable to get into action.

It had been in early August 1942 that the U.S. Marines landed on the island of Guadalcanal in the Solomon Islands, so the Third Fleet's Carrier Division 1 and the *Zuikaku* were ordered south to take part in operations in the eastern Solomons. The force would remain in combat in the Solomons area essentially continuously for the next two months, taking part in Guadalcanal operations and the Battle of Santa Cruz on October 26, where the *Zuikaku* was bombed, but undamaged. On October 30, she returned to Truk and then back to Yokosuka by way of the naval base at Kure.

For Tetsuzo Iwamoto, the Solomon Islands action would mark an end to his career as a carrier pilot, but he returned to the same area as part of the land-based Imperial Japanese Navy Air Force 281st Kokutai. In November 1943, he was transferred to the 204th Kokutai, based ashore at Rabaul, New Britain.

During his first month with the 204th Kokutai, Tetsuzo Iwamoto is credited with 15 victories and 5 probables, including three Curtiss SB2C bombers and a pair each of Lockheed P-38 and Bell P-39 fighters. On December 10, he claimed a pair of Vought F4U Corsairs and four bombers.

In February 1944, having painted another 25 kill marks on his Zero, Tetsuzo Iwamoto was reassigned to the 253rd Kokutai to fly air defense for the big Imperial Japanese Navy base at Truk. On March 6, he destroyed five Consolidated B-24 Liberator strategic bombers in one of the most dramatic attacks in the history of aerial combat. With one swift blow, Iwamoto dropped a phosphorous bomb on one Liberator, igniting its bombs in a fireball that consumed the other four aircraft.

After reassignment to Japan, where he was finally promoted to lieutenant, Tetsuzo Iwamoto was assigned briefly to the 252nd Kokutai in the Philippines in October 1944. Coincidentally, the *Zuikaku* was sunk on October 25, 1944, during the battle off Cape Engano. She had been the last surviving carrier of those that took part in the attack on Pearl Harbor.

By this time, Japan's home islands were starting to come under attack, and a man of Tetsuzo Iwamoto's skill was considered to be an important asset in their defense. He was assigned to the 203rd Kokutai, an air defense interceptor unit. By this time, attacks against Japan's major cities were an almost nightly occurrence. With the 203rd Kokutai, Tetsuzo Iwamoto would score 23 victories between February and April 1945, including seven American fighters on February 16 alone.

On April 6, 1945, when the Imperial Japanese Navy super-battleship *Yamato* was sent against the U.S. Navy forces off Okinawa, the 203rd Kokutai was assigned to provide air cover. The 64,000-ton *Yamato,* and her sister ship, *Musashi*, carried 18-inch guns and were the largest battleships ever built. The big ship was, ironically, sunk by U.S. Navy airpower before ever firing a shot at another capital ship, but during the air attack, Tetsuzo Iwamoto succeeded in shooting down three F4U Corsairs and three F6F Hellcats. He would not live to see the end of World War II, but his final combined score of 94 in China and the Pacific is generally accepted as having made him Japan's highest-scoring ace overall.

Not counting his 14 in China, however, Iwamoto's score of 80 during World War II is second to the 87 that were scored by Hiroyoshi Nishizawa, the top-scoring Japanese ace of World War II.

Nishizawa was a sullen loner. He was an unassuming man who was ill at ease on the ground, but when he got into the air, he was transformed. Almost sickly in appearance, Hiroyoshi Nishizawa was a man who one hardly noticed in a group, but when he got into the air, he suddenly became—as Saburo Sakai remembers—"The Devil." For him, flying was less second nature than *first* nature. He flew with the best units in the Imperial Japanese Navy Air Force during the intense early days of the war and achieved the best record of any pilot of any nation in the Pacific Theater of World War II.

This pilot who was called "The Devil" even by his comrades, was born on January 27, 1927, the son of a sake brewer in rural Nagano Prefecture. He left school in his mid-teens to work in a textile factory, but in 1936, he decided on a whim to volunteer as an aviation trainee with the Imperial Japanese Navy Air Force. He earned his wings in 1939 and served with several air groups in Japan over the ensuing two years, winding up in 1941 at the Chitose Air Base with the Chitose Kokutai (Chitose Air

Group). During these years, he never tasted the action that all the young men of his generation craved. He was never assigned to units that were then in combat in China, nor did he participate in the attack on Pearl Harbor in December 1941, or the subsequent offensive operations in Southeast Asia.

While the high-profile activities of the Imperial Japanese Navy Air Force were the carrier actions against Pearl Harbor and later at the battles of Midway and the Coral Sea, most of the Imperial Japanese Navy Air Force fighter groups were actually based on land in such areas as the Solomon Islands, New Guinea, and the Philippines. In January 1942, the Chitose Kokutai was assigned to the newly captured air base at Rabaul on New Britain. Now a petty officer first class, Hiroyoshi Nishizawa claimed his first aerial victory on February 3 in an A5M, although the Royal Australian Air Force Catalina that he thought he shot down had actually survived.

The unit would soon make the transition from the Mitsubishi A5M to the Mitsubishi A6M Zero. By March, the Zeros of the Chitose Kokutai were incorporated into the larger 4th Kokutai headed for New Guinea. Here, where the air war in the Southwest Pacific would soon be the most intense, Nishizawa was able to prove himself in several air battles, as 4th Kokutai Zeros tangled with USAAF and RAAF fighters.

Strategically, the Japanese high command had decided to capture the island of New Guinea as a stepping-stone to neutralizing Australia, and this set the stage for the vicious fighting that would result in many significant combat actions over the next two years.

In early March 1942, the Japanese captured Lae on the northern coast of the island, and established a major—albeit crude—air base. A further reorganization of the

Imperial Japanese Navy Air Force resulted in the fighter units of the 4th Kokutai being incorporated into the Tainan Kokutai.

During April and May, the Tainan Kokutai flew numerous missions—mainly against the big Allied base at Port Moresby on the opposite side of New Guinea—escorting bombers and conducting fighter sweeps aimed at drawing Allied fighters into dogfights. In the latter, the A6M Zeros of the Tainan Kokutai often achieved decisive victories over superior numbers of Allied P-39 Airacobras and P-40 Warhawks. Nishizawa would be an ace twice over by the summer of 1942, claiming five P-39s between June 1 and July 4 alone.

Meanwhile, on May 17, in an account that is vividly described by Sakai in his 1957 book, *Samurai,* he, Nishizawa, and Ota brazenly flew a series of aerobatic maneuvers—including six tight close formation loops—over the Allied field at Port Moresby. The Allied gunners, apparently stunned by this audacious display, didn't fire a shot at the trio.

The spring and summer of 1942 would be the best of times for the pilots of the Imperial Japanese Navy Air Force and its Tainan Kokutai. They flew a superior aircraft, they had better training, and they had the Allied air forces thoroughly outclassed in every regard. Japan was still on the offensive, and the eventual Allied superiority in numbers, equipment, and training had not yet begun to manifest itself.

Only the formidable Boeing B-17 Flying Fortresses, with their bristling defensive armament, proved to be an obstacle. By August, however, Nishizawa and Sakai developed the tactic of attacking them head-on, and after that, even the Fortresses were just huge sitting ducks for the Zeros of the Tainan Kokutai.

It was in early August 1942, when the U.S. Marines landed on the island of Guadalcanal in the Solomon Islands, that the Tainan Kokutai was relocated to Rabaul, New Britain. Initially, the level of air superiority that the Tainan Kokutai and the Imperial Japanese Navy Air Force had enjoyed in New Guinea would continue, but soon it began to fade, never to be seen again.

On August 7, in the Tainan Kokutai's first battle with U.S. Navy carrier-based fighters after arriving back at Rabaul, Hiroyoshi Nishizawa shot down six Grumman F4F Wildcats, primarily VF-5s, based on the USS *Saratoga*. The score for the Tainan Kokutai for the day included at least nine F4Fs and a Douglas SBD Dauntless dive-bomber.

The air battle raged over Guadalcanal through September and October, with Nishizawa and the Tainan Kokutai being forced to engage larger and larger numbers of U.S. Navy and U.S. Marine Corps aircraft. In November, the Tainan Kokutai was redesignated as the 251st Kokutai and strengthened for a struggle that would continue until February, when Japanese troops were finally withdrawn from Guadalcanal. It was a major psychological blow to the Japanese, who had, a year earlier, been virtually invincible.

After the evacuation of Guadalcanal, Nishizawa was out of action until May 7, 1943, when the 251st Kokutai was sent back to Rabaul. It was on June 7 that he shot down his first Vought F4U Corsair on a fighter sweep over Guadalcanal. In October, after a brief assignment to the 253rd Kokutai, Nishizawa was promoted to warrant officer and rotated back to Japan. He would remain in the home islands, essentially out of action, for a year. By this time, he is reported to have achieved a total of 85 aerial victories.

While in Japan, Hiroyoshi Nishizawa spent time training

recruits at Atsugi Air Base—a task he disliked, because there was no longer sufficient time to give them the level of training he had received—and patrolling the Kurile Islands north of Japan waiting for American air attacks from Alaska. These patrols were endlessly boring, because the attacks, which Japanese intelligence was sure were imminent, never came.

When American forces invaded the Japanese-occupied American Commonwealth of the Philippines in October 1944, Nishizawa was sent back into the fray at last. He was assigned to the 201st Kokutai, which was sent to the island of Cebu to help defend Japanese occupation forces being pounded by American bombers.

By now, the shortage of good pilots in the IJNAF, combined with ever-growing American strength, led the Imperial Japanese Navy to resort to the desperate measure of sending inexperienced pilots on suicide missions. Under the kamikaze (divine wind) doctrine, it was believed that the suicide pilots were religiously inspired heroes of the highest order. Experienced pilots were assigned to escort the novices on their one-way missions.

On October 25, Nishizawa was chosen to provide a fighter escort for what was to be the first kamikaze attack against American ships. The attack succeeded in sinking the carrier USS *St. Lo,* and Nishizawa shot down two Grumman F6F Hellcats in his first and last air duel with the U.S. Navy's premier fleet air defense fighter.

Later that day, Nishizawa reportedly had a premonition of his own death and requested to fly a kamikaze mission himself. His request was denied because the Imperial Japanese Navy Air Force still needed his skill as a fighter pilot.

The following day, October 26, 1944, Hiroyoshi Nishizawa and several other 201st Kokutai fighter pilots were to be ferried north to Clark Field on the island of Luzon to pick up several A6M Zeros, which they were to fly back to Cebu. Having imagined his own death, Japan's leading ace would be flying as a passenger in a transport and not at the controls of a fighter.

There are different versions of what happened that morning. Nishizawa may have been piloting the aircraft or he may have been just a passenger. The aircraft may have been a twin-engine Nakajima Ki-49 bomber, or (according to Saburo Sakai) an unarmed DC-3 airliner. In either case, it was attacked by a pair of Hellcats and shot down. There were no survivors.

Hiroyoshi Nishizawa was posthumously promoted to lieutenant (junior grade). The final score of Japan's top-scoring ace in World War II was 87 victories, 85 of them occurring between February 1942 and October 1943. As noted above, this placed him second in Japanese history to Tetsuzo Iwamoto. Though Nishizawa is often credited with as many as 202 kills, 87 is the most widely agreed final score.

Sakai: The Man Who Lived to Tell the Tale

Saburo Sakai was Japan's third (some sources would say fourth) highest-scoring ace in World War II, but he is best remembered for being the only major Japanese ace to live to tell about his experiences during the war.

He was born on August 26, 1916, in Saga, on Kyushu, the southernmost main island of Japan. Ironically, for a man who would be at home in the sky, he enlisted in the Imperial Japanese Navy, envisioning a life at sea. He was mustered in at Sasebo Naval Base in May 1933 as a sea-man recruit, and in 1935, he was assigned as a gunner's mate aboard the battleship *Haruna*. Two years later, as a petty officer third class, he applied for, and was accepted into, the naval flight training program at Tsuchiura. As noted above, Imperial Japanese Navy Air Force flight training was the most demanding in the world at this time. The numbers of students who passed the course were relatively few, but their quality was extremely high.

Saburo Sakai became a naval aviator in July 1937 and was assigned to various units within Japan before being sent into action in the Sino-Japanese War in May 1938. Based at Kiukiang in China, he flew the clumsy Mitsubishi A5M open-cockpit fighter, escorting bombers against targets such as Hankow. It was on one such mission that he scored his first victory, against a Soviet-built Polikarpov I-16 of the Kuomintang Chinese air force.

Sakai would spend the next year in Japan, leisurely training to fly the new Mitsubishi A6M Zero fighter. There was still no particular urgency to Japanese pilot training. In May 1941, he returned to Hankow for more missions against the Kuomintang. After scoring his first two victories in an A6M, Sakai was transferred to the Tainan Kokutai, which was being formed at Tainan on the island of Formosa. It was here that IJNAF units began to prepare for the invasion of the American Commonwealth of the Philippines.

On December 7, 1941 (December 8 across the International Dateline in Taiwan and the Philippines), the IJNAF attacked the United States Naval Base at Pearl Harbor, Hawaii, launching simultaneous raids from Taiwan against the Philippines. The Tainan Kokutai and accompanying bombers struck at Clark Field, the big American air base on Luzon, and Saburo Sakai scored his first victory against the Americans, a USAAF P-40 Warhawk.

Three days later, he shot down a B-17 piloted by Captain Colin P. Kelly, who had, according to American media reports, just sunk the battleship *Haruna,* coincidentally, the same ship on which Sakai had served as a seaman. In fact, the *Haruna* was not in the area and Kelly had missed, not sunk, the heavy cruiser *Ashigara,* off Aparri, Luzon. Nevertheless, Kelly would be posthumously awarded the first Congressional Medal of Honor of World War II, and he would become a patriotic rallying point for Americans.

After the Imperial Japanese Navy Air Force destroyed the USAAF units in the Philippines, the Tainan Kokutai was sent into the Netherlands East Indies to support the Japanese offensive in this area. Here, Sakai enjoyed a remarkable series of victories flying his A6M Zero against American and Dutch aircraft, mainly Brewster Buffalos and Curtiss P-36s and P-40s.

In April 1942, the Tainan Kokutai was sent to a crude airfield, recently captured at Lae, New Guinea. Strategically, the Japanese high command had decided to capture the island of New Guinea as a stepping-stone to neutralizing Australia, and this set the stage for vicious fighting that would result in many significant combat actions over the next two years.

As discussed above, it was at Lae that some of the best fighter pilots in the Imperial Japanese Navy Air Force were brought together in the Tainan Kokutai, transforming it into Japan's ultimate fighter unit.

During April and May, the Tainan Kokutai flew numerous missions—mainly against the big Allied base at Port Moresby on the opposite side of New Guinea—escorting bombers and conducting fighter sweeps aimed at drawing Allied fighters into dogfights. In the latter, the A6M Zeros of the Tainan Kokutai often achieved decisive victories over superior numbers of Allied P-39 Airacobras and P-40 Warhawks, as well as against B-25 Mitchell and B-26 Marauder medium bombers that ventured to attack Lae and other Japanese positions on New Guinea. Both Hiroyoshi Nishizawa and Saburo Sakai would be aces twice over by the summer of 1942.

In early August 1942, when the U.S. Marines landed on Guadalcanal, the reinforcements sent by the Japanese included the Tainan Kokutai, which was based at Rabaul, New Britain. On August 7, when the Tainan Kokutai was assigned to escort a bomber force headed for Guadalcanal, the force was attacked over the target by a large number of Grumman F4F Wildcats. They proved to be among the most skilled opposition that the Tainan Kokutai had encountered, but Nishizawa destroyed six and Sakai shot down a Wildcat and a Douglas SBD Dauntless, his 59th and 60th victories.

Sakai then engaged eight Grumman TBF Avenger torpedo bombers, which he had never seen before, and which he mistook for Grumman Wildcats, because of the general similarity that might be expected of two single-engine types from the same manufacturer. A principal difference, which he had not counted on, was that the Avengers had a rear-facing gunner that could fire at an attacker coming in from behind.

Sakai shot down two TBFs, but the rear gunners in the remaining six badly damaged his Zero, and the battering that he took knocked him unconscious. He regained consciousness before the aircraft hit the water, and managed to recover it, although he had been blinded in one eye and his vision in the other was seriously impaired. He suffered severe head wounds and the left side of his body was paralyzed, but somehow he managed to keep the Zero in the air, navigate for more than 500 miles, and land at Rabaul.

Having suffered wounds that should have killed him, Saburo Sakai was sent back to Japan, where a series of operations saved one of his eyes and repaired much of the remaining damage to his body. In April 1943, when he was finally released from the hospital, he begged to be allowed to fly again, and was assigned as an instructor at Omura Air Base.

Had the IJNAF not become desperately short of combat-experienced pilots, Saburo Sakai would probably never have seen combat again. A year after being released from the hospital, the partially blind ace was transferred to the Yokosuka Kokutai at the huge naval base at Yokosuka. This kokutai was sent to Iwo Jima in June 1944 to fend off the American invasion, which was expected imminently but which would not finally materialize until February 1945. Ironically, an invasion in June 1944 would have caught the Japanese totally unprepared, but by February, they had turned the volcanic island into a virtually impregnable fortress that would cost the Americans over 6,000 men killed.

It was on June 24 that Sakai had his initial opportunity to duel with the Grumman F6F Hellcat, the U.S. Navy fighter that was the first such aircraft to achieve a clear superiority over the Zero. A force or 40 Zeros engaged a large number of Hellcats. Sakai shot down one of the F6Fs, but barely eluded being shot down by others in what was his first aerial combat in nearly two years. In a further action, he shot down another Hellcat, but the Iwo Jima defenders were badly mauled by the U.S. Navy. They were withdrawn to Yokosuka to prepare for the defense of Japan.

Beginning in September 1944, Sakai, now promoted to ensign, test-flew a number of advanced fighter aircraft, including both the Kyushu J7W Shinden and the Mitsubishi J2M Raiden. In June 1945, he test-flew the successor to the great Zero, the Mitsubishi A7M Reppu. However, he was never to fly these aircraft, all designed to match or better the Hellcat, in combat. His last combat mission came on the night of August 13, 1945, less that 48 hours before the announcement of Japan's unconditional surrender. He was part of a ten-ship formation of Yokosuka Kokutai Zeros that downed what they thought was a Boeing B-29 Superfortress, but which was actually a Convair B-32 Dominator.

Saburo Sakai's final score—excluding the shared kill of the B-32—is listed variously as 62 or 64, although it may have been much higher. After the war, he worked as a day laborer for nearly a decade before scraping together the money to start a small printing company. The 1956 publication of his autobiography, *Samurai* (with Martin Caidin and Fred Saito), brought him worldwide notoriety and provided a valuable account of the Japanese side of the air war in the Pacific.

The choice of the word "samurai" was a good one. Nothing exemplifies the attitude of Japan's World War II fighter pilots better than the code of the samurai, the classical Japanese warrior. This code, known as Bushido, dates back to the twelfth century, and exemplifies the same kind of dedication to duty and honor as the code of chivalry that has defined European knighthood since the Middle Ages.

6

THE SOVIET UNION

WHEN RANKING THE AIR FORCES of World War II, that of the Soviet Union must be, without dispute, listed as "most improved." From the moment the Germans invaded in June 1941 to the moment of Germany's final surrender in May 1945, the Soviet air force (Voenno-Vozdushnie Sily or VVS) was transformed from a cadre of ineffective pilots in vulnerable, obsolete aircraft, into a well-oiled and formidable force. Part of the reason for the lack of preparedness on the part of the VVS at the beginning of the conflict lay at the feet of the enigmatic, capricious, and contradictory man who was the Soviet Union's absolute leader.

Josef Vissarionovich Djugashvili, who took the name "Stalin," meaning "man of steel," had a thirst for absolute power that led him to undertake a series of purges that resulted in the execution or imprisonment of tens of thousands of the best and the brightest individuals in Soviet society and government.

Stalin had emerged from the 1917–1922 Russian Revolution in control of the Bolshevik—later Communist—Party apparatus that would ultimately give him the power he so craved. When Vladimir Lenin died in 1924, Stalin pushed aside his various rivals, including the more radical Leon Trotsky, to seize absolute power within the party and the Soviet Union. Through the bloody purges that accompanied the three five-year plans that he launched in 1928, 1933, and 1938, he arrested, tried, and executed well over half of the party's Central Committee and Party Congress—as well as most of his competent military leadership.

During the 1930s, Stalin jailed and/or executed as many as 20 million people, mostly Russians. With his military forces, including his VVS, Stalin was jealous of its professional leadership and he purged anyone he perceived as a threat. This left the VVS without the tactical leadership it would later need.

In aviation, Stalin was a proponent of staging dramatic stunts rather than building a first-rate indigenous aviation industry. The 1930s in the Soviet Union are remembered for long, dramatic, record-setting flights and large, pretentious aircraft. This, he felt, was good publicity for the Communist economic experiment that he was compelling his people to endure. However, most contemporary Soviet aircraft never matched, or even approached, the level of quality seen in the frontline aircraft of Germany, Britain, and the United States in the late 1930s.

The Opening Shots

Even before World War II, the rivalry between fascism and Communism—and between two obsessive nationalists Adolf Hitler and Josef Stalin—erupted into warfare on and over the dusty, yellow hills of Spain. Stalin felt obligated to intervene in 1936, when Hitler sent covert forces to assist the fascists in the Spanish Civil War. The Voenno-

Vozdushnie Sily found itself fighting the Luftwaffe's Condor Legion in what was to be a dress rehearsal of the air combat that would take place on the Eastern Front during World War II. The Soviets, in their primitive, open-cockpit Polikarpov I-15s and I-16s, were no match for the German Condor Legion pilots in their Bf-109s, and Stalin was forced to withdraw the Voenno-Vozdushnie Sily in 1938.

This was not before several of the Polikarpov pilots achieved ace status flying against the fascists and their Condor Legion comrades. Anatoli Serov—better known as "Carlos Castejon"—the top-scoring Soviet ace, scored 16, including the first night fighter kill of the conflict. Pavel Rychagov—who flew under the name "Pablo Palencar"—had 15 victories. I. T. Yeremenko scored 14. Their scores should be considered in light of the fact that Werner Mölders, the top-scoring German experte in the Spanish Civil War, claimed just 14.

The highest-scoring Voenno-Vozdushnie Sily ace to add to victories in Spain with further kills in World War II was Vladimir Bobrov, who scored 13 victories against the Germans in the Spanish Civil War before increasing his count to 43 in the later conflict.

As for the other aces of the Spanish Civil War, "Carlos" Serov was killed in a crash in May 1939, while "Pablo" Rychagov returned home a hero, rose through the ranks to become a brigade commander, offended the wrong person, and was killed in a Stalinist purge. Boris Turshanski, a Polish nobleman's son who joined the VVS and scored six kills in Spain, also died in a purge.

In the little-known border conflict between the Soviet Union and Japan that took place in Mongolia during the summers of 1938 and 1939, the Imperial Japanese Army Air Force thoroughly outfought the VVS. Nevertheless, several Soviet pilots managed to achieve ace status. The highest-scoring among them was Grigori Kravchenko, who scored 15 kills flying a Polikarpov I-16. Another ace of note was Arseni Vorozheikin. He scored 6 kills in Mongolia and went on to score 46 against the Luftwaffe.

On August 24, 1939, Stalin stunned the world—especially his staunch socialist friends in the West who had supported him against the fascists in Spain—by signing a nonaggression pact with Hitler. This gave Stalin's rival the flexibility that he needed to initiate the mischief that rapidly became World War II. A week later, on September 1, the German army invaded Poland. Britain and France issued ultimatums because their mutual assistance treaties with Poland called for them to finally take action to halt Hitler's aggression. On September 3, Britain and France declared that a state of war had existed for two days. World War II had begun.

The Soviet Union quickly occupied half of Poland as its bonus for Stalin's pact with Hitler, but otherwise remained on the sidelines for nearly two years while the German juggernaut consumed Europe.

Despite Stalin's innate brutality and paranoia—not to mention his hatred for Hitler—the Soviet Union was totally unprepared when Germany suddenly launched its invasion on June 22, 1941. For the Soviets, World War II was now the Great Patriotic War.

Known as Operation Barbarossa, the German attack advanced swiftly on all fronts. The Voenno-Vozdushnie Sily lost over 4,000 aircraft in the first week alone, many of them on the ground. In the early days of the German onslaught, the Soviet defenders were brutally hurled back into Mother Russia and the Luftwaffe swept through the VVS like it was swatting flies. Flying relatively primitive Mikoyan-Gurevich MiG-3s and the Polikarpov I-16s, the Soviet Union's air arm was ill-equipped to deal with the

Luftwaffe's Messerschmitt Bf-109s. Nowhere were they able to challenge the Luftwaffe successfully.

It was to be the same story on the ground until December, when the severity of the Russian winter finally stalled the German invaders at the gates of Moscow. For the great Luftwaffe, the weather was so cold that engine oil congealed and the engines refused to turn over. The VVS crews used the unorthodox method of mixing gasoline with the oil to thin it.

The combination of the Russian winter and the armed resistance of the Russian military forced a retreat. However, in the spring of 1942, the Germans counterattacked, successfully regaining much—albeit not all—of what they had lost. The city of Stalingrad—named for the dictator himself—became the symbol of Soviet resistance. When the Soviets defeated the Germans and captured the entire German Sixth Army in January 1943, it was a psychological and military triumph that marked the turning point in the Great Patriotic War.

For the Voenno-Vozdushnie Sily, the initial losses in Barbarossa would cost it 74 percent of its combat strength, but most of its pilots survived because the aircraft were caught on the ground. At the same time, the VVS didn't lose very many first-rate, modern combat aircraft, because Stalin's ironhanded central economic planning hadn't produced very many. As for the operational leadership of the VVS, Stalin himself had already done more damage with his purges than the Luftwaffe could do.

Soviet Aces Strike Back

The Soviet army, aided by the respite afforded by the bitter Russian winter, was able to rebuild itself in time for the 1942 Spring Offensive, and so, too, was the Voenno-

Vozdushnie Sily. A number of factors contributed to the phoenixlike rebirth of the Voenno-Vozdushnie Sily. One was a pragmatic flexibility in developing tactics, and another was the ability of the VVS to replace losses. With virtually unlimited manpower and open space, the Soviet Union was able to quickly build new factories out of reach of the advancing Germans, and these turned out a new generation of warplanes—especially the fighter aircraft that had been designed by the Lavochkin and Yakovlev design bureaus.

At the same time, American Lend Lease aircraft were starting to make their way to the Eastern Front by way of Alaska by the summer of 1942. Notable among these were the Bell P-39 Airacobra, an aircraft that would ironically be more important to the VVS than to the U.S. Army Air Forces.

Finally, the VVS was able to rebuild itself through an influx of thousands of brave and dedicated men—and women—who became its combat pilots. Many of these people were merely schoolchildren during the purges of the 1930s, and felt an allegiance to their "Rodina" (Motherland) rather than to Stalin and his cronies. Indeed, many of the fighter pilots who became the top aces of the VVS were still in school when the Soviet Union was invaded in 1941.

In terms of air combat, the Luftwaffe fighter pilots completely overwhelmed the VVS in 1941, and continued to rack up incredible scores until near the very end, but the VVS pilots fought back bravely—and well.

There were at least 60—and possibly four times that number—Soviet aces during the Great Patriotic War, and at least 16 who matched or outscored America's top ace, Dick Bong, who had 40 victories. At the head of this list was Ivan Kozhedub, whose 62 kills made him the deadliest combat pilot of any nation who fought against the Axis in the global war that raged between 1939 and 1945.

The first Soviet pilot to achieve ace status through victories scored during the Great Patriotic War was probably Boris Safonov, a naval aviator whose unit was later incorporated into the VVS. He scored his first victory, a Heinkel He-111, on June 24, 1941. His unit converted from I-16s to Lend Lease Hawker Hurricanes and later American-made Curtiss P-40 Warhawks. On May 30, 1942, flying one of the latter, he scored two victories while flying top cover for a British convoy bound for Murmansk. This brought his score to 25, but it was the day his luck ran out. His engine was hit and he crashed into the Arctic Ocean. Safonov was the first fighter pilot to be awarded the Rodina's top decoration for bravery—the Hero of the Soviet Union—twice.

Pokryshkin and Rechkalov: The Penultimate Pair

The second- and third-highest scoring Soviet aces of the Great Patriotic War flew and fought together through much of the conflict. During 1941 and early 1942, both Aleksandr Pokryshkin and Grigori Rechkalov flew with the VVS 55th Fighter (Istrebitel'naya Aviatsiya Protivovozdushnoi or IAP) Regiment. On March 7, 1942, the 55th IAP received a "Guards" redesignation as the 16th Guards IAP. The "Guards" prefix was used to denote a unit that had distinguished itself valiantly in combat. By 1943, Pokryshkin was an escadrilli (squadron commander) with the 16th Guards IAP, and Rechkalov is often mentioned as having been his wingman on the Caucasus Front and during the Kuban battles in 1942 and 1943.

Aleksandr Ivanovich "Sasha" Pokryshkin is the man regarded as perhaps the premier Soviet air combat tactician of the Great Patriotic War. He was also the Soviet Union's second-highest-scoring ace, and one of a small number of top Voenno-Vozdushnie Sily aces whose combat career began with a victory on June 23, when the war was just hours old, and spanned the entire war.

Born in 1913, Sasha Pokryshkin joined the Voenno-Vozdushnie Sily in 1933 and survived the chaotic days of the Stalinist purges. He was on duty as a fighter pilot when the Germans launched Operation Barbarossa. The outclassed VVS defenders fought back bravely. Flying a MiG-3 with the 55th IAP Regiment, Senior Lieutenant Aleksandr Pokryshkin and his wingman engaged five Luftwaffe fighters over the Germans' Prut River bridgehead. Pokryshkin succeeded in shooting down a Bf-109, but he took a cannon shell in his right wing. He then went low and successfully managed to lose the Bf 109s that were chasing him.

This Bf-109 was not the only aircraft that Pokryshkin would claim during the war's first 48 hours. The 211th Attack (Bronirovanny Aviatsiya Protivovozdushnoi or BAP) Regiment assigned to the Odessa Military District had launched nine Sukhoi Su-2 ground attack planes to attack German forces crossing the Prut River. Only 75 of the still-classified Su-2s were in service and Pokryshkin, like most Soviet pilots, had not been briefed on the aircraft's existence.

When Pokryshkin observed the formation of unfamiliar aircraft, he assumed they were German and dove to the attack. He hit one of the aircraft but broke off from a second pass when he saw the red stars on the wings, and spent several frantic moments trying to wave off his squadron mates—without breaking radio silence—before they made the same mistake. It is believed that the crippled Su-2 managed a crash landing with no loss of life. The crisis of meeting the German invasion diverted attention from this faux pas and Pokryshkin was never reprimanded for the incident. A month later, he was, himself, shot down, but he managed to escape and make his way back to Soviet-held territory.

During the bitter winter of 1941–1942, as the Soviet Union fought its desperate battle for survival, the VVS braved extremely brutal weather conditions. As for Pokryshkin, he earned the nickname "Mustafa," because of the frozen cheeks that he suffered while flying an open-cockpit I-16.

By 1942, a Bell P-39D had become Aleksandr Pokryshkin's signature aircraft. He eventually graduated to the more powerful, Soviet-built Lavochkin La-7, but 48 of his 59 aerial victories would be scored in the American P-39 Airacobra.

Pokryshkin was also coming to be regarded as an extraordinary tactician. In that role, he is often compared with the great World War I French ace René Fonck and Adolph "Sailor" Malan of the Royal Air Force—men who were not only excellent combat pilots but who also developed air-to-air tactics they could teach to others to make them effective in combat as well.

After helping to defeat the Germans on the Kuban Front in 1943, the 16th Guards IAP Regiment was operational on the First, Second, and Fourth Ukrainian Fronts through 1944 and followed Soviet advances through Romania and Hungary toward the final victory in 1945.

In July 1944, Aleksandr Pokryshkin had been promoted to colonel and placed in command of the 9th Guards IAP Division. The units that he commanded contained 30 pilots who were awarded the Hero of the Soviet Union, the nation's highest military decoration. As for Pokryshkin himself, he was one of only three men to be awarded the Hero of the Soviet Union *three* times. The other two were fellow fighter ace Captain Ivan Kozhedub and Marshal Georgi Zhukov, the supreme commander of all Soviet armed forces in the Great Patriotic War.

Aleksandr Pokryshkin flew 550 missions, engaged in 139 air battles, and ended the war with 59 victories, second only to Kozhedub with 62. Some sources say that his score was actually 73 because of victories scored over German territory during the fighting around Kuban in 1943. During this period, enemy aircraft not downed over Soviet territory were not counted—possibly because it would suggest that the Soviet pilots were not defending Soviet territory.

Aleksandr Pokryshkin, a leading tactician in the history of the Red Air Force, and three times a Hero of the Soviet Union, died on November 13, 1985.

Close behind Pokryshkin, the third-place Soviet ace of the Great Patriotic War was his sometime wingman, the baby-faced Grigori Andreevich Rechkalov. He was born on February 9, 1920, in the village of Khudyakovo near the city of Ekaterinburg, which was known as Sverdlovsk between 1922 and 1991. By the time he joined the VVS in 1938, he had already learned to fly at the Sverdlovsk Aeroclub. He graduated from the Perm Military Air College in 1939, but was grounded by the flight surgeon when he was discovered to be color-blind. However, by 1941, this was no longer an issue, and he was assigned to a fighter squadron, the 55th IAP, based in the Soviet Republic of Moldavia (now Moldova), which was equipped with Polikarpov I-15s and I-16s. He flew 13 missions on the first two days of the Great Patriotic War and killed his first Bf-109 on June 27. By July, when he was shot down for the first time, he was flying an I-16.

In March 1942, when the 55th IAP received its "Guards" redesignation as 16th Guards IAP, it was reequipped with the newer Yak-1 fighters. Through 1942, Rechkalov's combat prowess had not yet begun to be demonstrated. He had scored three kills during the summer of 1941, but by the end of 1942, he was listed with just four victories, plus two shared. This would have given him five, enough to be classed an ace, however.

Through the winter, the regiment was reequipped with its Bell Airacobras, and by the spring of 1943, it had been reassigned to the North Caucasus Front for operations over the Kuban River area. On the unit's first operational sortie with Airacobras, Rechkalov and Pokryshkin shared a Messerschmitt Bf-109 in a fight over Krymskaya. By April, Rechkalov had started to hit his stride as a fighter pilot. Between April 15 and April 21, he claimed three Bf-109s and a Junkers Ju-88.

On April 21, Rechkalov was part of a six-ship patrol led by Pokryshkin when they encountered four Ju-87 Stukas escorted by four Bf-109s. Pokryshkin immediately attacked the Stukas and ordered Rechkalov to engage the fighters. Pokryshkin would claim a pair of Stukas, and Rechkalov a pair of Bf-109s. Rechkalov was awarded his first Hero of the Soviet Union decoration on May 24, 1943.

During the summer of 1944, as the 16th Guards IAP was shifted to the 4th Ukrainian Front in the Crimea, Rechkalov saw action over the Sea of Azov as well as in the Kishinev campaign, pushing his score up to 48, plus 6 shared, by the end of his 415th mission in June. However, by the time that he received his second Gold Star of the Hero of the Soviet Union on July 1, he was no longer on the best of terms with his commander. Pokryshkin had come to strongly disapprove of the brash, 21-year-old pilot's obsession with personal victories at the expense of unit cohesion.

When Aleksandr Pokryshkin was promoted to colonel

and placed in command of the 9th Guards IAP Division, it was assumed that Rechkalov would be promoted to head the 16th Guards IAP Regiment, but at Pokryshkin's urging, the corps commander brought in Boris Glinka from the 100th Guards IAP instead. However, when Glinka was badly wounded a few weeks later, Rechkalov, the deputy commander, became the de facto regimental commander.

By the autumn of 1944, the 16th Guards IAP had been transferred to the 1st Ukrainian Front for operations in the Lvov area and throughout Poland. The regiment was flying air cover when Soviet armies crossed the Oder River and plunged into Germany itself. By this time, they had transitioned from the Airacobras to Lavochkin La-7s, and it was in this type that Rechkalov scored his last victory over Berlin in April 1945. This is calculated to have been on his 450th mission.

Rechkalov is credited with 57 victories, although some sources record the number as 56 (with 5 shared) or as high as 61. In any case, he is easily ranked in the company of his former commander and the great Ivan Kozhedub. Of his score, 44 kills were made in the Airacobra, making him the highest-scoring Airacobra ace of any air force.

In addition to being named Hero of the Soviet Union twice, Rechkalov was awarded the Order of Lenin, the Order of the Red Banner (four times), the Order of Alexandr Nievski, and the Order of Patriotic War (First Class). After the war, Rechkalov remained with the VVS, retiring as a major general in 1959. He is also the author of two autobiographical books, *The Smoking Skies of War* and *In Moldavian Skies*.

Kozhedub: The Soviet Union's Ace of Aces

Born in 1920, Ivan Nikitich Kozhedub was part of the second generation of Soviet fighter pilots to see action during the Great Patriotic War. Only 21 years old when Germany invaded the Soviet Union in June 1941, Kozhedub was different from pilots who were just a few years older than he; unlike him, they had firsthand experience with Stalin's dreadful purges of the Soviet armed forces during the 1930s, and experienced the desperate battles of 1941–1942, when the Red Air Force was hopelessly outclassed by the German Luftwaffe.

Ivan Kozhedub had enlisted in 1940 and qualified for flight training in 1941, even as the German armies were sweeping eastward across the borders of the Soviet Union. Because of his natural abilities as a pilot, he was kept on as a flight instructor after his training. This was a source of great frustration and disappointment for him because of his eagerness to get into a combat unit, but it meant that by the time he actually did get into the field, the tide of the Great Patriotic War had turned in favor of the Soviet Union.

Kozhedub watched nearly two long years of war go by before he finally got his wish for a combat unit assignment in March 1943. However, his first major combat action did not come until July. This coincided with the great battles in the Kursk salient, which turned out to be some of the largest armed clashes in human history.

Ivan Kozhedub scored his first aerial victory on July 6, when his squadron, led by a Major Soldatienko, spotted a group of 20 Junkers Ju-87 Stuka dive-bombers attacking a Soviet ground position near Kursk. Kozhedub downed one of the Stukas that day and added another seven to his total through July 16. In August 1943, he was promoted to squadron commander, and by the first week of November, his score stood at 26. He was awarded his first of three Hero of the Soviet Union decorations on February 4, 1944.

Early in 1944, Kozhedub was transferred to the elite

176th Guards IAP, a rapid-reaction unit that was designed specifically to be moved at any time to any place on the front where air superiority was especially critical.

One such place where air superiority was especially critical was the sky over the Dnieper Front, and the 176th Guards IAP arrived to take charge of this aerial battlefield. It was here that Kozhedub was to down 11 German aircraft in the space of just ten days. In April 1944, he shot down three in one day, and his second Hero of the Soviet Union came on August 19, 1944, in the wake of his 34th victory.

By the beginning of 1945, the Soviet army and air force were clearly on the offensive. Ivan Kozhedub was now the vice commander of the 176th Guards IAP, and still taking his toll on the Luftwaffe. In February 1945, having traded his Lavochkin La-5 for the lighter, more powerful, and much improved Lavochkin La-7, he became possibly the first Soviet pilot to fight and shoot down a Messerschmitt Me-262 jet fighter.

When the war ended, Ivan Kozhedub had completed 326 missions and was the top-scoring Soviet ace. He was officially credited with 62 victories, although some sources suggest that his score may actually have been in excess of 70. The official total included 22 Focke Wulf Fw-190s, 19 Messerschmitt Bf-109s, 18 Ju-87s, and various bomber types, as well as the Messerschmitt Me-262. His third Hero of the Soviet Union was awarded on August 18, 1945.

After the war ended, Kozhedub remained in the Red Air Force and attended the Zhukovski Military Aviation Academy. Meanwhile, he also remained active as a fighter pilot, making the transition from the piston-powered Lavochkin to the MiG-15 jet fighter, which was arguably the best fighter in the world in the late 1940s.

Late in 1950, when China entered the Korean War against the United Nations forces defending South Korea, the Soviet Union sent a large number of its best wartime fighter pilots to fly against the United States Fifth Air Force. They flew MiG-15s in Chinese markings so as to disguise the fact that Soviet pilots were involved in the war. They were fighting against the United Nations while, at the same time, their country held a chair on the Security Council.

American and other United Nations pilots at the time suspected the presence of Soviet fighter pilots in the skies over Korea, but it was not until after the fall of the Soviet Union, four decades later, that Red Air Force involvement was confirmed. Because of his being the highest-scoring Soviet ace, and a superb aerial combat tactician, Ivan Kozhedub was sent east to command the shadowy Soviet regiments, but it is generally believed that he flew no actual combat missions himself.

The two top-scoring VVS aces of the Korean War, Nicolai Sutyagin and Yevgeny Pepelyaev, with over 20 kills each, are not known to have had any victories during World War II. Grigori Ulyanovich Okhai is the only man who is known to have been an ace in both wars, with 6 victories over the Germans, and 11 in Korea. All three of these men were undoubtedly mentored by Ivan Kozhedub.

Litvak and Budanova: Not All the Aces Were Men

Most of the air forces of the nations engaged in World War II had women in their ranks. The German Luftwaffe had its corps of "helferinnen," who played a major role in numerous tasks, including staffing the fighter control centers that managed air defense operations. The British Royal Air Force used women in a similar role, and in the United States, the Women Air Service Pilots (WASP) logged tens of thousands of hours ferrying every type of combat aircraft in the USAAF inventory to and from every corner of the country.

Only in the Soviet Union, however, did women fly regular, routine missions in live-fire combat. Of all the major air forces that were engaged in the war, only the VVS had units composed specifically of women. In the armies of the Soviet Union, over 58,000 women endured the harsh conditions at the front, fighting and dying next to their brothers, fathers, and sons.

Initially, as with other air forces, the Red Air Force maintained an all-male policy among its combat pilots. However, as the apparently invincible German juggernaut sliced through Soviet defenses like the proverbial hot knife through butter during the summer of 1941, the Red Air Force began to rethink its ban on women. By October 1941, authorization was forthcoming for three regiments of women pilots.

Credit for this policy change can be traced to a surge of volunteers from among the women who had been members of the prewar state-sponsored flying clubs—and to the vision of the great aviatrix Marina Raskova. As the story goes, she made a personal plea to Stalin himself to secure authorization for official all-female combat units.

In 1934, at the age of 21, Marina Raskova graduated from the Zhukovski Aviation Academy, the first Soviet woman to pass the navigation examination, and the following year, she earned her pilot's license. In 1937–1938, in the span of less than a year, she made a mark for herself as a crewmember on three record-breaking flights. In October 1937, she and Valentina Grizodubova set a Soviet women's distance record of 867 miles, flying a Yakovlev AIR-12. (The aircraft is better known as the UT-1. The AIR prefix stood for Communist Party official A. I. Rykov, who was killed in one of Stalin's purges, and the evidence of whose existence was erased.)

In July 1938, Raskova, Polina Osipienko, and W. Lomako flew a Polikarpov MR-1 flying boat a distance of 1,345 miles, and in September, she and V. Grizodubova and P. Osipienko made a nonstop flight of 3,545 miles in a Tupolev DB-2 (aka Ant-37) twin-engine bomber.

According to the legends that are told about her, the young Raskova was a very remarkable young woman. In addition to being an excellent pilot, she was a classical pianist, she spoke both French and Italian, and she was a charismatic leader. Because of her accomplishments in aviation, she was appointed to the People's Defense Committee and she moved in all the right circles in Moscow society.

When Germany invaded the Soviet Union in June 1941, there was an obvious and immediate need for qualified pilots, and thousands—male and female—volunteered. However, the Voenno-Vozdushnie Sily initially rejected the notion of using women pilots in combat, despite their qualifications and the fact that many were part of the Soviet Grazhdanski Vozdushny Flot (GVF), the civil air fleet. Raskova proposed that Stalin create all-woman units within the VVS that could be staffed by all the girls who had been in the prewar flying clubs. At first the answer was no, but that soon changed and the Stavka (Shtab Glavnogo/Verkhovnogo Komandovaniya, the Supreme High Command) okayed Raskova's plan.

The initial selection took place at the Zhukovski Aviation Academy, but training would be centered near the city of Engels on the Volga. The women were issued ill-fitting men's uniforms, and boots so big that they had to stuff them with paper. The female pilots were organized into three aviation regiments, which were numbered in the

"500" series, indicating that they were designated as reserves under the control of the Soviet State Committee for Defense, the GKO (Gosudarstveny Komitet Oborony). The units were the 586th IAP, the 587th BAP, and the 588 NBAP (Night Bomber Regiment).

Commanded by Major Tamara Kazarinova, the 586th IAP first saw action on the Moscow Front in the spring of 1942, flying Yak-1 fighters. On September 3, 1942, Lieutenant Valeria Ivanovna Khomyakova had the distinction of being the first woman pilot to down a German aircraft, a Junkers Ju-88 bomber. Before joining the VVS, she had been an engineer and a flight instructor.

Because of the losses being suffered in the Battle of Stalingrad and the general lack of trained male replacements, many women fighter pilots were transferred from the 586th IAP to all-male IAPs. On the ground, and in the air, the women endured the torment and ridicule of their male counterparts, who did not like the idea of them invading their profession, and initially, they refused to fly with them. Reluctantly, however, they incorporated the female pilots into their combat formations. Soviet fighters flew in cells of four, with two "shooters" at the number-one and number-three slots. Initially, the women were assigned to a three-man cell in the number-four slot.

Gradually, the women began to prove themselves, and as the all-female units got into action, they demonstrated that they were capable of the task at hand. Eventually, the 587th BAP, flying Petlyakov Pe-2 twin-engine bombers, became the 125th Guards BAP. The 588th NBAP became the 46th Guards NBAP—both with the coveted "Guards" designation.

The 46th Guards NBAP was the legendary women's night bomber regiment that came to be known to the Germans as the much-feared "Night Witches," because of their combat effectiveness flying Polikarpov Po-2 biplanes against German positions in the darkness of night. The Night Witches produced over 20 pilots who were awarded the Hero of the Soviet Union decoration.

Meanwhile, the pilots of 586th IAP flew an average of over 3,000 combat sorties between 1942 and 1945 in Yakovlev Yak-1s, Yak-3s, and later Yak-7s. They are credited with at least 38 victories, and with playing an important role in the defeat of the German Sixth Army at Stalingrad.

Of all the women fighter pilots who flew with the 586th IAP and other units within the Voenno-Vozdushnie Sily, perhaps none proved themselves more effectively than Lidiya Vladimirovna "Lilya" Litvak and her friend and comrade Yekaterina (Katarina) Vasilyevna "Katya" Budanova. With 12 and 11 victories respectively, they are confirmed as having been the highest-scoring female aces of all time.

While these scores are generally accepted as exact, some sources credit Litvak with as many as 20 victories, and others suggest that Olga Yamshchikova had as many as 17 victories. Whatever the numbers, Lilya Litvak was probably the highest-scoring woman ace. Given the diminishing level of intensity in aerial combat, she is likely to retain this distinction in perpetuity.

Litvak's story, for all its glory—and for its status as a milestone of feminist accomplishment—is not a happy one. She grew up in the shadow of her father, who was on the unlucky side of one of Stalin's mad purges, and she never lived to see the ultimate victory in which she played a small but important role.

Lidiya Vladimirovna was born in Moscow on August 18, 1921, amid the chaos and confusion of the consolidation of power that followed the Bolshevik Revolution of 1917. In the course of Stalin's purges, Lidiya's own father was discredited and put to death as an "an enemy of the people." This would have eventually hampered her own career had she not gone to great lengths to keep it a secret.

She took an early interest in becoming a pilot, and despite her family difficulties, she soloed at the age of 15 at the Chkalov Aeroclub. In 1940, having graduated from high school, she became a flight instructor, first at the Kherson Flight Academy and later with the Osoaviakhim, the Society for the Support of Defense and Aviation.

Best remembered by her nickname "Lilya," meaning "Lily," Litvak began her training as a military pilot at the Engels Training Center near Stalingrad on October 15, 1941. In January 1942, she was assigned to the 586th IAP, then based at Saratov, also near Stalingrad.

The women flew without rank insignia, identification, or parachute, because it was assumed that any who survived being shot down behind enemy lines would suffer a cruel death. The women themselves decided that if they ever survived a crash behind German lines, they would have to shoot themselves.

By the summer of 1942, the initial inclination of the Red Air Force not to take the women's regiments seriously had dissipated as the women proved themselves in combat. Meanwhile, the tactical situation had deteriorated to the point where the Red Air Force wanted its best pilots—regardless of gender—flying the most essential missions. In September 1942, several of the best women fighter pilots—including Starshina (Senior Sergeants) Lilya Litvak and Katya Budanova—were ordered to join the previously all-male 296th IAP Regiment, flying Lavochkin La-5s on the Stalingrad Front.

Flying her second mission with the 296th IAP on September 13, Lilya Litvak shot down a Messerschmitt Bf-109 and a Junkers Ju-88. Two weeks later, she added a third victory, shooting down another Ju-88. By the time she was awarded the Order of the Red Banner on February 17, 1943, her unit had transitioned to the nimble Yakovlev Yak-1, and she had added another score to her tally, as well as a shared victory over a Focke Wulf Fw-190, then considered to be the Luftwaffe's best operational fighter.

On March 1, Litvak and Budanova, flying as half of a four-ship flight, intercepted a dozen Fw-190s on a ground support mission near Stalingrad. Two of the Focke Wulfs were shot down, one of them claimed by the guns of Lilya Litvak's Yak-1. The Germans broke off the fight, and the Russians promptly engaged and mauled a flight of Ju-88s. Lilya Litvak claimed one of the four Ju-88s that were shot down, and returned to base with an overall score of 6.5.

Promoted to junior lieutenant, and now an ace, Lilya Litvak was a rising star in the Red Air Force. Meanwhile, the fact that she was a female ace was not lost on the hero-hungry Soviet media, and soon her name became well-known. It also didn't hurt the image of the Soviet Union's new star that Litvak was a very colorful character. She wore long silk scarves made of parachute cloth, carried bouquets of fresh-cut wildflowers in her cockpit, and although she was blond, she bleached her hair white.

As a reference to her nickname, she painted a large white lily on the side of her Yak-1. The Germans, who mistook the flower for a rose—but knew through the rumor mill that this pilot was a woman—started calling her "The White Rose of Stalingrad."

She is recalled in anecdotal accounts as a strikingly beautiful woman, although the handful of photographs that exist show her as somewhat plain. Nevertheless, she caught the attention of fellow fighter pilot Alexei Salomatin, an ace with a dozen victories of his own, and with whom she often flew in the wing position. The couple fell in love and were engaged to be married, a turn of events that delighted the Soviet media, which was keen for tales of patriotism to punctuate its reporting from the battle-fronts of the Great Patriotic War.

By then, word had come through that Marina Raskova was dead. She was one of several women pilots who had volunteered to help ferry a group of Pe-2 bombers to the Stalingrad Front. On the night of January 4, 1943, during a blinding blizzard, Raskova crashed into the cliffs over-looking the Volga River, north of Stalingrad.

On March 15, during a mission on which she downed a pair of Ju-88s, Lilya Litvak was badly wounded, but she managed to bring her Yak-1 back to base. By the time she recovered from her wounds to return to action, her regi-ment had been redesignated as the 73rd Guards IAP. The heroism that warranted the "Guards" designation included the continued bravery of Lilya Litvak, who claimed her ninth solo victory on May 5.

To add to the evolving legend of the White Rose of Stalingrad, Lilya Litvak—now promoted to senior lieuten-ant—would be shot down behind enemy lines twice during the ensuing weeks. Both times she was unhurt, and both times she escaped to fly again—once by evading the Ger-mans on foot, and once when a fellow pilot landed behind enemy lines to rescue her.

On May 21, the storybook romance with Salomatin ended tragically when he was shot down and killed, but Lilya Litvak continued to fly and fight, adding an obser-vation balloon to her tally of victories on May 31.

By July 18, Katya Budanova and Lilya Litvak were aces twice over, tied with ten victories each. Then tragedy again visited Litvak. Katya Budanova was attacked by a pair of Messerschmitt Bf-109s and shot down. She managed to take one of the Germans with her before she herself was killed. This final victory made Budanova the top-scoring Soviet female ace, with 11 victories to Lilya's 10 (plus 3 shared victories).

On August 1, 1943, Lilya Litvak was flying her 168th mission as part of a flight of eight Yak-1s escorting a flight of Il-2 Sturmovik bombers on a ground attack mission, when they were bounced by a large number of German fighters. As the story goes, eight Messerschmitt Bf-109s ganged up on the Yak-1 with the white lily on the side, as though determined to put the legend to an end, once and for all.

According to the final chapter of that legend, Litvak took two of the Messerschmitts with her, to end her life and career with 12 victories.

The White Rose of Stalingrad fell near the village of Dmitriyevka. Like Katya Budanova, a few days earlier, she apparently survived the crash only to die in her wildflower-bedecked cockpit, and was buried under the wing of her aircraft. Two weeks later, she would have turned 22.

In the coming months, the legend of the White Rose of Stalingrad faded, pushed from the headlines by other stories of defeat, victory, and heroism in the global war. Amazingly, the location of Litvak's grave was forgotten when the wreckage of the Yak-1 was removed, and her body was not recovered for 46 years.

The fact that she was officially "missing" through all those years also precluded her being posthumously awarded the USSR's highest decoration, that of Hero of the Soviet Union, a distinction she had certainly earned. This error was rectified on May 5, 1990—during the Soviet Union's final days—in a decree signed by Mikhail Gorbachev. Three years later, on October 1, 1993, President Boris Yeltsin officially designated Lidiya Vladimirovna "Lilya" Litvak as a Hero of Russia.

7

ITALY

OF THE AXIS LEADERS OF World War II, Benito Mussolini was the first to come to power. He was named prime minister of Italy in 1923 and ruled as a dictator from 1926 to 1943. As a socialist newspaper editor, he had, at first, opposed Italy's involvement in World War I. However, he changed his mind and even enlisted in the army. In 1919, Mussolini and other war veterans founded a revolutionary, nationalistic group called the Fasci di Combattimento, named for the ancient Roman symbol of power, the fasces—an ax in a bundle of reeds. The group, which became a political party, were known as "fascists." This term would subsequently be applied to the Nationalists in Spain, the National Socialists (Nazis) in Germany, and the Imperial Nationalists in Japan. Strongly nationalistic, the fascists were equally outspoken in their denunciation of unions, socialists, Communists, and Catholics. By 1922, they had become so powerful that King Victor Emmanuel III asked Mussolini to form a coalition government. By 1926, the coalition had evolved into a single-party, totalitarian dictatorship.

In terms of foreign policy, Mussolini imagined himself

as a reconstituted Roman emperor and set out to rebuild what he could of the Roman Empire. In northern Africa, he had inherited Italian Somaliland and Libya, and he conquered Ethiopia in 1936. In Europe, he annexed Albania in 1939. He aided the Spanish Nationalist leader, General Francisco Franco, in the Spanish Civil War and he allied himself with Nazi Germany. On October 25, 1936, Hitler and Mussolini formally created the alliance called the Rome-Berlin Axis. Japan joined with Germany and Italy to form the Rome-Berlin-Tokyo Axis on September 27, 1940, when it signed the Tripartite Pact or Triple Alliance with the first two Axis powers.

In the course of recreating his Roman Empire, Mussolini recreated his Roman Legions by building up the Italian army, navy, and air force. By 1939, the latter, known as the Regia Aeronautica, had been built into a sizable, modern force. It was, with the exception of the Luftwaffe, a match for any air force in continental Europe.

No air-to-air combat was involved in conquering Ethiopia or Albania, so the first time Italian pilots would see action between the world wars was during the Spanish Civil War. Both Hitler and Mussolini sent airpower to aid their friend Franco in defeating the Spanish republic. Mussolini sent a selection of Regia Aeronautica pilots organized as the Aviazione Legionaria, and Hitler sent a selection of Luftwaffe pilots organized as the Condor Legion. They would fight alongside Nationalist Spanish pilots, against Republican Spanish and Soviet pilots from July 1936 to March 1939.

Italy did not enter World War II until June 1940, when Germany invaded France. The first Regia Aeronautica actions were against France's Armée de l'Air in the south of France, but the Regia Aeronautica would see extensive action against the Royal Air Force (and later the USAAF) in

North Africa and the Mediterranean region from 1940 through early 1943.

In terms of air superiority fighters, the Regia Aeronautica began World War II with such types at the Fiat G-50 and the Macchi MC-200, both durable, low-wing monoplanes having top speeds of about 300 mph. The best Italian fighter to see widespread service with the Regia Aeronautica during World War II was certainly the Macchi MC-202, which was introduced into squadron service in 1941. It was powered by the German-made Daimler-Benz DB-601 engine, of the same type used in the Messerschmitt Bf-109, which gave the MC-202 a top speed of 373 mph. In the hands of a good pilot, the nimble MC-202 was as capable as anything flying in the Mediterranean Theater during the early years of its deployment.

The year 1943 would be a turning point for Italy. By that time, Mussolini had lost the African portion of his empire, and on July 9, the Allies invaded Sicily. The war had come home to Italian soil. On July 25, the king fired Mussolini, and on September 3, the Allies invaded Italy proper. Italy surrendered unconditionally five days later and the Germans occupied the country, which would remain a battleground until the war ended in May 1945. Mussolini fled to the northern, German-occupied portion of Italy and formed a puppet government under the name Repubblica Sociale Italiana. Mussolini himself lived under German protection until April 28, 1945, when he was captured by partisans as he and his mistress tried to escape to Switzerland. He was executed and hanged by his heels.

Many die-hard fascist members of the Regia Aeronautica continued to fight on as part of the air force of the Repubblica Sociale Italiana, but the majority surrendered and some actually fought alongside the Allies.

Meanwhile, Italian warplane development ended in

1943, but at that time several promising air superiority
fighters had just been introduced. All were powered by the
newer Daimler-Benz DB 605 engine, which made possible
a class of fighters with top speeds in the 400mph class.
These aircraft, the Macchi MC-205, the Fiat G-55, and the
Reggiane Re-2005, had just begun to reach frontline
squadrons when Italy quit the war. This would leave the
Macchi MC-202 as the definitive Italian fighter of the war.

Italy's Top Aces

Italy produced over 120 aces during World War II, 4 of
them with scores in excess of 20 (including shared victories). Like the French Armée de l'Air, the Regia Aeronautica gave full scores for shared victories. However, none
of the Italians in World War II topped the score of Francesco Baracca, who was Italy's top-scoring ace in World
War I with 34—and possibly as many as 36—victories.

The highest scoring Italian ace of World War II was
Adriano Visconti, with 26 victories, although this score
was equaled by Franco Lucchini, who scored 5 in the
Spanish Civil War, plus 21 in World War II for a total of
26. All of Visconti's victories were scored in World War
II.

Next in line are Teresio Martinoli, who scored all of his
23 victories in World War II, and Leonardo Ferrulli, who
scored 22 in World War II, plus 1 in the Spanish Civil
War. Mario Bonzano and Adriano Mantelli were the
highest-scoring Italian aces in the Spanish Civil War, with
15 each. Only Bonzano would add to his score in World
War II, for an overall total of 17.

Adriano Visconti scored his first victory in North Africa
while flying as a reconnaissance pilot in 1940, but he later
qualified to fly fighters. He was active with 7 Gruppo

(Group) of the Regia Aeronautica's 54 Stormo in combat over Malta in 1941 and 1942. During this period, he would claim a pair of Bristol Blenheim bombers and a pair of Hawker Hurricane fighters.

At the end of 1942, Visconti moved to 16 Gruppo and scored 14 victories against the Allies during the final campaign in Tunisia and the battles over Sicily in August 1943. During the latter campaign, he was among the first to operate the new Macchi MC-205 in combat. When Italy capitulated in September 1943, Visconti did not. He flew north to continue fighting the Allies under the banner of the Repubblica Sociale Italiana. Flying his MC-205 for the new fascist Italian government's 1 Gruppo, Visconti claimed seven victories, including a Lockheed P-38 and three Republic P-47 Thunderbolts.

As was the case with Benito Mussolini, Adriano Visconti met an ignominious end. After surviving dozens of difficult combat missions across the length of the Mediterranean, he was shot in the back by a partisan on a Milan street corner on April 29, 1945.

Lucchini: Baracca Della Segunda Guerra Mundial

More than just being the highest-scoring Italian ace of World War I, Francesco Baracca is an Italian folk hero. He died a hero's death in June 1918, and he is still revered in his native Lugo—where the airport bears his name— and throughout the Italian aviation community. In World War II, he was the man who was emulated by the Regia Aeronautica fighter pilots. For a pilot to be called "Baracca Della Segunda Guerra Mundial" (The Baracca of World War II) is the highest honor that could have been bestowed, greater than any award or decoration. Franco Lucchini was known as Baracca Della Segunda Guerra Mundial.

Having scored 5 victories to become an ace in the Spanish Civil War, Lucchini scored 21 more in World War II while flying with the Regia Aeronautica's 10 Gruppo. Born in Rome on Christmas Eve in 1917, he joined the Regia Aeronautica as a reserve officer and earned his wings at the Foggia training base in July 1936. He was initially posted to the 91 Squadriglia (Squadron) of 4 Stormo, and in July 1937, he volunteered with the Aviazione Legionaria for duty in the Spanish Civil War. At the time, Spain was the place to go for Europe's aspiring young knights of the skies. Over the course of a year, Lucchini flew 122 sorties in that country, flying Fiat CR-32 biplanes with 19 Squadriglia of 23 Gruppo. In 1938, he was shot down twice; the second time, in July, he would remain a prisoner of war for six months until he was able to escape.

Back in Italy, Lucchini returned to 10 Gruppo, where he was serving with 90 Squadriglia when war was declared against Great Britain and France in June 1940. At first, 90 Squadriglia was assigned to Libya and equipped with Fiat CR-42s. Lucchini had two shared victories during June 1940, a Gloster Gladiator and a Short Sunderland flying boat, and scored his first solo kill, a Royal Air Force Gladiator, on August 4. Through the end of the year, Lucchini would fly 94 missions and score 3 confirmed victories, 4 probables, and 15 shared victories.

Early in 1941, 10 Gruppo rotated back to Italy for conversion to the new Macchi MC-200 fighter. Its members were then assigned to Sicily to take part in the offensive against the British garrison on the Mediterranean island of Malta. Lucchini's first confirmed victories of the Malta campaign came on July 11 during a major Regia Aero-

nautica attack against the island. He shared two Hawker
Hurricanes in aerial combat and participated in destroying
or damaging five Vickers Wellingtons and three Bristol
Blenheims on the ground.

Another major assault on Malta came on July 17, when
three Regia Aeronautica groups launched 49 MC-200s.
The Royal Air Force claimed two MC-200s destroyed,
while 10 Gruppo claimed four Hurricanes. One of these
was a shared victory for Lucchini. On August 19, it was
the turn of the Royal Air Force to go on the offensive, with
a dozen Hurricanes intercepting a dozen MC-200s over Sicily. Lucchini would claim a probable shared victory.

Late in 1941, 10 Gruppo reequipped with the MC-202,
and after a training period, they were reassigned to Sicily
in April 1942. On May 9, Lucchini claimed his first Spitfire over Malta. Six days later, in another battle over Malta,
he scored against a second Spitfire and damaged a third.
The last 10 Gruppo mission over Malta, which came on
May 19, was uneventful for Lucchini.

On May 26, 10 Gruppo was sent back to North Africa.
Over the next five months, Lucchini flew 59 missions and
scored six victories, two probables, and shared eight kills.
Most of these would be Curtiss Tomahawks, but he did
shoot down another Spitfire on the last day of August. On
October 24, he claimed another Tomahawk and a Douglas
Boston, but he was shot down himself and badly injured.

When Lucchini was finally released from the hospital to
return to 10 Gruppo, the Axis had been defeated in North
Africa and the focus was on defending Sicily from the
impending Allied invasion. On July 5, having already
flown seven sorties since his recuperation, Lucchini was
on an air intercept mission against a strike force of American B-17 Flying Fortresses. He succeeded in shooting
down one of the escorting Spitfires and started to attack

the bombers, when he was hit by fire from the bombers and went down in a plume of black smoke. His body was found at the crash site two days later.

Franco Lucchini had flown at least 262 missions and had been awarded the Medaglia d'Argento al Valore Militare (Silver Medal) five times, four War Crosses, and a German Iron Cross during his career. He was posthumously awarded the Medaglia d'Oro al Valore Militare, Italy's highest decoration.

Ferrulli: Flying with Lucchini

Leonardo Ferrulli, Italy's next-highest-scoring ace, flew with and, by bizarre coincidence, died on the same day as Franco Lucchini. Born in Brindisi on the first day of January 1918, Ferrulli earned his wings with the Regia Aeronautica in March 1936, four months ahead of Lucchini, and he was assigned to 4 Stormo ahead of Lucchini. Ferrulli volunteered for the Aviazione Legionaria in February 1937, five months ahead of Lucchini, but he didn't actually get into the Spanish Civil War until May, and he remained only through October 1937. While in action, he claimed one enemy aircraft.

When Italy entered World War II in June 1940, Ferrulli was assigned to 91 Squadriglia of 10 Gruppo and Lucchini was assigned to 90 Squadriglia of the same group. Both squadrigli were equipped with Fiat CR-42s and sent to Libya. Lucchini scored three confirmed victories in the latter half of 1940, but Ferrulli's first did not come until January 4, 1941, when he claimed a Royal Air Force Hawker Hurricane Mk.I near Tobruk.

Beginning in July 1941, Ferrulli, like Lucchini, was flying Macchi MC-200s with 10 Gruppo in the Axis offensive against Malta. During the major attacks on July 11 and

July 17, both Lucchini and Ferrulli shared victories. After the two aces flew together in North Africa between May and August 1942, Ferrulli was sent to the Air Academy in Caserta, while Lucchini remained in the desert until he was shot down in October.

Fate brought Ferrulli and Lucchini together one last time on July 5, 1943. Ferrulli managed to claim a pair of USAAF warplanes before his Macchi MC-202 was blown out of the skies over Sicily. Like Lucchini, he was awarded the Medaglia d'Oro al Valore Militare posthumously.

Bordoni-Bisleri: Italy's Best in the Desert War

Outside Italy, most of Mussolini's new Roman Empire lay, as had much of the original Roman Empire, in northern Africa. Before World War II, Mussolini dreamed of an imperial domain. After the reality of the war began to sink in, however, he turned to trying to save what he had. In the 1940–1942 period, the war to save the new Roman Empire would be waged in and around Libya—an Italian possession since 1911—in North Africa.

In this make-or-break war to preserve the new Roman Empire, Italy's army fared poorly, but the Regia Aeronautica fought bravely. The highest-scoring Italian ace of this period was Franco Bordoni-Bisleri. He was born in Milan on January 10, 1913, and grew up in the shadow of the family business, which produced a patent medicine called Ferro-China Bisleri. The label on the bottles of this popular potion featured a lion and the word "robur," meaning "strength" in Latin. During World War II, Bordoni-Bisleri would paint the lion and its legend on his aircraft.

In 1937, after earning a civilian pilot's license, Bordoni-Bisleri joined the Regia Aeronautica as a bomber pilot before being reassigned to fighters. In June 1940, when Italy went to war, he served in the initial offensive against southern France with 18 Gruppo. In September 1940, during the Battle of Britain, the group was part of the Italian contingent that joined the German attack on Britain.

At the end of January 1941, 18 Gruppo was sent to Libya, where Bordoni-Bisleri flew Fiat CR-32s with 83 Squadriglia through the end of August. He would later write that the CR-42 was a good aircraft, easy to fly and maneuverable, but that it lacked sufficient speed and armament. The only aircraft against which it wasn't outclassed were Gladiators, Blenheims and Wellingtons.

Bordoni-Bisleri's first victory, against a Royal Air Force Bristol Blenheim, was scored on March 10. The first fighter that he shot down was a Hawker Hurricane on April 14 over Tobruk Harbor. After reequipping with Macchi MC-200s late in 1941, 18 Gruppo participated in the conquest of Greece. May 1942 found the group back in Libya, but Bordoni-Bisleri did not return to North Africa until July.

His first victory during the second phase of his North Africa career came in October, after 18 Gruppo had started to receive MC-202s as replacements for lost MC-200s. He shot down a Royal Air Force Boston on October 20 over Fuka, and he claimed six Curtiss Kittyhawks between October 26 and November 7—including one during the pivotal Battle of El Alamein on October 30. Though he was injured in a car wreck on November 19 and taken out of action, Bordoni-Bisleri's 12 victories made him the top-scoring Italian fighter pilot of the desert campaign. He was a four-time recipient of the Medaglia d'Argento al Valore Militare, the Silver Medal, Italy's penultimate decoration, as well as the German Iron Cross.

When Bordoni-Bisleri returned to duty in May 1943, central Italy, from Naples to Rome, was coming under increasing pressure from USAAF heavy bombers, with raids on important railroad yards and industrial centers. Bordoni-Bisleri was assigned to air defense operations and was one of the first to receive the new Macchi MC-205. His initial victory in the fighter was a Boeing B-17 Flying Fortress, which he shot down over Rome on July 30. On August 11, he claimed a pair of the big heavy bombers north of Rome, between Terni and Viterbo. A week later, while flying a Macchi MC-202, Bordoni-Bisleri shot down a Martin B-26 medium bomber over Largo Ostia.

The remainder of his victories would be against USAAF B-17s in the final days before Italy's unconditional surrender. He claimed one over Naples on August 21 and another on August 30. His 19th and last victory, and his fifth heavy-bomber kill, was scored over Civitavecchia on September 5, three days before the surrender.

After the war, Franco Bordoni-Bisleri went back to the family business and took up sports-car racing as a hobby. In 1953, he won the Italian championship in his racing class. He also continued flying as a private pilot and became president of the Milano-Bresso Aeroclub. He died as he had earned his glory, in the crash of his Siai-Marchetti SF-260 aircraft in the Apennines on September 15, 1957, during a thunderstorm, on a flight to Milan from Rome. His son, age ten, was also killed in the crash.

8

FRANCE

BEGINNING WITH ROLAND GARROS, THE first, French pilots were among the most colorful and storied aces of the First World War. The tales of their exploits are some of the greatest stories from the war that was then known simply as the "Great War.". France produced 158 aces, men whose names were household words throughout the world in the early years of the 20th century, and which are still well known icons of military aviation history. Throughout the largest cities and tiniest villages in France, there are streets and squares that bear their names.

At the top of the list of French aces is the name of the great ace of aces, René Paul Fonck, who scored 75 victories, more than anyone in World War I except the "Red Baron," Manfred von Richthofen. Also on the list are Georges Guynemer, with 54 victories; Charles Nungesser with 45; Georges F. Madon with 41; Maurice Boyau with 35; and Michel Coiffard with 34.

For all the hardship that France suffered, it was a victor in World War I. Its capital was never occupied and it never tasted defeat. In World War II, however, France was defeated in a month and a half.

Germany invaded Poland on September 1, 1939, and two days later, Britain and France declared that a state of war had existed for two days. Poland was defeated in three weeks, but Allied and German troops sat and stared at one another across the heavily fortified Franco-German border until the spring of 1940, when Germany defeated all of Western Europe in three months. Compared with the years of stalemate that had occurred in World War I, the German victories came with blinding speed.

On May 10, the Germans began a great offensive to the west that was similar to their advance on Belgium and France in 1914 at the beginning of World War I—except that in 1940, they were not stopped. By May 28, Luxembourg, Belgium, and the Netherlands had surrendered and German forces were pouring into France. By June 14, Germany had seized control of Paris, having accomplished in five weeks what it had been unable to do in four years of protracted fighting in World War I.

France finally surrendered on June 22, but in the meantime, the French forces put up a resistance that was, at times, noble. Certainly the squadrons of the French air force, the Armée de l'Air, were among the most heroic of French combat units. Just as the French equipment was outclassed by that of the German armies on the ground, so, too, were French fighter aircraft. The Messerschmitt Bf-109 was easily superior to the Armée de l'Air's French-made Dewoitine D520s and American-made Curtiss Model 75 Hawks (equivalent to the P-36 in American service).

There were many Armée de l'Air aces during the brief Battle of France, but this is due in part to its method of counting victories. During World War I, the French had been more strict about crediting scores for shared victories than they were in 1940. Full scores were given for assists and for probables to the point where all the aircraft on the scene when an enemy was shot down received a full point for their overall tally. This created inflated scores, and more aces than there actually were, but it was certainly a propaganda measure which ensured that good news about the battles would be reported in the French media. However bracing this was for French morale at the time, it has left a great deal of uncertainty for historians of aviation.

The top-scoring French ace of the short Battle of France was Edmond Marin la Meslée, who is credited with 20 victories while flying a Curtiss Hawk with the Escadrille (Squadron) 5 of the Armée de l'Air's Groupe de Chasse (Pursuit Group) I. Indeed, Groupe de Chasse I/5, which was based at Rheims, in northeastern France, was the highest-scoring Armée de l'Air unit of the Battle of France, with 111 credited victories. Having scored a shared victory before the Battle of France, Marin la Meslée claimed a pair of Ju-87 Stukas on May 12. By June 7, his score stood at 20, including 4 probables and 10 shared kills. He would later join the Free French air force, with which he was flying P-47 Thunderbolts in the Alsace campaign when he was killed in action on February 4, 1945. He is credited with no victories while flying with the Free French.

The leading French ace to be killed in action during the battles on the Western Front was François Morel, who also flew with the Armée de l'Air's Groupe de Chasse I/5. He was credited with 12 victories when he died on May 18, 1940.

When France surrendered, so, too, did the Armée de l'Air. Some of the pilots remained in France with the air force, which was taken over by the new Vichy government, a puppet regime set up by the Germans. Others fled to Britain to carry on the war against the Germans alongside the British. These became the nucleus of the Free

French forces under Charles de Gaulle. The Free French pilots would ultimately fly British and American aircraft and operate under the Anglo-American command structure through the end of the war.

Other French pilots went east after the surrender to join the Soviet Voenno-Vozdushnie Sily. They would ultimately be organized into the famed Normandie-Niemen group under the VVS command structure. Two of the most important of the Normandie-Niemen pilots were Marcel Albert, who is credited with 16 victories while flying with the Armée de l'Air, plus 5 with the Normandie-Niemen, and Jacques André, who had only 1 with the Armée de l'Air, but 11 with the Normandie-Niemen group. Roland de la Poype, who was apparently scoreless with the Armée de l'Air, had one with No.602 Squadron of the Royal Air Force, and six—plus nine probables—with the Normandie-Niemen.

Pierre LeGloan was probably the leading French ace who did not fight the Germans in the Battle of France. He had two shared victories against Dornier Do-17 bombers early in the war, but he was flying D520s with Groupe de Chasse III/6 in the south of France in May-June 1940, so he fought against the Italians during that period. After the surrender, he stayed with Groupe de Chasse III/6 as it came under Vichy control. Here he found himself fighting France's former allies, the British. Flying for the Vichy government in Syria, he shot down four Hawker Hurricanes and a Gloster Gladiator. This brought his score to 18, including 3 probables, which the Armée de l'Air counted as full scores. Most of these had been scored against the Italian Regia Aeronautica. In 1943, Group de Chasse III/6 switched sides and joined the Allies, but LeGloan would score no more kills. He died on September 11, 1943, when his D520 suffered an engine failure while he was returning from a mission.

Clostermann: In the Shadow of René Fonck

In World War II, France's leading ace would not enjoy the glory and celebrity of the great René Fonck, who scored 75 victories in World War I, but he was, nevertheless, a colorful character who worked hard and made France—and his native Alsace region—proud.

Generally regarded as France's leading ace in World War II, Pierre Clostermann would score all of his victories while flying with the British Royal Air Force, although the number is uncertain. Some sources credit him with as few as 19, while in his autobiography, *The Big Show,* he recounts a total of 33.

Clostermann fled to Great Britain in 1940, but did not became a pilot with the Royal Air Force until early 1943, when he was assigned to No.341 "Alsace" Squadron, which was composed entirely of Free French airmen flying the Supermarine Spitfire Mk.IX. In August 1943, Clostermann shot down a pair of Focke Wulf Fw-190s, his first two victories. He was subsequently transferred to the No.602 "City of Glasgow" Squadron, composed of Belgian, Australian, Norwegian, Canadian, and English—as well as French—pilots. On January 17 1944, the squadron was transferred to the Orkney Islands, where they would fly air defense for the naval base at Scapa Flow using Spitfire Mk.VIIIs.

As time for the June 6, 1944, invasion of northern France drew close, No.602 Squadron was reassigned to attacking German antiaircraft positions in Normandy, a task which Clostermann despised. After the invasion, however, the squadron was able to go back to air-to-air work and he scored three victories in one day. For this, he was awarded the Distinguished Flying Cross by the Royal Air Force. In the meantime, he and fellow pilot Jacques Remlinger were the first Free French airmen to land in France.

After he received his Distinguished Flying Cross, Clostermann was taken out of combat and given a desk job because he was diagnosed as suffering from battle fatigue. This lasted until December 1944, when he requested and received another combat assignment. This time, he found himself back on the continent, specifically with No.274 Squadron, which was flying Hawker Tempest Vs from a base at Volkel in the Netherlands. On May 3, 1945, after four months with No.274 Squadron, Clostermann was given command of No.122 Wing, but the war was over within a week.

As he describes in his autobiography, Clostermann flew 293 offensive missions, 97 ground attack missions and 42 defensive missions. He ended the war with 33 aerial victories, many of them scored in 1945. These included 19 Focke-Wulf Fw-190s, 7 Messerschmitt Bf-109s, a pair of Dornier Do-24 flying boats, a Fiesler Fi-156, a Junkers Ju-88, a Junkers Ju-252, a Junkers Ju-290, and a Heinkel He-111. He also lists 12 probable kills of Focke-Wulf Fw-190 and Messerschmitt Bf-109 fighters, and 24 aircraft destroyed on the ground. Other ground targets that he destroyed include 5 tanks, 225 other vehicles, and 72 locomotives. He also participated in a successful attack on a German U-boat.

9

POLAND

WORLD WAR II BEGAN WITH Germany's sudden Blitzkrieg invasion of Poland in the predawn hours of September 1, 1939. The Polish air force was the first Allied air force in action during the war, but for Poland, it would last just three weeks. After the country's defeat, many of its best pilots escaped, some to the Soviet Union, but most to Britain. As for the Soviet Union, it should be recalled that on September 17, its army *also* invaded Poland. Resistance had ceased by this time, and under the terms of the Hitler-Stalin pact of August 24, the Soviet invasion amounted to "dividing the spoils." Most of the Polish territory occupied by the Soviet army in 1939 remained part of the Soviet Union until its collapse in 1991. It is now within the borders of Belarus, not Poland.

Many of the Polish pilots who escaped would fight again, flying as part of the Royal Air Force, the VVS, or the USAAF, and there were ultimately over 40 Polish aces in World War II. The top three, Stanislaw Skalski with 22 victories, Witold Urbanowicz with 18, and Eugeniusz Horbaczewski with 16.5, all flew with the Royal Air Force—and Urbanowicz flew with the USAAF as well. Boleslaw

"Mike" Gladych scored 14 kills with the USAAF, and Victor Kalinowski was the top-scoring Polish ace with the Voenno-Vozdushnie Sily, winning 9 victories.

After the war, the Polish pilots would again find themselves ensnarled in the coils of fate. After bravely defending their country during the war, they continued to fight the enemy of their country after the war. However, when those who fought Germany from Britain returned home, they faced prison, not a hero's welcome.

After German forces occupied Poland in 1939, the Polish government chose to set up a "government in exile" in Britain. This government in exile was recognized by Britain and the United States, along with many other countries, as the legitimate government of Poland. Why wouldn't they? It was the same government that had been recognized previously. It was assumed that when the Germans were driven out, this government would go back to Warsaw and take up where it had left off.

Poland was liberated by the armies of the Soviet Union, however, not those of Britain and the United States, and Josef Stalin had another agenda. In the process of defeating the Germans, the Soviets occupied all of the previously independent states from Poland to Bulgaria. Stalin announced that he had no intention of withdrawing his forces from these territories, using the pretext that he wanted to maintain a buffer zone between Germany and the Soviet Union so that never again would Germany be able to do what it had done in 1941. To accomplish his goal, Stalin used the force of his army to install local Communist governments that answered to his whims. The Polish government in exile was never allowed to return, and those who had fought for it from bases in Britain were now considered to be enemies of the new Polish state.

Josef Stalin's paranoia and vindictiveness infected the

political leadership of every nation in which he installed a client government. The decade after the end of World War II was a dangerous time, and Poland would be a dangerous place for anyone who the Communists decided was politically incorrect.

The Polish Air Force at War

On the eve of the war, the Polish air force had seven fighter squadrons (Dywizjon Mysliwski), each equipped with about 20 aircraft, mainly PZL P-7s and P-11s produced by the Polish State Aircraft Factory (Panstwowe Zaklaty Lotnicze). These were assigned primarily to support the field armies. Only two reinforced squadrons, under the command of Colonel Stefan Pawlikowski, a World War I veteran pilot, were tasked with the air defense of Warsaw when the first attacks came.

The PZL-series aircraft were gull-winged single-seat fighters powered by British-made Bristol Jupiter or Mercury engines. Generally, they were armed only with a pair of 7.7 mm machine guns, although later aircraft had four such weapons. The P-11 had a top speed was 186 mph at sea level and 242 mph at 18,000 feet. Its range was typically under 600 miles and it could climb to 16,400 feet in six minutes, but this would prove inadequate for intercepting German bombers. While the P-11 was very maneuverable, the German fighters were generally superior in every other way. By 1939, the more advanced P-24 had been developed, but only for the export market. None of these faster, cannon-equipped fighters was in service with the Polish air force when the Germans attacked. Romania, Bulgaria, and Greece all had them, however.

At about seven o'clock on the morning of September 1, airplane spotters alerted the Polish air-force air defense units that a German bomber force was headed for Warsaw. Interceptors were launched, and the first Allied aerial victory of World War II, a Heinkel He-111, would be claimed by Lieutenant Alexander Gabszewicz. Hieronim Dudwal, in turn, scored what was to be the first of four for him in the Polish campaign. Though the Luftwaffe fighters escorting the bombers took their toll on the Polish defenders, many of the bombers were forced to abort and the initial attack on Warsaw was less than a resounding success. Few bombs actually fell on the capital the first day, and the Luftwaffe suffered more than a dozen bombers lost. In the coming weeks, however, the Germans overwhelmed the Polish air force, and Warsaw suffered the terror of aerial bombing that would be visited upon many major cities across the world over the coming six years.

Although the first Allied aerial victory of World War II occurred on the morning of September 1, it is not certain who exactly scored it, because the first two may have come more or less simultaneously. Wladyslaw Gnys is reported to have shot down a pair of Dornier Do-17s at approximately 5:30 A.M., although his own after-action report gives the time as seven o'clock. Obviously, the second of the pair would have gone down several minutes after the first. Meanwhile, Stanislaw Skalski downed a Henschel Hs-126 on a reconnaissance mission at 5:32. The fourth victory was probably the Heinkel He-111 claimed by Lieutenant Alexander Gabszewicz at or about seven o'clock.

Skalski: The First and Finest

The first Allied ace of World War II, and the man who went on to be the highest-scoring Polish ace of the war, was Stanislaw Skalski, the pilot who may also have shot down the first Axis aircraft. He scored his second and third victories—two Do-17s—on September 2, and scored his fifth on September 4 to become Poland's first ace.

Born in October 1915 in Kodyma, Skalski earned his wings in 1938, and was assigned to the 142nd "Wild Ducks" Fighter Squadron in Torun. Flying P-11s with the Wild Ducks, he is credited with downing two Do-17 bombers, two Hs-126s, a Ju-86 bomber, and a Ju-87 Stuka. He also damaged three and had a shared victory. When he flew his last mission with the Polish air force on September 16, his total stood at 6.5.

With Poland's ultimate defeat now certain, a number of Polish air-force pilots escaped from their country via Romania, hoping to regroup and fight the Germans from Britain and France. Skalski eventually made his way to Britain, where he joined the Royal Air Force in January 1940. He was assigned to No.501 Squadron, which was equipped with Hawker Hurricanes. Skalski was in combat against the Germans in August 1940, during the Battle of Britain. In his first weeks back in action, he managed to down three enemy aircraft, bringing his total to 9.5. It must have seemed like déjà vu.

On September 5, Skalski's unit intercepted a strike force of He-111s, one of which was promptly claimed by his guns. He also managed to claim a pair of Messerschmitt Bf-109s, but his own Hurricane was shot down. He bailed out, but severe burns would keep him hospitalized for six weeks. The first Allied ace of World War II was also now probably the first man to achieve ace status with two separate air forces.

During 1941, the Royal Air Force had so many expatriate pilots within its ranks that it was possible to form entire squadrons of pilots who had formerly been with a specific air force. Skalski was assigned to No.306 (Polish) Squadron as a flight commander in June 1941, and it was with this unit that he scored five victories during the summer. By now, Skalski was the recipient of the Royal Air Force Distinguished Flying Cross, as well as the Silver Cross (Virtuti Militari)—Poland's highest decoration—and the Cross of Valor.

In April 1942, Skalski was placed in command of No.317 (Polish) Squadron for five months before being reassigned to the North African Theater. In Tunisia, between March and May 1943, he commanded the Polish Fighting Team, flying Spitfire Mk.IXs as an autonomous component of No.145 Squadron. The Fighting Team, which came to be known as "Skalski's Circus," claimed a large number of German aircraft, and Stanislaw Skalski added four to his own total. The first of these was a Ju-88 downed on March 28. Between April 2 and April 6, 1943, the Circus claimed eight Messerschmitt Bf-109s, two of which were shot down by Skalski. Skalski's fourth in North Africa came on May 6, 1943, on the last day of combat for the Circus. A week later, the Germans surrendered in North Africa and withdrew to Italy.

Skalski was promoted to command the Royal Air Force No.601 "County of London" Squadron, becoming the first Pole to command a Royal Air Force fighter unit. With this squadron, he took part in Operation Husky, the invasion of Sicily on July 9–10, 1943, and the subsequent invasion of Italy at Salerno, which began on September 9.

Stanislaw Skalski returned to England in December 1943, where he would be placed in command of No.131 Wing, which contained the Polish No.302 Squadron, No.308 Squadron, and No.317 Squadron. For exactly four months, starting on April 3, 1944, he was in command of the No.133 (Polish) Wing, which contained one British squadron, No.129 Squadron, and two Polish units, No.306 Squadron and No.315 Squadron. As commander of No.133

Wing, Skalski participated in the operations surrounding the Operation Overlord invasion of France on June 6. On June 24, he would score two victories in an intense battle over Rouen that netted the unit a total of six confirmed kills. From August until the middle of October, Skalski commanded No.1 (Polish) Wing.

Stanislaw Skalski spent the final months of the war as an instructor at the Royal Air Force Advanced Gunnery School at Catfoss that was headed by the legendary Royal Air Force ace Adolph Gysbert "Sailor" Malan. Skalski ended the war as a national hero in Poland, with three Distinguished Flying Crosses and a Distinguished Service Order awarded by the British. His final official score was 22 confirmed victories and one probable.

Returning to Poland after the war, Stanislaw Skalski found that his British decorations and his stellar career did not hold him in good stead with the Soviet-controlled Communist government. In 1949, after the Communists consolidated their power, they decided that Skalski was a spy for the West and threw him into prison. When he was finally released in 1956, the decorated hero of the skies wound up as a taxi driver in Warsaw.

Urbanowicz: A Polish Flying Tiger

Witold Urbanowicz was born in March 1908 in Olszanka and joined the Polish air force in 1930. After a stint as an observer with a bomber squadron, he applied for pilot training. Between 1933 and 1936, he served as a fighter pilot before being assigned as a flight instructor. When the war began, he was in Romania, helping to deliver to Poland new aircraft recently purchased from Britain and France. The two major Western European nations declared war on Germany after the invasion of Poland because of the tripartite defense alliance that they had with the country, and one of the provisions of that alliance had been the promise to supply the Polish air force with late-model fighters, including Hawker Hurricanes.

Urbanowicz and his team failed to deliver the aircraft in time to make a difference, and he was captured. He managed to escape and, along with many other Polish pilots, made his way to Britain. In January 1940, he was among the first group of Polish pilots to join the Royal Air Force.

During the early days of the Battle of Britain, Urbanowicz flew with the Royal Air Force No.145 Squadron, with whom he scored his first two aerial victories. On August 21, he was transferred to No.303 (Polish) "City of Warsaw" Squadron, and on September 6, 1940, he shot down the Bf-109E flown by Joachim Schlichting, then a staffel commander with the Luftwaffe's JG 27. The following day, when No.303 Skalski's commander, Major Zdzislaw Krasnodebski, was injured, Urbanowicz was chosen as his replacement.

On September 15, 1940, No.303 Squadron claimed 16 kills, with Urbanowicz himself claiming a pair of Dornier Do-217s. Three days later, the commander of all Polish forces in England awarded him the nation's highest decoration, the Silver Cross (Virtuti Militari).

In October, after adding four victories to his score, Urbanowicz was reassigned to a desk job. After a short stint between April and June 1941 as commander of No.1 (Polish) Wing, he was sent as assistant air Attaché to the Polish embassy in Washington, D.C. In the United States, Urbanowicz was offered a unique invitation. It was to join the USAAF on temporary duty and fly with the 75th Fighter Squadron of the USAAF 14th Air Force in China, the successor to the old American Volunteer Group, the legendary "Flying Tigers."

Urbanowicz accepted the offer in September 1943, and he traveled east to Kunming, where he found himself assigned as wingman to the legendary David Lee "Tex" Hill. Flying Curtiss P-40s with the 75th Fighter Squadron, Urbanowicz had soon claimed two Mitsubishi A6M Zeros, one of them in a spectacular battle over Hong Kong at rooftop altitude. These would be his last 2 of 17 (some sources credit him with 18).

In December 1943, his temporary duty concluded, Urbanowicz rejoined the Polish headquarters within the Royal Air Force and later took a second diplomatic assignment in Washington. When he returned to Poland in 1946, he was promptly arrested by the Communist government because of his having served with the Polish government in exile in Britain in a diplomatic role. He was later released, but still faced prison or possible execution at the hands of the Soviet-supported Communists. Taking no chances, he promptly relocated to the United States, where he would live until his death, by natural causes, in August 1996.

Horbaczewski: On Skalski's Wing

Poland's third-highest-scoring ace was an interesting character. He was a Ukrainian-born Pole who chose to fight for Britain after the fall of his native Poland, and in the course of his career with the Royal Air Force, he was part of the group that flew with Stanislaw Skalski through much of the war. Eugeniusz Horbaczewski was actually the pilot who had the highest score while flying with the Polish Fighting Team—"Skalski's Circus"—in North Africa. If the four V-1 cruise missiles that he shot down were added to his ultimate score of 16.5 aircraft, he would have been second only to Skalski among Polish aces.

Horbaczewski was born in Kiev, the capital of the Ukraine, in 1917. He grew up in Poland with an interest in flying and earned a Class-C (highest) glider rating at age 18. The next step was powered flight, and he joined the Polish air force. He went on to become an aviation cadet at Deblin under Witold Urbanowicz, and he was part of the group who, along with Urbanowicz, was trying to get advanced fighters delivered to the Polish air force when the Germans attacked on September 1, 1939.

Along with Urbanowicz and Skalski, Horbaczewski escaped to Britain and joined the Royal Air Force. However, he was a relative latecomer. While Skalski, Urbanowicz, and most other Polish pilots had been in combat during the Battle of Poland in 1939, and certainly during the Battle of Britain in 1940, Horbaczewski was not actually in combat until October 1941. He was assigned initially to No.303 (Polish) "City of Warsaw" Squadron, a Spitfire unit which had earlier been involved in the heat of the Battle of Britain, and which had been previously commanded by Urbanowicz.

Horbaczewski's first "probable" victory came on October 6, when the squadron was attacked by Messerschmitt Bf-109s while escorting bombers over France, but he would not get a confirmed kill until April 4, 1942, during another bomber escort mission over France. He attacked a Focke Wulf Fw-190 that was on the tail of another Spitfire, opening fire at close range. The second victory came quickly. During another mission over France on April 16, he downed a Bf-109, again using close-in fire.

On August 19, Horbaczewski was in one of the Spitfires that was flying cover for the ill-fated Allied raid against Dieppe on the French coast. No.303 Squadron intercepted a group of Fw-190s bent on attacking the landing craft and cut them apart. The unit ended the day with eight victories, one of them claimed by Horbaczewski.

In March 1943, Horbaczewski was sent to the North African Theater and assigned to the Polish Fighting Team, commanded by Stanislaw Skalski ("Skalski's Circus"). Ultimately, Horbaczewski would claim five victories as part of the team, more than anyone else, including Skalski himself. The first of these, a Ju-88 bomber, came on March 28, the unit's first day of combat. On April 2, he added a Bf-109. Four days later, the tables were turned, and Horbaczewski found himself alone in a fight with five Messerschmitt Bf-109s. He was hit, but managed a crash landing. Fortunately, he was over Allied territory at the time, and he was soon back in combat.

Horbaczewski's final action with the Circus came on April 22, when he downed a pair of Bf-109s in a massive dogfight over the Bay of Tunis. His combat record led to his promotion to command No.43 Squadron, making him the second Polish ace, after Skalski, to command a Royal Air Force fighter squadron. Like Skalski's No.601 Squadron, Horbaczewski's No.43 Squadron was involved in Operation Husky over Sicily, and in subsequent activities over Italy. At one point, he would shoot down two Bf-109s in less than a minute.

Having been sent back to Britain early in 1944, Horbaczewski was assigned to command No.315 (Polish) Squadron, which was named "City of Deblin," after the Polish metropolis where many of the Polish aces in the Royal Air Force had originally earned their wings. Based at Coolham, it was also part of No.133 (Polish) Wing, which was commanded by Stanislaw Skalski. In March 1944, the City of Deblin Squadron became operational with the Spitfire Mk.V, as well as the American-made

North American Mustang III, the equivalent of the USAAF P-51C.

Horbaczewski and No.315 Squadron took part in operations leading up to and following the June 6, 1944, Normandy Invasion. On June 22, he was involved in a rather dramatic display of heroism. When a squadron mate was forced to make a crash landing in Normandy after a strafing operation, Horbaczewski landed his own aircraft and picked up the wounded pilot—who was unable to walk—and flew him back to Britain for medical attention.

Operationally, the squadron had a varied workload during the summer of 1944. In addition to their missions over Normandy, on June 30, they escorted a group of bombers against targets in Norway. Here, a large number of Luftwaffe fighters jumped them. Although the Germans were much closer to their bases and the Polish pilots were at the limit of their range, the Poles managed to shoot down eight, and they suffered no losses. Horbaczewski himself shot down one Bf-109 before his guns jammed.

The summer of 1944 was also the time when the Germans began launching barrages of jet-propelled V-1 cruise missiles against Britain. While actual damage from the unguided "buzz bombs" was minimal, the morale implications in Britain were considerable, so all available resources were devoted to shooting them down. No.315 Squadron was one of those resources. They managed to take out 53, including 4 downed by Horbaczewski himself.

Early on the morning of August 18, 12 City of Deblin Mustang IIIs were again on patrol over northern France when they surprised and engaged a larger group of Fw-190s belonging to JG 26. They shot down 16—possibly 17—of the Focke Wulfs, 3 of them claimed by Horbaczewski. However, the defenders struck back, with three confirmed kills. One of these was Eugeniusz Horbaczewski's Mustang.

The stone marker that still stands near the site of his death outside the French village of Vellennes records the fact that he was awarded Britain's Distinguished Service Order and Distinguished Flying Cross. It also notes that he was 26 at the time of his death.

Gladych: Five Air Forces and Three Lives

While most of the Polish pilots who escaped after their country's capitulation wound up flying in "Polish" squadrons in Britain's Royal Air Force, Boleslaw Michel "Mike" Gladych began his expatriate career flying in a "Finnish" squadron in the French Armée de l'Air. His fourth and fifth air forces would be the Royal Air Force and the USAAF.

Boleslaw Gladych was born in May 1918 in Warsaw and joined the Polish air force in 1938. He had learned to fly the PZL P-VII and PZL P-XI at Deblin when the war started, but he had not yet officially transitioned into a combat unit. He fled to Romania, where he was briefly interned at Turnu Severin, from which he escaped. When he arrived in France, he joined the Groupe de Chasse I/145, a French squadron that was being sent to Finland to fight the Soviet forces. Designated as "Finnish," it also contained Polish volunteer pilots. While Finland was technically neutral in World War II, it had been attacked by the Soviet Union at the end of November 1939, two months after the Soviets occupied the eastern half of Poland. For Poles in 1939 and 1940, the Soviet Union was almost as much an enemy as Germany.

Groupe de Chasse I/145 would actually wind up fighting the Luftwaffe on the Western Front when the Germans launched their offensive against France in May 1940. Gladych first faced the enemy, flying an aging Caudron Cr-714 against Bf-109s, on June 10. As the story goes, the Messerschmitt pilot shot up Gladych's outclassed Caudron Cyclone, then dipped his wings and flew away, allowing the future ace to live to fight another day.

Gladych escaped to Britain when France fell and eventually joined the Royal Air Force's No.303 (Polish) "City of Warsaw" Squadron, which was commanded by Stanislaw Skalski, and which was the home, at one time or another over the coming years, to many major Polish aces. Gladych's first action with No.303 Squadron came on April 26, 1941. This time, he was in the cockpit of a Supermarine Spitfire instead of a Caudron Cyclone, and his first victory was forthcoming. Statisticians recall his first kill as the 250th by a Polish pilot flying with the Royal Air Force.

After being injured in June, Gladych was back in action in October with another victory. Beginning in July 1942, he transferred to No.302 "City of Poznan" Squadron, where he became a flight leader early in 1943. A few months later, a very strange thing happened. During a dogfight over northeastern France, Gladych was attacked by an Fw-190 pilot who shot up his Spitfire, but dipped his wings and flew away. It was a replay of the incident that had occurred over France three years earlier. This time, Gladych noticed a "13" on the side of the German aircraft and thought he recalled the same number from the previous incident.

In the autumn of 1943, Gladych was grounded by the Royal Air Force after he accidentally almost shot down the aircraft carrying British Prime Minister Winston Churchill. This led to his volunteering for his fifth air force. When he was with No.303 Squadron, Gladych had met Francis

"Gabby" Gabreski, a Polish-American pilot who had volunteered with the unit before the United States entered the
war. Now Gabreski was flying Republic P-47s with the
USAAF 56th Fighter Group. With Gabreski's help, Gladych arranged a temporary duty transfer to the 56th Fighter
Group, and was soon flying combat missions with the
group's 61st Fighter Squadron.

On March 8, 1944, the 61st Fighter Squadron was escorting bombers on a strike deep into Germany, when Gladych had the strangest experience of his life—a *third*
encounter with the German pilot with the mysterious "13."
Gladych had shot down one of the Fw-190s that attacked
the bomber stream, but he had almost run out of ammunition and had become separated from the rest of the
squadron. Two Fw-190s cornered him and indicated that
he should land at a nearby airfield. One of them was numbered "13."

Gladych came in low, followed by the two Focke Wulfs,
and lowered his landing gear. When he was over the field,
he opened fire, as though he was on a strafing run, and
gave his P-47 Thunderbolt full throttle. German antiaircraft
gunners returned fire, but they hit the Fw-190s instead of
Gladych. On the way home, he ran out of fuel and had to
bail out over southern Britain. His action earned him an
American Silver Star.

Boleslaw Gladych's ninth and tenth—his last—victories
scored with the USAAF 56th Fighter Group were a pair
of Fw-190s that he shot down on September 21, 1944. This
would bring his final score to 14. His friend Gabby Gabreski, meanwhile, had the distinction of being the
number-two top-scoring USAAF ace in the European
Theater, with 28.

When the war ended, Gladych emigrated to the United
States, rather than returning to Poland, thus probably sav-

ing himself some prison time as a guest of the Soviet-sponsored Polish government. His having volunteered to assist the Finns in fighting the Soviets would not have been well received. In 1950, however, he did travel to Europe, where he happened to be in Frankfurt, Germany, when a meeting of former German fighter pilots was taking place.

As would happen if the story were fiction—and truth can be as contrived as fiction—Mike Gladych found himself face-to-face with the man who had worn number 13 on *all three* previous encounters. Gladych finally shook the hand of Georg-Peter Eder, who had ended the war as an ace with 78 victories.

10

THE OTHER ALLIED AIR FORCES

Czechoslovakia

Of all the countries that were directly involved in World War II, Czechoslovakia had the distinction of being the only one (except Austria, which became part of the Reich in 1938) that was defeated and occupied without a shot before the war had even started. Czechoslovakia was created in 1918 as a union of Bohemia, Moravia, and Slovakia, which had been part of the Austro-Hungarian Empire before its collapse in 1918. During the next two decades, the country evolved as the most democratic and economically developed nation in Central or Eastern Europe. However, Adolf Hitler used the presence of a sizable German-speaking population in the Sudetenland area of western Bohemia as an excuse to foment trouble. He demanded the Sudetenland, and France and Britain agreed at the famous Munich Conference in September 1938 that he could have it if he made no more demands. Czech president Eduard Benes also acquiesced to Germany's demands and surrendered the Sudetenland. In turn, Slovakia seceded from Czechoslovakia and allied itself with Nazi Germany.

Then, in March 1939, Hitler sent troops to occupy Bohemia and Moravia in violation of the Munich Treaty.

The Czechoslovakian military ceased to exist, and as would be the case with the Poles six months later, many Czech airmen escaped to fight the Germans in the uniforms of other nations. Some escaped to Poland; most eventually reached France and then moved on to Britain when France surrendered. Their story is an amazing odyssey of pilots escaping the collapse of two or three independent nations while serving in the air force of each as they went.

Two of the first Czechs to become aces flew with the French Armée de l'Air. Despite the Armée de l'Air's policy of giving full credit to assists and probables as well as confirmed victories, both men probably really were aces, with at least five solo victories. Frantisek Perina scored 13 (by Armée de l'Air calculations) with Groupe de Chasse (Pursuit Squadron) I/5, the French unit with the most kills during the Battle of France of May-June 1940. He then went on to score one with the Royal Air Force's No.312 (Free Czech) Squadron before he was killed in action.

Josef Stehlík had the distinction of flying with three air forces after he left Czechoslovakia. His first victories were with the Armée de l'Air's Groupe de Chasse III/3 in 1940; a total of seven, including five solo kills. In 1941, he had at least one shared victory with the Royal Air Force's No.312 (Free Czech) Squadron, and in 1944, he scored one with the 1st Czech Regiment of the Soviet Voenno-Vozdushnie Sily.

The highest-scoring Czech ace would be Karel Miroslav Kuttelwascher. He scored three with the Armée de l'Air's Groupe de Chasse III/6 before being forced to evacuate to Britain. With the Royal Air Force, Kuttelwascher scored 18 victories while serving with both No.1 Squadron and No.23 Squadron.

The second-highest-scoring Czech ace with the Royal Air Force was Josef Frantisek, who scored 17 victories with No.303 (Polish) Squadron before being killed in a flying accident on October 8, 1940. There are unconfirmed reports that he scored as many as 11 victories with the French Armée de l'Air before reaching Britain. If true, this would make him the highest-scoring Czech ace.

Born at Otaslavice near Prostejov in October 1913, Frantisek joined the Czech air force in 1934 and earned his wings at Prostejov in 1936. He was initially assigned to the 5th Observation Flight of the 2nd "Dr. Eduard Benes" Regiment at Olomouc. He was later picked for fighter pilot training because of his exceptional skill, and in June 1938 he was assigned to the 40th Fighter Flight. Based near Prague, the unit was equipped with Czech-manufactured Avia B-534 fighter aircraft, with which the Czech capital would have been defended if Czechoslovakia had not surrendered without a fight in March 1939.

Frantisek left his homeland for neighboring Poland, from which he had intended to move on to France, as did many Czech pilots from his former unit. In July 1939, he had accepted an opportunity to join the Polish air force. When the Germans attacked in September, Frantisek was assigned to an observation unit and saw no combat. On September 22, 1939, he was one of three Czech pilots who participated in an operation aimed at evacuating Polish aircraft to Romania to avoid capture by the Germans.

Frantisek was interned briefly in Romania, but he escaped to Marseilles via Beirut, reaching France on October 20. In France, he became part of a Polish unit within the Armée de l'Air. Some sources state that he scored as many as 11 kills during the Battle of France, but official documentation, if it ever existed, has been lost. One story suggests that he changed his name while he was in France to prevent German reprisals against his family in Czechoslovakia. If so, his Armée de l'Air victories may have been scored under this unknown assumed name.

When France fell in June 1940, Frantisek escaped again, this time to England. On August 2—still traveling with Polish pilots with whom he had been flying in two other air forces—he arrived at Northolt and reported for duty with the Royal Air Force's No.303 (Polish) Squadron. Soon he would be deep in the events of the Battle of Britain.

Frantisek scored his first victory with the Royal Air Force on September 2 over Dover, downing a Bf-109 in a Hawker Hurricane Mk.I. He scored a second on the following day, and five on September 6. His amazing success in so short a time suggests that he was not a beginner and that he must have had at least some previous combat successes, probably with the Armée de l'Air. On September 15, when No.303 Squadron scored 16 victories, Frantisek was credited with a Bf-110.

During September, Frantisek would score a total of 17 confirmed, plus 1 probable. This made him the top-scoring ace in No.303 Squadron during the Battle of Britain, which, with 126 kills, was the highest-scoring squadron. He was also one of the leading aces in all the Royal Air Force. He was a pilot with amazing skill and enormous potential, but he also had a tendency to break formation to hunt alone, which did not please his commanders.

On October 8, his flight was on patrol over Surrey when, as had become his habit, he peeled off to fly alone. Nobody saw what happened. His Hurricane crashed near the village of Ewell, but there was no evidence that he had been shot down. His body was found near the crashed aircraft with no visible injuries except the broken neck that was the cause of his death.

Denmark

At the start of World War II, Denmark remained neutral, hoping that this stance would protect it as it had done in World War I. The nation's army aviation section—there was no independent air force—had just 48 combat aircraft out of a total fleet of 92, and the government felt that any attempt to acquire more would be hopeless and might provoke the Germans. On April 8, 1940, when the Germans began laying mines between Denmark and Norway, the commander of army aviation asked the Danish general staff for permission to deploy his aircraft to dispersed landing fields. The general staff refused, not wanting to initiate any troop movements that could be taken as a provocation by the Germans.

The following day, the Germans crossed the Danish border in force. Most of the 48 combat aircraft were destroyed on the ground and Denmark was occupied within days. The Danish air force was allowed to exist on paper during the early years of the occupation, but in August 1943, the Germans occupied all Danish military facilities and interned all the officers.

A small number of Danish pilots escaped to Britain, where they joined either the British Royal Air Force, the Royal Navy Fleet Air Arm, or the Royal Norwegian Air Force. Another 25 ended up in Sweden, which would remain neutral throughout the war. In Sweden, they were secretly trained and equipped by the Royal Swedish Air Force. On May 4, 1945, they were prepared to attack the German occupation forces. However, the Germans in Denmark surrendered the next day, and all German armies capitulated two days later.

There were only two Danish aces during World War II. Peter Horn scored 11 victories flying with the enemy—the

Luftwaffe's JG 51. Another Dane to fly with the Luftwaffe was Poul (Paul) Sommer, who had flown previously with the Finns during the Winter War against the Soviet Union. Sommer scored at least three victories with JG 27. On the opposing side, Kaj Birksted was the only Danish ace with the Allies, scoring 10.5 victories flying with the Royal Air Force. Initially, he was assigned to No.43 Squadron, but he later moved to No.331 Squadron. He ended the war with the Bentwaters Wing.

On July 31, 1945, Lieutenant Colonel Kaj Birksted was named to head the postwar Danish Office for Military Aviation Matters, which became the Air Military Committee in December. He would become the architect of Denmark's postwar military aviation policy and the father of the independent Danish air force.

Iceland

Independent of Denmark after 1918, Iceland shared a king—Christian X—with its former mother country until the German occupation, when Iceland declared itself as a republic. The country was never occupied during World War II—by the Germans, that is. Both the British and Americans set up bases on the remote and rocky—but very strategic—island. During the war, the USAAF used it as a vital refueling stop for ferrying aircraft to Britain. Without Iceland, the great Allied air offensive that broke the back of German industrial might would not have been possible.

Iceland itself had little involvement in the war, but some Icelanders did serve with the Allied forces. The country had one ace, Thorsteinn Elton Jonsson, who scored eight victories while serving with the Royal Air Force in No.17 Squadron, No.111 Squadron, and later, No.65 Squadron.

Norway

Like Denmark and Sweden, Norway remained neutral in World War I and hoped to do so in World War II. However, like Denmark, it was invaded on April 9, 1940. Sweden, unlike the others, had prepared for war and was not attacked. Both Denmark and Norway were overwhelmed, and the capitals of both countries were captured in a matter of days. British troops landed in the north of Norway and held on until June, when they were forced to withdraw. Norway's King Haakon VII, who had fled to Britain, formally surrendered his country on June 9.

Many Norwegian pilots escaped to join the Royal Air Force, and among them was Svein Heglund, who flew with No.331 Squadron and No.85 Squadron. He become Norway's only World War II ace, with 14.5 victories.

Netherlands

World War II began with Germany's thrust to the east against Poland, and it was assumed to be only a matter of time before Hitler turned west to attack France, which German armies had invaded twice since 1870. However, between the two lay the "low countries" of Luxembourg, the Netherlands, and Belgium. Luxembourg and Belgium were badly mauled in World War I, but the Netherlands had remained neutral and, like the Scandinavian countries, hoped to do so again. However, the Netherlands' very name, which means "low country," explains why it is virtually indefensible. It is flat, with no natural barriers to invasion. The terrain is naturally suited to the kind of Blitzkrieg tactics that the Germans had developed and used so effectively in Poland.

When the German invasion of Western Europe began

on May 10, 1940, Belgium and the Netherlands were attacked first. The Dutch city of Rotterdam was flattened by the Luftwaffe and the Netherlands army surrendered after just four days. Following the defeat, many of the former Royal Netherlands Air Force pilots went to Britain to fly with the British Royal Air Force. One, Gerald Kesseler, became an ace with 16 victories. In 1944, when Germany launched its air offensive against Britain with the V-1 cruise missiles, a number of Dutch pilots were involved in the interception effort. Ironically, a large number of V-1 launch sites were in the Netherlands. Two of the highest-scoring Dutch pilots during this phase of operations were J. L. Plesman, who is recorded to have shot down 12 of the "buzz bombs," and R. F. Burgwal, who claimed 21.

Belgium

In both world wars, Germany saw Belgium as merely a stepping-stone to France, and in both wars, Belgian resistance to the invasion lasted but a few weeks. In World War II, Belgium was invaded on May 10 and surrendered on May 28. Through most of both world wars, Belgian pilots found themselves fighting the invader of their country from the outside, after their homeland was occupied by German armies. In World War I, the Belgian air force retired to France to fight for four long years. There were several important Belgian aces during the first war, with the highest scoring, by far, being Willy Omer François Jean Coppens, who scored 37 victories while flying with Escadrilles 1, 4, 6, and 9 of the Belgian Air Service.

In World War II, Belgian pilots, like those of many other nations, fled to Britain. Among these was Count Rodolphe Ghislain Charles Henricourt de Grunne, who had previously scored ten victories during the Spanish Civil

War—while flying alongside the Germans, and with the
Nationalist Air Force in 1938–1939.

Henricourt de Grunne is not known to have scored any
victories during Belgium's brief resistance to the German
invasion. When the country collapsed, he joined the British
Royal Air Force, where he was assigned to fly Hawker
Hurricanes with No.32 Squadron. His score against the
Germans is variously reported, from one victory plus a
shared kill, to three victories plus three probables. By the
time that he was killed in action on May 21, 1941, Henricourt de Grunne had been transferred to No.609 Squadron.

The Belgian ace to achieve the highest score during
World War II was another nobleman, Yvan Georges Ar-
sène Felician du Monceau de Bergandael. He fought
briefly against the German offensive during the spring of
1940, and later escaped to Britain by way of Gibraltar. He
joined the Royal Air Force and was assigned initially to
No.253 Squadron, but was soon instrumental in helping to
organize the Belgian contingent within No.609 Squadron.
He later served with both No.349 and No.350 Squadrons.
Referred to by his squadron mates as "Duke," because of
his family's nobility, Monceau de Bergandael scored a total of eight victories.

Next behind the Duke among Belgian aces was Rémy
van Lierde, who also flew with Royal Air Force N.609
Squadron. His score was six aircraft, plus 40 V-1 cruise
missiles shot down in 1944. After the war, van Lierde
worked for many years as a helicopter pilot in the Belgian
Congo before it became independent in 1960. A curious
footnote to his later career came in 1959, when he pho-
tographed a python in the Congo that was estimated to be
50 feet in length. Had the snake not attempted to attack

his helicopter, van Lierde would have been able to confirm its length. At 50 feet, it would have been nearly twice as long as the longest snake ever officially recorded.

Greece

Because their kings were related, Greece had a close relationship with Britain in the years leading up to World War II. When Italy invaded the country on October 28, 1940, Britain sent in both army and Royal Air Force contingents to reinforce the Greek military. The Italians were held off until spring, when Mussolini asked Hitler for help and the Germans invaded. Germany committed superior numbers on both land and sea, and by the end of April, it was all over. Greece had surrendered and the British had withdrawn.

The highest-scoring Royal Air Force ace of the brief Battle of Greece was Marmaduke St. John Pattle, who scored at least 15 kills during the campaign (see British Commonwealth), while the highest-scoring pilot to fly with the Royal Hellenic (Greek) Air Force was Epaminindas Dagoulas, with 4 victories. Pattle was flying a Hawker Hurricane, while Dagoulas was flying with No.22 Mira (Squadron), which was equipped with the clumsier, Polish-made Panstwowe Zaklaty Lotnicze (State Aircraft Factory) P-24s.

After the fall of Greece, many pilots relocated to Britain to fight with the British Royal Air Force. Among these, the highest-scoring ace was Basilios Michael Vassiliades. He scored 7.83 victories flying with No.19 Squadron and later No.3 Squadron. He was shot down and killed on March 25, 1945.

China

Though China did not technically become one of the Allies until the Cairo Declaration of December 1, 1943, it had been at war with Japan since 1931. After the incident at Mukden in 1931 in which Japanese troops clashed with Chinese troops, Japan took over the province of Manchuria. In 1932, they declared it a puppet kingdom under the Japanese Empire and called it Manchukuo. During this time, Japan announced its intention to incorporate most of Asia into its empire as the "Greater East Asia Co-Prosperity Sphere." In 1937, Japan launched a full-scale invasion of China, thus beginning the Sino-Japanese War, which would rage for four years before becoming the Asiatic Theater of World War II.

On September 27, 1940, having occupied the main Chinese ports, Japan became part of the Axis. The empire signed the Tripartite Pact, or Triple Alliance, with Germany and Italy to form the Rome-Berlin-Tokyo Axis. The United States gave matériel support to China over the next few months as relations between the United States and Japan deteriorated. After the United States entry into World War II in December 1941, the United States and Britain immediately formalized the de facto alliance that had previously existed and they recognized both the Soviet Union and China as allied with them in the fight against the Axis. There were numerous competing factions within China, but the one that wielded the most power at the time, and thus the one recognized by the other Allies as the "official" Chinese government, was the Nationalist, or Kuomintang, faction headed by General Chiang Kai-shek. On December 1, 1943, after President Franklin Roosevelt met with him in Cairo, the Declaration of Cairo called for Japan's unconditional surrender and stated that all Chinese territories occupied by Japan would be returned to China.

In the field, Japan's initial successes in China during 1937–1938 devolved into a bloody stalemate that lasted until the end of the war. During this time, the British, and especially the Americans, continued to supply matériel, but their primary contribution to actual combat operations in Asia was in terms of airpower.

The Chinese air force itself was never a match for the Imperial Japanese Navy Air Force or Imperial Japanese Army Air Force, which were both equipped with superior aircraft and better-trained pilots. The Chinese were flying Curtiss Hawk biplanes and Russian-made Polikarpov I-16s against such aircraft as the Mitsubishi A5M. When the Imperial Japanese Navy Air Force started flying the Mitsubishi A6M Zero, there would be no match at all.

Most records of the victories of Chinese aces were lost, so their scores are based on thirdhand sources. Comparison of various sources gives what is probably a fairly accurate picture of the most important aces.

The first Chinese ace of the Sino-Japanese War was Liu Che-Sheng, a pilot with the 4th Fighter Group of the Kuomintang air force, who scored his first victory on August 14, 1937, the first day of the war. He scored his second, flying an I-16 against an A5M, in February 1938. The lag between scores indicates how difficult things would be for the Chinese. Through 1941, Liu Che-Sheng scored a total of 11 kills plus one-third of a shared victory.

Li Kwei-Tan, who also flew with the 4th Fighter Group, is recognized as the highest-scoring ace of the entire period from 1937 through 1945. He had a total of 12, although records indicate that all of his victories were scored after 1941. Both Lo Chi and Liu Tsui-Kan are reported to have scored 11 victories between 1941 and 1945. Wang Kuang-Fu is regarded as another of the highest-scoring Chinese aces. He scored 6.5 kills while flying with the USAAF 7th Fighter Squadron, but he is widely believed to have scored during the Sino-Japanese War as well. Some sources list his total as 8.5 victories, but it isn't clear whether this includes the 6.5, or whether it is in addition to the 6.5. The former is probably the case, but if the two are combined, it would make him the highest-scoring Chinese ace of the period, with 15.

Two additional Chinese aces who scored their victories while flying with USAAF units are Tan Kuan, with five, and Tsang Tsi-Lan, with six.

Four other aces are listed as having eight victories apiece in the Sino-Japanese War, but this total score may encompass the period from 1941 through 1945 as well. These men are Yuan Pao-Kang, Kao Yu-Chan, Kuan Tan, and Kao Yu-Hsin.

Since all of the above pilots flew with the USAAF or the Nationalists, it is probable that none of them saw action with the Chinese People's Liberation Army Air Force during the 1950-1953 Korean War.

11

THE OTHER AXIS AIR FORCES

THE TERM "AXIS" ORIGINALLY DEFINED the alliance of Germany and Italy, which, under the like-minded nationalist dictators Adolf Hitler and Benito Mussolini, joined forces as the "Rome-Berlin Axis" on October 25, 1936. On September 27, 1940, Japan signed the Tripartite Pact or Triple Alliance with Germany and Italy to form the "Rome-Berlin-Tokyo Axis." These three were the principal, and certainly the most militarily powerful, of the Axis powers during World War II. However, they were not the only Axis powers.

In November 1941, Hungary and Romania both became signatories to the Axis pact, as did Slovakia, which had expressed pro-German sympathies since 1938, when it seceded from Czechoslovakia. Bulgaria also joined the Axis, as did Croatia, which was independent of Yugoslavia between 1941 and 1944.

Spain, which was ruled by nationalist General Francisco Franco during World War II, did not join the Axis, despite the extensive support both Germany and Italy had given him during the Spanish Civil War, which he won in 1939. Spain did, however, supply troops to the Axis cause, and these fought extensively on the Eastern Front. The French government centered in Vichy, which was established after the defeat of France by Germany in June 1940, supported, but did not actually join, the Axis. However, Vichy French troops fought against the Allies in French North Africa and the Vichy government gave Japan military control of southern French Indochina.

All of the "second tier" Axis powers had troops in the field during World War II, and they had air forces in the air. Among these air forces were a number of pilots who had the distinction of becoming aces.

Slovakia

Czechoslovakia was carved out of the Austro-Hungarian Empire in 1918 as a confederation of Bohemia, Moravia, and Slovakia (see Other Allied Air Forces). However, the Slovak people felt estranged from the Czechs of the other two regions. In 1938, as it would again in 1993, Slovakia seceded. The catalyst was the Munich Conference in September 1938, in which Czech president Eduard Benes reluctantly agreed to surrender the Sudetenland to Germany in exchange for peace. Slovakia then took itself out of the Czechoslovak Republic. In March 1939, Bohemia and Moravia were incorporated into the German Reich and Slovakia declared itself an independent ally of Nazi Germany. It was to be ruled by Jozef Tiso, head of the Slovak People's Party.

When the war began six months later, the pilots of the former air force of Czechoslovakia went two ways. The now-stateless Czech pilots went—by way of Poland and/or France—to Britain to fight against Germany with the Royal Air Force. The Slovaks formed their own air force— the SVZ (Slovak Air Arm)—which was equipped by Germany and placed under the operational control of the Luftwaffe.

By 1944, however, when it was clear that Germany was going to lose the war, a movement got under way to change sides. This was idealistic as well as pragmatic. Slovakia could see that it was going to be occupied by Soviet troops and it was obviously better to be an anti-German country "liberated" by the Soviets than a pro-German country "defeated" by the Soviets. In August, a Slovak National Council was formed, and an uprising against the Tiso government began.

The Slovak National Uprising was declared on August 29 and it allied itself with the Czechoslovakian government in exile in Britain. Many of the pilots of the SVZ, who had fought with the Luftwaffe, switched sides and began fighting against the Luftwaffe. German forces, however, were superior to those of the Slovak National Council, and the uprising was contained. However, this complicated Germany's defense of the Carpathian Mountains region, by forcing it to divert troops and resources from fighting the Allies to containing the Slovaks. Slovakia was occupied by Soviet forces in 1945, and reunited with Czechoslovakia until 1993.

Though records are incomplete, it is known that there were at least 14 aces in the SVZ. All of them flew under Luftwaffe group (JG) control, and almost all of their victories were scored against the Soviet Voenno-Vozdushnie Sily. The highest-scoring aces were all under the control of JG 52. Jan Reznak was the top Slovak ace. He is credited, according to various sources, with 32 or 33 victories while flying with JG 52. In second place was Izidor Kovarlk, who scored 29 kills with JG 52 before being shot down and killed on July 11, 1944, a month before the

Slovak National Uprising. Third highest among Slovak
aces was Jan Gerthofer, who scored 27.

Rudolf Bozik presents an interesting case. He shot down
eight aircraft while flying with JG 52, although one of
these turned out to be a Messerschmitt Bf-110 that he
would claim was a USAAF B-24 Liberator. In 1944, he
switched sides during the Slovak National Uprising and
scored 2.5 against the Luftwaffe.

Hungary

In the early years of World War II, Hungary was probably
the most staunchly loyal of the second-tier Axis powers.
The strongly nationalistic dictator of Hungary, Admiral
Miklos Horthy de Nagybanya, enthusiastically emulated
Hitler and Mussolini. He saw an alliance with them as a
good route to restoring the national pride that had been
lost when the Treaty of Trianon in 1920 took away nearly
three-quarters of the territory Hungary had occupied as a
kingdom within the old Austro-Hungarian Empire. Horthy
had been the last commander-in-chief of the Austro-
Hungarian navy and he became regent of Hungary in 1920,
ruling with the proverbial iron fist until 1944. In that year,
sensing that Germany would lose to the Allies, he attempted, through secret negotiations, to switch sides. However, the Germans got wind of his plans and jailed him.
After the war, he retired to Portugal, where he would live
until his death in 1957.

Ironically, Hungary stood by Hitler longer than any
other Axis power in Europe, fighting on until May 1945.
Long after the others—including Italy—had given up or
changed sides, Hungary remained loyal.

During World War II, Horthy's armed forces fought
alongside the Germans, first against the Soviet Voenno-

Vozdushnie Sily, and later against the USAAF. Ironically, the admiral could contribute only land and air forces, because landlocked Hungary had no navy. In the air, the Royal Hungarian Home Defense Air Force had at least 10 aces, and possibly quite a few more.

Hungary's first ace was Imre Panezel, who scored his five victories during 1942 before he was declared missing in action during a mission on January 11, 1943. Another important ace during the early part of the war was Miklos Kenyeres, who had 18 victories (some sources say 19) when he was shot down and captured on February 6, 1944.

The leading Hungarian ace was Dezso Szentgyorgyi, who scored at least 32 (some sources say 34) victories. He first saw action on the Eastern Front in 1942, flying Italian-made Reggiane Re-2000s, but his 5/1 VSzd (Squadron) transitioned to Messerschmitt Bf-109Fs in the summer of 1943, and it was with this type that he scored his first victory on June 5, 1943.

During 1944, Hungary itself started to come under air attack by long-range heavy bombers of the USAAF Fifteenth Air Force, based in Italy. With this, the Royal Hungarian Home Defense Air Force had to reorient its priorities to air defense of the homeland rather than offensive operations against the Soviet Union. During this period, Szentgyorgyi flew with 2 VSzd of 101 Regiment and claimed five USAAF aircraft, four of them B-24 Liberators.

The air defense mission soon also included the Soviet Voenno-Vozdushnie Sily, as Soviet aircraft began flying over Hungary by winter. Szentgyorgyi continued to fly against the Soviets until Hungary capitulated early in 1945, scoring 20 victories against Soviet aircraft. For this, he was imprisoned by the Soviet Union for many years, but he was eventually "rehabilitated." He went on to fly as an airline pilot until his death in an air crash in 1971.

He is honored today by the modern, post-Communist Hungarian air force, who named a regiment after him. The 59th "Dezso Szentgyorgyi" Tactical Fighter Regiment based at Kecskemet is considered to be the most important unit in the air force. Tasked with the air defense of eastern Hungary, it contains two squadrons operating MiG-29 fighters.

Hungary's number-two ace, Gyorgy Debrody, fought in several of the same units as Szentgyorgyi, and scored 26 victories. The two aces first saw action on the Eastern Front in 1942 with 1/5 VSzd, but neither scored against the Soviets until the unit switched to Messerschmitts in 1943. Debrody's first came on July 5, less than two weeks after Szentgyorgyi's. He would score 6 more kills against Soviet foes during the summer, and by the spring of 1944, his total stood at 19, placing him ahead of Szentgyorgyi, who had 6 at that time. Like Szentgyorgyi, Debrody went back to Hungary to fly with 2 VSzd of 101 Regiment against the USAAF Fifteenth Air Force. His score would include three American bombers and three fighters.

During the final stages of the war, Debrody once again fought the Soviets. In his final combat mission on November 16, 1944, he downed a pair of Soviet Yak-9s, but was badly wounded. By the time that he was able to fly again, the war was nearly over, and he saw no more action.

At the time of his death in 1944, Laszlo Molnar had been the highest-scoring ace in Royal Hungarian Home Defense Air Force, with 25 victories, but he would be out-scored by both Szentgyorgyi and Debrody, and is recorded by posterity as the number-three ace. He was killed in action on August 7 during a dogfight with USAAF escort fighters.

The fourth Hungarian ace was Lajos Toth, who scored

24 victories, 11 against the Soviets in 1943–1944, 4 against the USAAF, and 5 against the Soviets in the final battles of 1945.

Romania

Like Hungary, Romania entered World War II ruled by a powerful nationalist faction that sympathized with the goals and philosophy of Nazi Germany and fascist Italy. Beginning in 1938, King Karol II attempted to rule as an absolute monarch, but in 1940, the government was taken over by the fascist Iron Guard under General Ion Antonescu, who retained Karol as a mere figurehead. Antonescu joined the Axis when Romania was forced to cede Bessarabia and Bucovina to the Soviet Union and northern Transylvania to Hungary. When Germany invaded the Soviet Union in June 1941, Antonescu supplied troops that took a full and active part in offensive operations.

Romanian forces fought shoulder to shoulder with the Germans until 1944, when the Soviet counteroffensive finally pushed them out of Soviet territory and into Romania itself. Facing the most unpleasant prospect of occupation by the Soviet army as a conqueror, King Michael (Karol's son) formed a coalition with the Romanian Communist Party and other factions to successfully overthrow Antonescu. In August 1944, the country joined the Allies, but in March 1945, King Michael was forced to accept a Communist-dominated Soviet puppet government, and eventually to abdicate when the monarchy was abolished in 1947.

Between 1941 and 1944, the Royal Romanian Air Force produced as many as 20 aces on the Eastern Front and in the air defense of Romania against USAAF Fifteenth Air Force long-range bombers. The actual number is unclear for a number of reasons, loss of accurate records being one. Another is the strange and complicated Royal Romanian Air Force practice of awarding multiple points depending on the type of aircraft shot down. This practice, which was probably not instituted in its final form until 1944, called for awarding three "victories" to a pilot who claimed a four-engine bomber, and two victories for downing a twin-engine aircraft. Shooting down a fighter in a dogfight, however, merely counted as one. The purpose of this practice was obviously domestic consumption, to keep morale up when the big bombers started showing up over Romania's major cities.

The highest-scoring Romanian ace also has the distinction of being the highest-scoring ace of noble birth. The colorful Count Constantin Cantacuzine (or Cantacuzino) was an extraordinary pilot who had flown in aerobatic meets before the war and who would do so again after the war, well into the 1950s. The count's actual total, however, is uncertain because of the usual discrepancies in record keeping and the complex method of counting multiple-engine victories mentioned above. He is often listed with as many as 56 to 60 victories, but his actual number is probably closer to the 43 that is often suggested.

The second-highest-scoring Romanian ace was probably Alexandru Serbanescu, who was killed in action on August 18, 1944. He is credited with between 47 and 53, but his actual number of aircraft shot down should probably be scaled back to between 30 and 35. Next in line are Ion Milu and Florian Budu, who are credited with 45 and 40 respectively. Budu was killed in action on May 31, 1944.

Bulgaria

Though it was a member of the Axis, Bulgaria was less aggressive than either Hungary or Romania in contributing to the Axis war effort. King Boris III ruled with a strong hand internally, but his death in 1943 left the country with a power vacuum. The Soviet Union invaded in September 1944 and occupied the country in a matter of months.

As with the Royal Romanian Air Force, the Bulgarians adopted the practice of awarding multiple points depending on the number of engines in an enemy aircraft. However, the Bulgarians took this a step further, not only awarding three "victories" to a pilot who claimed a four-engine bomber but giving him two victories just for damaging it.

The leading Bulgarian ace was Stoyan Iliev Stoyanov, who flew with the 682 Jato (Squadron). He is credited with 14 victories under the Bulgarian system, but is believed to have actually shot down 4, shared in a 5th, and damaged 4.

Croatia

Croatia took advantage of Germany's invasion of Yugoslavia in 1941 to declare its independence, and remained so until 1944. It would return to the Yugoslav federation after World War II but again declare its independence in 1991. Between 1941 and 1944, Croatia was ruled by the cruel nationalist Ante Pavelic, who allied himself closely with fascist Italy, and gladly associated himself with Nazi Germany. During those years, Croatian pilots fought against Serb, Greek, and Soviet forces. They were organized into special Croatian squadrons within the Luftwaffe, especially Kroaten-Staffeln 15 of the Luftwaffe's JG 52, and were equipped with Messerschmitt Bf-109s.

The leading Croatian ace was probably Cvitan Galic, who flew with Kroaten-Staffeln 15 until he was killed in action on April 6, 1944. He is credited with 36 victories, although some sources list him with 38. Croatia's number-two ace was Mato Dukovac, who also flew with Kroaten-

Staffeln 15. He is credited with 34 victories, although some sources list him with as many as 40. Dukovac was declared missing in action on September 20, 1944, and is said to have defected to the Soviet Voenno-Vozdushnie Sily—a supposition that his family vehemently denied after the war. Two Croatian aces credited with 18 victories each are Dragutin Ivanic and Mato Culinovic, both of whom flew with Kroaten-Staffeln 15.

Spain

Between 1936 and 1939, the Spanish Civil War tore the country apart, with bloodshed on a scale that exceeded any European conflict of the twentieth century except the two world wars. The two sides became so polarized that they invited the killing machines of Germany, Italy, and the Soviet Union to come to Spain and kill other Spaniards. The Nationalist leader, General Francisco Franco, won the war with the help of Germany and Italy, but he never officially intervened in World War II to return the favor.

The Spanish Civil War began in July 1936 with a rebellion against the Spanish republic by conservative military elements led by Franco, and over the ensuing three years, Germany and Italy aided him extensively with supplies and manpower, notably 70,000 ground troops supplied by Italy. In terms of the air war, Franco's Nationalist forces were aided by volunteers from Germany's Luftwaffe, who operated as the Condor Legion, and from Italy's Regia Aeronautica, who operated as the Aviazione Legionaria.

The Spanish Republican forces were, in turn, aided by Soviet Voenno-Vozdushnie Sily units and by actual volunteers from 53 nations, especially France, but also including the United States. The highest-scoring aces on both sides, however, would all be Spanish, over 20 of them Nationalists. The Republican side in the Spanish Civil War produced fewer than ten, but the top man, Leopoldo Morquillas Rubio, outscored all of the non-Spanish aces fighting on the Republican side.

Technologically, the Luftwaffe and the Regia Aeronautica—and to a lesser extent, the Voenno-Vozdushnie Sily—used the Spanish Civil War as a proving ground for the weapons and tactics that would be used in World War II.

The Republicans successfully defended Madrid, but could not launch an offensive against the Nationalists, so a stalemate developed during the winter of 1936–1937. Soviet supply shipments declined in 1938, giving the Nationalists the upper hand during the winter of 1938–1939. Franco then captured Barcelona and isolated Madrid, which finally fell on March 28, ending the war.

The three highest-scoring Spanish aces of the Spanish Civil War were also the three highest-scoring aces of any nation in the war, and they all flew with Franco's Nationalist air force. They were Joaquin García-Morato y Castaño, who scored 40 kills; Julio Salvador Díaz-Benzumea, who scored 24 (some sources say 23); and Manuel Vasquez Sagastizabel with 21.33. The former two were members of the Patrulla Azul (Blue Patrol) and later of Grupo 2-G-3. Sagastizabel flew only with Grupo 2-G-3.

García-Morato y Castaño had served with the Republican air force in Spanish Morocco in the early 1930s, but he quickly joined the Nationalists when the Spanish Civil War broke out. He scored his first victory on August 12, 1936, flying an old Nieuport-Delage 52. When Germany started supplying the Heinkel He-51 biplanes, he was one of the first to fly one, although he preferred the Italian Fiat CR-32 until the Germans started supplying Messerschmitt

Bf-109s. He was instrumental in founding the elite Patrulla Azul, and in organizing the Nationalist air arm into an effective fighting force. On January 3, 1937, already with 15 victories, he brought down a pair of Soviet-built Tupolev SB-2 bombers, which were a fast and sophisticated aircraft for the time. His best day of the war came almost two years later, on Christmas Eve in 1938, when he downed three Polikarpov R-5 attack bombers. His 40th and last victory, which came on January 19, 1939, was the 12th Polikarpov I-15 fighter that he downed. On April 3, while performing an aerobatic routine at a photo opportunity for newsreel cameras, he experienced engine failure and crashed to his death.

When World War II began, Franco remained on the sidelines in terms of a declaration of war—especially against Britain and France. In June 1941, when Germany invaded the Soviet Union, however, he was anxious to get back at his old enemy, and he supplied ground troops in the form of the famous Spanish Blue Division. A number of Spanish pilots also served in the Luftwaffe. The Blue Division was finally withdrawn from combat late in 1943. The Nationalists, who, as we said, had over 20 aces in the Spanish Civil War, had 16 with the Luftwaffe during World War II.

Meanwhile, former Republican pilots offered their services to the Voenno-Vozdushnie Sily. The Republican side produced fewer than ten aces in each war, but the highest-scoring Spaniards in World War II were Republicans and many of them fought in both wars.

While a large number of Nationalist Spanish pilots served with the Luftwaffe, especially JG 51, during World War II, only one would add to his total victories in World War II. Angel Salas-Larrázabal, who had 16.33 victories in Spain, added 7 to his score in World War II. The two highest-scoring Nationalist Spanish aces of World War II were Gonzalo Hevia Alverez-Quinones, who claimed 12 Soviet aircraft, and Marinao Cuadra Medina, with 10. Both flew with the Luftwaffe's JG 51, and neither had scored in the Spanish Civil War.

Leopoldo Morquillas Rubio, the leading Republican ace during the Spanish Civil War, with 21 victories, would not add to his total in World War II. However, Antonio Arias, who scored 12 (9 solo plus 6 shared) in the Spanish Civil War, added 10 while flying with the Soviet Voenno-Vozdushnie Sily, and Manuel Claver, who shot down 11 (some sources credit him with as many as 23) in the Civil War, added 7 in World War II.

Meanwhile, there were two Republican aces who scored relatively lower numbers in the Spanish Civil War but went on to successful careers with the Soviet Voenno-Vozdushnie Sily in World War II. Juan Lario Sanchez, who flew with the Voenno-Vozdushnie Sily 960 IAP, was the highest-scoring Spanish ace of either side in World War II, scoring 27 kills against the Luftwaffe on the Eastern Front to add to the 8 he had scored in Spain. Francisco Meroño Pellicer, who also flew with the Voenno-Vozdushnie Sily 960 IAP, scored 20 in World War II to add to his 7 from the Spanish Civil War.

Another Spanish 960 IAP ace, Vincente Beltran, who is believed to have had no victories in the Spanish Civil War, scored 20 against the Germans in World War II. In fourth place was José Pascual Santamaria, who is credited with having shot down 14 enemy aircraft while flying with 283 IAP and 788 IAP. He was killed in action during the autumn of 1942, but the exact date is unknown.

12

FINLAND

DURING WORLD WAR II, FINLAND had the distinction of being the only country actively engaged in intense fighting that changed sides. It was also unique in being the only small country in Europe that successfully resisted both the Soviet Union and Germany. As Josef Stalin, whose armies defeated Germany but not Finland, said in 1948 with a great deal of irony, "Nobody respects a country with a poor army, but everybody respects a country with a good army. I raise my toast to the Finnish army."

The Finnish air force, known as the Ilmavoimat, also had the ace who outscored the top aces of every country in the world except Germany. With a score of 94.17, Eino Ilmari Juutilainen had more confirmed kills than any non-Luftwaffe ace. (Japan's Hiroyoshi Nishizawa and Tetsuzo Iwamoto may have had additional victories that put them over the 100 mark, but these were never officially validated.)

Juutilainen was also the only non-Axis ace to exceed the World War I score of 80, achieved by the "Red Baron," Manfred von Richthofen.

Finland had nearly 100 aces, more than any country

other than the biggest three Allied and biggest three Axis nations. Behind Juutilainen, the leading Finnish aces were Hans Henrik Wind, with 75 victories; Eino Antero "Ekka" Luukkanen (a boyhood friend of Juutilainen), with 56; Urho Sakari Lehtovaara, with 44.5; Oiva Emil Kalervo Tuominen, with 44; Risto Olli Petter Puhakka, with 42; Olavi Kauko Puro, with 36, and Nils Edvard Katajainen, with 35.5. It should be added that, both Juutilainen and Jorma Sarvanto (16.83 total victories) scored six in one day.

A Swedish protectorate for centuries, Finland became part of the Russian Empire in 1809 and finally emerged as an independent country in 1917 when the Russian Empire collapsed. Stalin, who imagined his greater Soviet Union as the inheritor of the territorial scope of the old Russian Empire, wanted Finland back, and actively—albeit unsuccessfully—encouraged revolution there throughout the 1920s and 1930s.

The famous "secret protocol" to the Hitler-Stalin non-aggression pact of August 24, 1939, stated that Finland, Estonia, Latvia, and Lithuania belonged to the Soviet sphere of interest. In October, the latter three decided to become part of the Soviet Union rather than risk war, and so they would remain for 51 years. Finland rejected Stalin's demands, and on November 30, the Soviet army attacked. During the ensuing "Winter War," as it was called, the Soviet forces captured the Carelia and Salla areas, but the Finns fought them to a standstill. A cease-fire signed on March 13, 1940, would remain in place and Finland would remain officially neutral.

On June 25, 1941, three days after the German invasion of the Soviet Union, Finland was again attacked. With the help of Germany, Finland managed to continue to resist the Soviet armies for more than three years. For Germany and Finland, it was a marriage of convenience rather than an alliance. The Soviet Union was a common enemy. Finland never joined the Axis, and was never at war with any Allied power other than the Soviet Union.

During the "Continuation War," as the conflict after 1941 was called, Germany supplied Finland with matériel, including Messerschmitt Bf-109s for the Ilmavoimat, and Finland allowed Germany access to facilities in Lapland— the far north of the country—which was adjacent to German bases in occupied Norway. For Germany, the value of having Finland on its side lay in the Finns' tenacity and effectiveness as fighters, who kept sizable numbers of Soviet troops and aircraft tied down and unavailable for combat against the Germans.

As we said, the Soviet Union was never able to defeat the Finns. On June 9, 1944, the Soviets launched a massive invasion of the Isthmus of Carelia. The attack was timed to coincide with the Anglo-American invasion of Normandy; this would force the Germans to divert forces away from the Eastern Front, permitting the Soviets a bit of breathing room to finish off Finland. Nevertheless the offensive failed. On September 4, 1944, another cease-fire was signed and the Soviet Union withdrew from its war with Finland.

Germany reacted by attempting to bring Finland back onto its side through force. The same German troops who had been aiding the Finns in their war against the Soviets would continue to fight the Finns through the end of 1944, but this fighting was at a relatively low level because by the end of 1944, the territorial integrity of Germany itself was threatened and the German forces were very much on the defensive everywhere.

Juutilainen: Finland's Ace of Aces

The ace with the greatest score of anyone outside Germany was born on February 21, 1914, in Lieksa and grew up in Sortavala, where there was an Ilmavoimat base. Eino Ilmari Juutilainen's interest in military aviation came from watching aircraft at this base as a youngster. When it came time for his required military service at age 18, he was assigned as a mechanic with the 1st Separate Maritime Squadron, but he learned to fly on his own and joined the Ilmavoimat in 1933. After his initial military flight training, he went through intensive training at a fighter pilot school at Utti, which, if the performance of the Ilmavoimat in World War II is any indication, was one of the best in the world.

In March 1939, Juutilainen was assigned to Lentolaivue 24 (Squadron 24), also at the base at Utti, the squadron with which he remained until 1943. On the eve of the war, Lentolaivue 24 was equipped with Dutch-made Fokker D-21s, which did not represent the leading edge in fighter aircraft technology.

By October 1939, as the Soviet Union began to demand territorial concessions from Finland, war was seen as inevitable. Finnish military units were put on alert and prepared for combat. Lentolaivue 24 was deployed to Immola so as to be close to the border with the Soviet Union, and camouflaged shelters were constructed. When the Winter War began at the end of November, the Ilmavoimat was as ready as it could be to meet the Soviet offensive. The Fokker D-21s were inferior to the Soviet Polikarpov I-15s and I-16s, but Finnish pilot training was superior.

Most aerial combat in the Winter War was governed not by hardware, but by the weather. For much of the first two weeks of the war, aircraft on both sides were grounded.

Juutilainen's combat action did not take place until December 19, when an element of Lentolaivue 24 intercepted a strike force of Ilyushin DB-3 bombers. When attacked, the bombers turned to run and Juutilainen quickly shot one down. The others were damaged, but the Fokkers turned back when their ammunition was exhausted and did not observe the Soviets crash. Four days later, Juutilainen participated in another intercept, and on New Year's Eve, he found himself in his first dogfight. The Soviet I-16 had the technical advantage, but Juutilainen outflew him and, through superior marksmanship, outgunned him as well.

When the Winter War ended in March 1940, the Ilmavoimat had been molded into a very effective force. It was certainly respected by the Soviet Voenno-Vozdushnie Sily. Finland attempted to acquire better aircraft from Britain and France, but the latter were gearing up for their coming fight with Germany, so the best that Finland was able to obtain was a small number of Gloster Gladiators. Next, they turned to the United States, from whom they were able to acquire 44 Brewster Model B-239 Buffalos, a type that had entered United States Navy service under the designation F2A-1. The Finns would retrofit their Buffalos with extra armor aft of the cockpit that was not present in the stock F2A-1. Today, the Buffalo is remembered as a cumbersome and inferior aircraft, but in 1940, it was a major improvement to the Ilmavoimat fighter force.

Between March 1940 and June 1941, the Soviet Union kept up its diplomatic pressure on Finland, and it was widely believed that the cease-fire that ended the Winter War was temporary. The Finnish armed forces prepared accordingly. Most Ilmavoimat fighter squadrons, including Lentolaivue 24, upgraded to the Buffalo. Germany, meanwhile, offered covert aid, which was accepted.

On June 22, 1941, Germany launched its massive invasion against the Soviet Union, and three days later, Voenno-Vozdushnie Sily bombers appeared over Finland. The so-called Continuation War had begun. Now based at Rantasalmi Air Base, Lentolaivue 24 first saw action on July 9, when it was tasked with intercepting a Voenno-Vozdushnie Sily bomber force. It was on the morning of this day that Juutilainen flew in his first combat action of the war, and his first with a Brewster Buffalo. He attacked an element of Polikarpov I-153s that had been escorting the bombers and shot one down only to be attacked by another. He evaded the second I-153, which turned off, formed up with a second Soviet fighter, and started running for the border. Juutilainen chased the two enemy fighters and brought down one as the other escaped. In its first day of combat in the resumed war, Lentolaivue 24 downed nine enemy aircraft, two of them by Juutilainen.

His next victories came on August 18, when Lentolaivue 24 was involved in a huge aerial battle over the Gulf of Finland. In the early stages of the fight, Juutilainen shot down an I-16, which was his fifth victory, the one that made him an ace. However, the fight was not yet over. He was attacked twice more by aggressive I-16 pilots, both of whom fell to the Buffalo's guns. If the Polikarpovs were superior to the D-21, they were clearly outclassed by the Buffalos. Lentolaivue 24 would claim 16 aircraft for the day, and the new ace, Ilmari Juutilainen, had 3 of them.

On September 20, Juutilainen shot down a fighter that was absolutely superior to the Buffalo. By this time, the British had delivered Hawker Hurricanes and a small number of Supermarine Spitfires to the Voenno-Vozdushnie Sily, and the aircraft that Juutilainen shot down on this date is believed to have been one of these Spitfires.

Juutilainen experienced engine trouble during a fight

and was making his way back to base when the aircraft
thought to be a Spitfire attacked from behind. Juutilainen
waited until the last possible moment, when he expected
the Soviet pilot to open fire, and then threw the Buffalo
into a quick roll. This unexpected maneuver caught the
enemy off guard and he overshot Juutilainen, who then
came in behind and opened fire, sending the Spitfire down
in flames. Another Spitfire attacked, but Juutilainen outmaneuvered him and he broke off the attack.

As Juutilainen continued to nurse the crippled Buffalo
toward his base, he was bounced by a MiG-1. After a tight,
turning fight, which was at slow speed because that was
all the Buffalo could muster, Juutilainen saw an opportunity for a shot and took it. He had now scored twice in a
malfunctioning aircraft.

Juutilainen's skills—and his growing number of victories—attracted a great deal of attention, both from the Ilmavoimat community and from a grateful nation. On April
26, 1942, he was awarded the Mannerheim Cross, Finland's highest decoration for bravery. He was also becoming well known in the Soviet Union as well. After the war,
he would learn that Voenno-Vozdushnie Sily pilots considered him to be a pilot to avoid.

The Brewster Buffalo had been good to Juutilainen, and
to the Ilmavoimat, but as the months wore on, it was
clearly becoming obsolete. The Ilmavoimat high command
knew that a new generation of fighters would be coming
on-line in 1943 and negotiated with the Germans to acquire the aircraft with which the Luftwaffe was tearing the
Voenno-Vozdushnie Sily to shreds, the Messerschmitt Bf-
109.

In February 1943, the Ilmavoimat organized a new
squadron, Lentolaivue 34, to operate the new fighters, and
naturally, Juutilainen was assigned to be one of the pilots.

He was also among those Finns who were sent to Germany to familiarize themselves with the aircraft, specifically the Bf-109G-2 model, and to begin flying them back to Finland. The Messerschmitt was vastly superior to the Buffalo, and in the hands of the well-trained and battle-hardened Finnish pilots, it became an extraordinary weapon. The Bf-109G-2 made it possible for Juutilainen to bring his score into the 80s and 90s, and for the Ilmavoimat to keep the much larger Voenno-Vozdushnie Sily at bay.

It was not until the Voenno-Vozdushnie Sily started deploying the Lavochkin La-5 and the Yakovlev Yak-9 that a Soviet-built warplane could again challenge the Messerschmitts in the skies over Finland. On August 31, 1943, Juutilainen first encountered the Lavochkin fighter. For him, being attacked by an La-5 was just like fighting an I-15 in a Buffalo. It was a turning battle in which he kept the Voenno-Vozdushnie Sily pilot from getting a clear shot until he managed to get behind the Soviet aircraft and line it up in the gunsight.

Juutilainen's best day of the war came on June 30, 1944, when he succeeded in shooting down six enemy aircraft in a single day. First came a battle in which he claimed a pair of P-39 Airacobras, and next a pair of Yak-9s. The Lentolaivue 34 formation was just running low on fuel when they encountered a bomber strike force, escorted by La-5s, headed for Viipuri. The Finnish Bf-109s made the intercept and Juutilainen downed a Sturmovik attack bomber and one of the Lavochkins.

By the autumn of 1944, the Soviet Union was locked in its massive life-and-death Great Patriotic War with Nazi Germany. The sideshow war with Finland—which was neither "great" nor "patriotic"—had reached a stalemate that offered little more than a drain on resources, so Stalin made the decision to call it off.

The war would officially end on September 4, and Juutilainen's last combat mission—and 94th victory— came the day before. His patrol was bounced by a Voenno-Vozdushnie Sily fighter over Carelia, possibly hoping to get a kill before the war ended, but the fighter broke off after one pass, and in the course of looking for him, Juutilainen encountered and shot down a Lisunov Li-2 transport. It was a rather anticlimactic close to a stellar career.

In 437 missions, Juutilainen scored 54 victories in the Messerschmitt Bf-109G-2, 36 in the Brewster Buffalo, and his first 4—plus a shared victory—in the old Fokker D-21. He was awarded his second Mannerheim Cross on June 28, 1944, making him one of only four people to be awarded two. One of the others would be Hans Wind, Finland's second-highest-scoring ace.

Juutilainen retired from the Ilmavoimat in May 1947 and pursued a career in commercial aviation, while flying his own private plane on the side. He would live to see the collapse of his old nemesis, the Soviet Union. He died on February 21, 1999, in Tuusula.

Wind: Finland's Second-Highest-Scoring Ace

Hans Henrik "Hasse" Wind was born on July 30, 1919, in Tammisaari and joined the Ilmavoimat as a reserve pilot in 1938. A shortage of aircraft kept him out of action during the Winter War, but he joined the active Ilmavoimat in 1941, so he was on hand when the war resumed in June 1941. This was less than a week after he received his commission as a lieutenant.

In August 1941, he was transferred to Lentolaivue 24, where he would fly Buffalos alongside Juutilainen. His first victory, against a Polikarpov I-15, came in September, but he progressed rather slowly, adding only two kills through

July 1942, when Lentolaivue 24 was transferred to Rompotti on the Gulf of Finland. At this point, things began to pick up for Hasse Wind. He achieved ace status on August 14, shooting down a pair of Hawker Hurricanes. Four days later, Lentolaivue 24 tangled with a large force of Voenno-Vozdushnie Sily aircraft, and Wind claimed another Hurricane and two I-16s.

Wind's ninth came on October 10, when a dozen MiG-3s attacked his three-Buffalo patrol. One of them got on his tail and he was unable to outturn him to get into firing position, so he maneuvered the turning battle lower and lower until the Soviet fighter crashed into the ground. By the end of 1942, his score stood at 14.5.

The Messerschmitt Bf-109s entered service with the Ilmavoimat in February 1943, but Wind remained with Lentolaivue 24 and continued to fly the Buffalo. He had become certainly the best Buffalo pilot in the world. American and British Commonwealth pilots who were using the plane against the Japanese in the Far East at this same time were completely overwhelmed by the Mitsubishi A6M Zero.

On April 5, 1943, Wind shot down three Il-2 Sturmovik attack bombers, which were considered to be very difficult because they were so heavily armored and because they had a rear-firing gunner who made attacks from behind difficult. Nine days later, he managed to shoot down a pair of Supermarine Spitfires, an aircraft that was far superior to the Buffalo—but, of course, only in the hands of a superior pilot.

On his 24th birthday in July 1943, Hasse Wind was awarded his first Mannerheim Cross. His score now stood at 33.5, and in October, he was promoted to captain. Over the winter, he added another sort of achievement to his résumé. In the course of training new pilots, Wind wrote a manual that would remain in use at the Ilmavoimat for the next three decades.

Lentolaivue 24 had begun to convert to Bf-109G-2s in the summer of 1943, but Wind continued to fly his Buffalo until May 1944. His first victory in the Messerschmitt came on May 27, when he claimed a pair of La-5s. When the Soviet offensive in the Isthmus of Carelia began on June 9, a badly outnumbered Lentolaivue 24 and Lentolaivue 34 were tasked with intercepting the Voenno-Vozdushnie Sily bombers that accompanied the ground attack.

Flying as many as seven missions a day, the Ilmavoimat pilots were nearly overwhelmed by this effort to inflict a final defeat on Finland. But the Ilmavoimat took its toll. June 13 was not a lucky day for the Voenno-Vozdushnie Sily in the sector patrolled by Hasse Wind's flight of six Messerschmitts. During the morning, they sighted a force of Petlyakov Pe-2 bombers and quickly shot down eight— three of them claimed by Wind—one after another in quick succession.

The day was not over. During the afternoon, Wind's patrol shot down four more Pe-2s out of a flight of six— with Wind claiming two for himself—and escaped before the escort fighters could even engage them. It was days like June 13 that made Stalin decide to give up on Finland.

Hasse Wind was on a roll. Over the next 11 days, he subtracted more of Stalin's assets while adding 25 kill marks to the tail of his Bf-109G-6—3 more Pe-2s, a Sturmovik, 2 DB-3s, 2 Spitfires, 3 Airacobras, 2 Yak-7s, 5 Yak-9s, and 7 La-5s. In a span of less than two weeks, Wind shot down 30 Voenno-Vozdushnie Sily aircraft, and he'd had three days on which he shot down five.

Streaks like this never last, though, and time was running out for Hasse Wind. He claimed another three Yak-

9s on June 26, but two days later, it all came to an end. He and his wingman, Nils "Nipa" Katajainen (an ace with 30 victories to Wind's 72), were ordered to undertake an armed reconnaissance deep into enemy territory south of Vyborg. Nearing the target, Wind led an attack on seven Yak-9s, only to be bounced by another 20 VVS fighters.

Wind managed to shoot down three of the Yaks, but he was, in turn, fired on by an Airacobra. A 37mm shell exploded in the cockpit, badly wounding him. The Messerschmitt was on fire and spiraling down. To the Soviets, it probably looked like a kill for their side. However, Wind managed to pull out and struggle back to his base at Lappeenranta. He assumed that Katajainen had been shot down.

When he landed, Wind was so weak from loss of blood that he had to be lifted from the cockpit of his Messerschmitt. He would not know, until he woke up in the hospital a week later, that his wingman had also survived the melee. On June 26, Katajainen had also assumed that Wind was dead. After he saw Wind's Bf-109 go down, Katajainen had claimed one of the Airacobras, and on his way home, he surprised a flight of Sturmoviks and shot down two. Five days later, he was, himself, badly wounded, and he wound up in the hospital bed next to Wind.

His last battle earned Wind his second Mannerheim Cross. His final score was 75 victories in 302 missions. Second only to Eino Juutilainen among Finnish aces, Wind still had a higher score than any ace in the opposing Soviet VVS. He was also the highest-scoring Buffalo ace in any air force, earning 39 of his kills flying the Brewster B-239.

Wind recovered from most of his wounds, but the small splinters from the shattered cockpit glass remained a painful legacy for the rest of his life. He was married on August 26, 1944, and resigned from the Ilmavoimat in May

1945. He went on to attend the Helsinki School of Business. For most of his life, he did not discuss his wartime exploits, but he finally did consent to a biography by Borje Sjogren that was published in 1990. He passed away at Tampere on July 24, 1995.

INDEX

ABOUT THE AUTHOR

WILLIAM YENNE is the San Francisco–based author of more than a dozen books on aviation and space-related topics, such as *The World's Worst Aircraft* (Dorset, 1990), which CJCA-Radio (Edmonton) called "a real masterpiece," and *"Black '41": The West Point Class of 1941 and the American Triumph in World War II* (Wiley, 1991), which WOAI-Radio (San Antonio) called "the epitome of the best war story you'll ever hear."

He was also a contributor and aviation consultant to *The D-Day Encyclopedia* (Simon & Schuster, 1993).

His repertoire includes *Superfortress: The Story of the B-29 and American Air Power in World War II* (with General Curtis E. LeMay, McGraw Hill, 1988) and *The History of the U.S. Air Force* (Simon & Schuster, 1984, updated 1992).

Among his other aviation titles are histories of America's great aircraft manufacturers: *Rockwell: The Heritage of North American* (Random House, 1989); *Lockheed* (Random House, 1987); *McDonnell Douglas: A Tale of Two Giants* (Crown, 1985) and *Boeing: Planemaker to the World* (with Robert Redding, Crown, 1983).

His space exploration books have included *The Encyclopedia of U.S. Spacecraft* (Simon & Schuster, 1986); *The Astronauts: The First 25 Years of Manned Space Flight* (Simon & Schuster, 1986); *The Atlas of the Solar System* (Simon & Schuster, 1987); *The Pictorial History of NASA* (W. H. Smith, 1987); *Atlas of the Universe* (with Kevin Krisciunas, Random House, 1991), *Solar System* (Random House, 1991) and the 1988 book *Interplanetary Spacecraft*, which describes the process of designing, building, launching and operating an unmanned interplanetary spacecraft using readily available, off-the-shelf components.

He has also written extensively on history and the history of technology. Of the books *100 Inventions That Shaped World History* and *100 Events That Shaped World History* (Bluewood Books, 1993) the Texas USA Radio Network said, "If you are a student of history, you are going to want these books. If you are not, you are going to *need* these books."

In 1995, Yenne was commissioned by General Dynamics Corporation to write a history of their Convair Division that was entitled *Into the Sunset: The Convair Story*. The book earned Mr. Yenne recognition from the San Diego Aerospace Museum, and in thanking Mr. Yenne for the work, General Dynamics called it "marvelous" and reported that employees were "very, very proud to have it as a keepsake." General Dynamics went on to say that they had received "numerous compliments from libraries and dignitaries . . . acknowledging the creation of a fine publication."

In 1999, Mr. Yenne was named to the board of directors of the Michael King Smith Evergreen Aviation Education Center, the air museum whose collection contains many milestone aircraft from the history of aviation, including Howard Hughes's HK-1 *Spruce Goose* and a flyable Messerschmitt Bf-109G, which is painted in the markings of history's leading ace, Erich Hartmann.